PUBLIC

WORKS

Image of Ardnacrusha Control Room.
Reproduced by kind permission of ESB Archives
(Electricity Supply Board, Ireland).

PUBLIC

INFRASTRUCTURE, IRISH MODERNISM, AND THE POSTCOLONIAL

WORKS

MICHAEL RUBENSTEIN

University of Notre Dame Press

Notre Dame, Indiana

Library of Congress Cataloging-in-Publication Data

Rubenstein, Michael, 1971–
Public works : infrastructure, Irish modernism, and the postcolonial /
Michael Rubenstein.
p.   cm.
Includes bibliographical references and index.
ISBN-13: 978-0-268-04030-7 (pbk. : alk. paper)
ISBN-10: 0-268-04030-3 (pbk. : alk. paper)
1. English literature—Irish authors—History and criticism.
2. English literature—20th century—History and criticism.
3. Public utilities in literature.   4. Infrastructure (Economics) in literature.
5. Modernism (Literature)—Ireland.   6. Postcolonialism in literature.
I. Title.
PR8755.R83   2010
820.9'3556—dc22

2010024336

♳ *This book is printed on recycled paper.*

CONTENTS

ACKNOWLEDGMENTS

This project was supported in part by funding from a President's Research Fellowship in the Humanities and from a University of California Humanities Research Fellowship. A series of Junior Faculty Research Grants enabled travel to archives and experts in Ireland.

Earlier versions of this work were first published elsewhere, and I am grateful to *Novel: A Forum on Fiction* and *Social Text* for permission to reprint them here.

Pat Yeates and Brendan Delany at Ireland's Electricity Supply Board Archive provided timely information, supplemental literature, and the permissions to reprint the images in the book and on its cover.

My book owes its strengths to the many colleagues and friends who read, commented on, and discussed it with me over the years. For six years the English department at Berkeley has continuously nurtured, sharpened, and challenged me and my work, particularly in the persons of Elizabeth Abel, John Bishop, Mitch Breitweiser, Ian Duncan, Cathy Gallagher, Steve Goldsmith, Celeste Langan, and Colleen Lye. These are just the ones that I know read all my work, even early drafts that must have been torturous, and provided thoughtful criticisms and guidance. That they applied their impressive intellect and energy to my project was a gift—occasionally terrifying, ultimately invaluable—of insight, motivation, and collegiality.

Others at Berkeley who read and commented on portions of my work and to whom this project owes, and I myself owe, much: Kea Anderson, Ann Banfield, Dorri Beam, Stephen Best, Eric Falci, Anne-Lise François, Kevis Goodman, Bob Haas, Abdul JanMohamed, Steven Justice, Chris Nealon, Geoffrey G. O'Brien, Genaro Padilla, Joanna Picciotto, Scott Saul, Sue Schweik, Namwali Serpell, Janet Sorensen, and Bryan Wagner.

Dan Blanton and Maura Nolan introduced me to Barbara Hanrahan and thus to the University of Notre Dame Press. Thanks to all three for their help and encouragement.

I thank friends and colleagues from around the profession whose work and conversation have amply sustained my intellectual life over the years and who, therefore, have had incalculable impact on the merits of the present work: Nancy Armstrong, Sophia Beal, Joe Cleary, Joshua Clover, Mike Cronin, Richard Dienst, Greg Dobbins, Enda Duffy, Brent Edwards, Luke Gibbons, Geoffrey Gilbert, Liz Ho, Marjorie Howes, Karen Leibowitz, Saikat Majumdar, Francine Masiello, Patrick Mullen, Lionel Pilkington, Michael Sayeau, Joey Slaughter, Moynagh Sullivan, Nirvana Tanoukhi, Joe Valente, Kevin Whelan, Alex Woloch, Edlie Wong, and Patricia Yaeger.

The students in the introductory graduate course I facilitated in Fall 2008 made for one of my most memorable and cherished teaching experiences to date: Adam Ahmed, Shannon Chamberlain, Alek Jeziorek, Ella Mershon, Jonathan Shelley, Luke Terlaak Poot, Rachel Trocchio, and David Vandeloo. Their intelligence, generosity, and friendliness were a revelation.

I thank my research assistants, Bahareh Brittany Alaei-Johnson, Annie McLanahan, and Sarah Townsend. Sarah's timely editorial work, and her critical engagement with my project and her own, have made mine an immeasurably better book.

Bruce Robbins has been an inspirational and formative presence in my professional life generally and in the production of this book particularly. I thank him for believing in and encouraging my work from the beginning.

John Bishop daily demonstrated for me the meanings of passionate engagement, scholarly expertise, intellectual integrity, and good citizenship.

Very special thanks go to my closest friends whom at one point or another I was compelled to call upon for weekly, daily, and occasionally hourly counseling, back when this book, as I was often convinced, was trying to kill me: Natalia Brizuela, Jeremy Glick, Seán Kennedy, Johnny Lorenz, and Kent Puckett. Their understanding and support were crucial to my survival, their company and humor to my flourishing. In the final stages of the manuscript Doctor Puckett made a few emergency house calls, as a result of which the patient's condition improved dramatically. And Clara O'Brien stuck with me through the hardest parts.

I dedicate this book to my parents, David and Shirley Rubenstein.

CHAPTER

THE POSTCOLONIAL COMEDY OF DEVELOPMENT: PUBLIC WORKS AND IRISH MODERNISM

ONE

Public Works is centrally about a brief span of time—1922 to 1940—in the literary, cultural, political, and technological history of Ireland. This was roughly the eighteen-year period of the Irish Free State, a political body that emerged in 1922 from colonial union with Great Britain and transformed itself, with the ratification of Éamon de Valera's constitution in 1937, into Ireland or Éire. In that time, James Joyce published *Ulysses* and the Free State planned, funded, and built the world's first state-controlled national electrical grid.[1] Joyce's monumental achievement in *Ulysses* is widely acknowledged; Ireland's technological and political achievement with their electrical grid is far less well known, even in specialized histories of science and technology.[2] *Public Works* seeks to describe the counterintuitive but profound connections between these two seemingly unrelated historical facts, one a milestone of literary modernism and the other a milestone of technological modernization. The term *public works* I use as a kind of synthetic summation of my argument:

that works of art and public works—here limited to water, gas, and electricity—are imaginatively linked in Irish literature of the period for reasons having to do with the birth of the postcolonial Irish state.

Chapters 2, 3, and 4 of *Public Works* make the case for the connection between literary acts and public utilities in the cultural milieu of the Irish Free State. Each of these chapters focuses on a literary text: Joyce's *Ulysses* in chapter 2, Flann O'Brien's posthumously published novel *The Third Policeman* in chapter 3, and Denis Johnston's play *The Moon in the Yellow River* in chapter 4. Joyce published *Ulysses* at the dawn of the Free State era; O'Brien wrote *The Third Policeman* looking immediately back on it; and Johnston staged *The Moon in the Yellow River* right in the middle of it, one year after the state's Shannon Hydroelectric Scheme began producing electricity for the first time. Taken together as a selection of Irish authors—Joyce the famous high modernist and Catholic exile, Johnston the representative "West Briton," and O'Brien the state functionary, native Irish speaker, and struggling author—they represent a diachronic slice of Irish cultural production in the new period of state sovereignty immediately following the partially successful Irish revolt against British colonialism. My chapters are organized thematically, however, not chronologically. Chapters 2 and 3 form Part I, "Water," and deal with Joyce and O'Brien: because they both thematized the waterworks and because O'Brien's novel is in my reading a direct response to Joyce's *Ulysses*. Chapters 4 and 5 form Part II, "Power," and deal with literary thematizations of electrification; chapter 4 treats Johnston's play depicting the construction, and destruction, of a hydroelectric power plant in Dublin. My last chapter departs from Ireland and follows the public utility to Martinique and to the end of the twentieth century. My central text there, Patrick Chamoiseau's 1992 novel *Texaco*, depicts the struggle of an officially unrecognized shantytown to obtain electrical supply from the municipal authorities of Fort-de-France. By thus moving, via a shared thematic concern for electricity, from early twentieth-century Ireland to the late twentieth-century Caribbean, my book makes two further arguments: first, that Irish modernism ought to be studied in the context of comparative postcolonial literary studies, and second, that the argument of *Public Works* is a portable heuristic that yields new insights into a multiplicity of postcolonial literatures.

In the later sections of the present chapter I sketch a brief history of what made public utilities so prominent in the minds and the works of the Irish writers I treat, tracing public works in Ireland back to a critical moment during the Irish Famine in the mid-nineteenth century; I offer a brief reading of a literary text from the Famine era, John Mitchel's *Jail Journal*, that focuses on the Famine works and prefigures later literary concerns with the public utility; I survey a small selection of high modernist reactions to the expansion of public utilities in the early twentieth century; and finally I deal with Irish literary modernism's representations of the public utility, bringing my argument to the historical period of the Irish Free State and to the next chapter on James Joyce. There are several theoretical arguments to set out, however, before I return to the Irish question. In the first parts of this chapter I will be defining the terminology that I use throughout *Public Works*; making a general case for public utilities as a critical problem for modernist and postcolonial literary studies; and mapping some of the literary-critical terrain upon which I situate my work.

DEFINITIONS

What do I mean by *public works*? I take a fundamental aspect of my definition from Adam Smith's *The Wealth of Nations*, where he identifies what he calls the "publick works" as "the third and last duty of the sovereign or commonwealth," coming after "defence and justice." That duty consists in "erecting and maintaining those publick institutions and those publick works, which, though they may be in the highest degree advantageous to a great society, are, however, of such a nature, that the profit could never repay the expence to any individual or small number of individuals, and which it, therefore, cannot be expected that any individual or small number of individuals should erect or maintain."[3]

In Smith's description the public works are loosely defined as a kind of social imperative, a set of necessary institutions for any "great society." He assumes a domain within the system of capitalism that is at once outside of capitalism (public works are in his conception beyond the profit motive because they cannot, strictly speaking, realize a profit, except perhaps a profit on so grand a social scale, and in so unquantifiable a way, that it could no longer be called a profit in any capitalist sense) and one of the most basic enabling institutions of capitalism (the facilitation of civil society by way of works that no single or corporate actor in civil society would, under the assumed constraints of self-interested capitalist motivation, undertake).[4] Public works are for Smith a part of, yet apart from, the capitalist system: a supplement, to borrow a term from Jacques Derrida.[5] Proposing public works as a supplement to civil society, Smith differentiates his thinking from the many latter-day distortions—whether neoliberal or neoconservative—of his understanding of the freedom of the free market. As Amartya Sen argues, while Smith "rejects interventions that exclude the market," he does not reject "interventions that include the market while aiming to do those important things that the market may leave undone."[6] "Important things that the market may leave undone": that is the domain, or the part of the domain, of Smith's public works that most interests me in this book. I will be emphasizing throughout that Smith's definition of the public works opens up a productive—and, in the literary texts I deal with, much contested—ambiguity for thinking broadly about public works: on the one hand those "things" that are prerequisite for the existence of the "great society," and on the other those "things" that result from the existence of the "great society." Within this ambiguity, Ulysses and the Irish national electrical grid both fall under Smith's definition of public works.

That Smith defines the public works as beyond private enterprise does not mean that they should ring synonymously with the state either. By separating public works out from defense and justice, and by rejecting interventions that exclude the market, Smith is already intimating something like the distinction that would emerge between certain kinds of public works and the state. And few kinds of public works better outline this ambiguous space than what I am calling "public utilities": water, gas, and electricity. These public utilities began and persist as a complicated admixture of the state and the market, that is, of both public and private sources, for their invention, financing, maintenance, and ownership. When he defines them in a nineteenth- and twentieth-century Irish context, Colin Rynne drops the "public" from "public utilities" and makes the indistinction a central part of his description:

The origin of utility industries in European cities arose from the need to regularise and control the basic amenities required for urban life beginning, in antiquity, with the provision of water supplies and sanitary services. As the fundamental nature and extent of these services expanded and evolved, the consumer-producer relationships associated with them became more direct. By the eighteenth century this already required intricate planning on the part of municipal authorities. Ideally, essential services such as water supply were kept under public control, but this was by no means always possible, while gas and electricity companies invariably began their operational lives in private hands. Yet regardless of ownership these industries, more than most others, owing to the fact that their product was supplied were obliged to keep pace with technological change. This was a consequence of their expanding customer bases and, as long-term demand for water, gas, and electricity could nearly always be expected to increase (both for industrial and domestic customers), the networks designed for their operation also had to cater for daily peaks in demand.[7]

I follow Rynne's definition of utilities here, but I use *public utilities* to denote them, mainly as a way to keep in mind the wishful thinking and utopian possibilities that they embody as a discrete function of Smith's public works. The term is also, for my purposes, a shorthand reference to water, gas, and electricity. Known as part of the category of "utilities" in Great Britain and "services publiques" in France, *public utilities* is an Americanism that actually means a great deal more, in the language of civil engineering, than just water, gas, and electricity. Here, however, I limit myself to these three because they represent a discrete epistemic change in the way that political power might be exercised and felt in the private sphere, particularly in the domestic sphere, and more broadly on and in the psychic life of the individual. The subject and the subject's relationship to power was, I argue, radically transformed with the advent of public utilities, in ways just as profound as, and in other ways even more intimate than, some of the other technological transformations wrought by modernization. Public schools, railroads, and the automobile: these things did not enter the home and the domestic sphere so intrusively, or, in an important paradox that I will explain shortly, so forgettably. They did not, like water taps or gas mains or electrical lines, restructure the home architecturally or demand a profound restructuring of the domestic habitus. New media like photography, telegraphy, and film had a tremendous impact on modern consciousness, and plenty of scholarly work proves this beyond a doubt. But again, they did not change the built environment to the same degree and, in the cases of telegraphy and film, were dependent on electricity in the first place. The radio and the telephone certainly had an impact on the home something like the one I am claiming for public utilities, but we know this already too, and again we have two technologies whose use presupposes electrical supply. I am, however, interested in public utilities precisely because they do not normally receive the same kinds of cultural-critical attention, and in this book I seek to understand why they escape that critical attention, to explain why they should receive critical attention, and to show that in the literary texts I examine they are being attended to in fascinating and unstudied ways that reveal much about their often subtle, and often profound, impact on the sense of self in fiction and in fact.

This progressive networking of the built environment through subsequent inventions of new utilities—electricity was the most prominent and controversial in the early twentieth century—was part of a modernizing drive that led to the conceptualization and construction of the welfare state, and ultimately to the electronic networked society to which we are so accustomed to referring, and which tends generally, I think, to obscure and even render invisible the simpler, older network of public utilities I wish to investigate in this project. We inherit the term *infrastructure* from these processes. *Infrastructure* really comes into the English language after Roosevelt's New Deal during the era of the Great Depression and is therefore an anachronism in the historical and literary contexts in which I employ it. When I use the term I mean to signal the ways in which, in the years of the development of national electrical grids, there was no precise term for what was happening because there was little precedent for it. *Infrastructure* later became the term that described phenomena that had far less settled, and far less certain, denominations as they were being built. The terminological lack was also a conceptual one in that the nature, context, meaning, and portent of the national electrical grid was unknown and mysterious for those who lived through its construction. It was a novel thing, and this is why, in the Irish and other fictions I discuss, it was also mystified, idealized, reviled, ignored, and scrutinized. Fiction was thus a place not so much to fix its meaning as to speculate about it: to imagine a concept that, by the 1930s, would come to be known colloquially as infrastructure.

GOVERNMENT IS GOOD

The public utility, then, is a specific subcategory of public works whose construction and upkeep exceed the capitalist motivation for profit, while at the same time generally subtending the goals of capitalism. In that supplemental role, and in their neither/nor relationship to the state and the market, public works might signify a collective institution whose political form threatens—weakly at times, strongly at others—to break away from the dominant political form of the state (whatever state-form that happens to be, and in whatever specific historical and geographical circumstances that state-form exists) or to break free of the market, or both at the same time. Ambiguously a part of the state, ambiguously part of private enterprise, the public works, especially in the form of the public utility, stand on the verge of being dominated by one or the other, or of being both at the same time, or—and these are the occasions I am most interested in—of being neither, that is, of exceeding the state and the market and claiming for themselves the status of a utopian alternative to both. In other words, the aspects of public utilities that most interest me in this book are their supplemental and utopian aspects, aspects that emerge in the modernist literature that concerns itself with them. In the works of fiction that I present here, I include both utopian and dystopian representations of public utilities, but the thrust of my general argument is toward a Benjaminian, redemptionist, weak-messianic story about the development of public utilities as the development of a common good. Though I present research into the historical backgrounds of two important public utilities projects in Ireland—the Vartry Waterworks and the Shannon Hydroelectric Dam—my interest always folds back into their representation in fiction. I have chosen this line of argument because as I see it all the questions that attend the provision of what Rynne calls "basic amenities" like water and power—to whom, where, using what method, and at what price—are also some of the most pressing questions shaping our

global political and economic situation in the present. It is an argument
I take up again in a moment.

The proliferation of public utilities in Europe and the United States
at the turn of the twentieth century came about mostly as a result of col-
laboration between municipal authorities and private interests, and as
part of the contemporaneous popularity of the discourse of town planning and its civic improvement schemes. According to Daniel T. Rodgers,
however, the public works schemes of town planning were also precur-
sive forms of the institutions of the welfare state that emerged later, in
the 1920s and 1930s.

> Investing boldly in public works, urban business-class progressives had
> engineered a major shift in the line between city and private enterprise.
> They had established for turn of the century cities a new set of collec-
> tive tasks, which, spinning out from concerns with public health, de-
> fied determinate limits. Long before the "welfare state" was more than
> a cloud in the sky of the nation-state, they began to elaborate a net-
> work of locally administered public services and socially priced goods.
> They had, however tentatively, experimented with cross-class politi-
> cal alliances.[8]

In the sense that public utilities might be understood as a metonymic,
miniature, and peculiarly concrete subset of public works, and to the
extent—following Rodgers—that the public works of the period were
the precursors of the modern welfare state, I see my work on the literary
representation of the public utility as part of a strand of recent literary-
critical scholarship that is reevaluating literary representations of the
welfare state—and, indeed, the welfare state's relationship to literature.
Amanda Claybaugh identifies the general argument of this critical trend
with the wry tagline "Government Is Good" and includes in its ranks recent books by Michael Bérubé, Sean McGann, Bruce Robbins, and Michael Szalay, as well as talks and essays by John Marx and Lisi Schoen-
bach. Claybaugh finds these authors' revalorization of the welfare state in
literary studies refreshing because, as literary critics, they are all "writing
from within an academic culture that automatically criticizes the welfare
state from two sides at once: from a Foucaultian position that describes

the institutions of welfare as totalizing and coercive and from a leftist position that describes them as compromised and inadequate."[9] In the cases of Robbins and Szalay, the goal is to perform the trick of making the state visible in literature (and in life), or, as Claybaugh puts it, of "perceiving government," which is a notoriously hard trick to pull off. Szalay's figural stand-in for the welfare state in *New Deal Modernism* is the mutual insurance company, a figure that works by invoking the welfare state as a kind of social insurance policy.[10] Robbins, in *Upward Mobility and the Common Good,* concentrates on the relationships engendered through the institutions of the welfare state: the social worker and the patient, or the professional mentor and the apprentice, for example. From Robbins's work in particular I borrow my use of the term *common good.* To the extent that the networking of public utilities in the early twentieth century presaged the European welfare state, I find Robbins's definition of the common good, as "a profound shift in moral sensibility that is both a cause and an effect of . . . the rise of the welfare state," to give an accurate account of what I wish to argue about the rise of public utilities.[11]

But by contrast to Szalay and Robbins, I am focused on a rather minute segment of the material culture of the state: the public utilities. In them I discover moments in fiction where the state—or rather, that ambiguous, ideal, and fictive institution that magically supplies "basic amenities"—becomes visible through the unnoticed rituals of daily life: rituals that are, though we would rarely stop to think of it, underwritten by the provision of public utilities through municipal and state authorities. These are moments in which a virtual relationship with the state— as opposed, say, to Robbins's focus on face-to-face relationships—occurs hundreds of times a day, whether we know it, or think of it, or not: instances of what Christopher Bollas in the context of psychoanalysis calls the "unthought known," "something known about, indeed deeply informative of any self's being and relating, but something which must be experienced and can only meagerly be described."[12] Such repetitive moments of communion with the state can be thought of as a peculiar spin on Benedict Anderson's concept of the imagined community.[13] Rather than communing with the mystical nation (when we read the newspaper, to use Hegel's example), we commune with the material culture of the state, encountering its power and, when things are in working order, its benevolent provision. And this kind of communion becomes much more prevalent in the beginning of the twentieth century with the advent of indoor plumbing and electricity. It's not common to think of our communion with the state as mystical at all, let alone benevolent, and least of all pleasant or pleasing. And it's certainly not safe to stop our thinking there; that would put an end to criticism altogether. But following Szalay and Robbins, et al., it is worth thinking about because, as Claybaugh has pointed out, it cuts so clearly against the grain of the habitual thinking in most schools of literary criticism. Along with the works of the other members of the "Government Is Good" school of criticism, my book is a necessarily incomplete, partial archive of literary works that cut against that grain as well.

This is, again, very far from saying that Foucauldian concepts like discipline and governmentality do not serve in an analysis of public utilities in literature: quite the contrary. Panopticism is for example a crucial concept for my reading, in the next chapter, of the "Wandering Rocks" episode in Joyce's *Ulysses*. But I am less concerned there with panopticism's policing or surveilling function than I am with what it enables Joyce to do with the narrative point of view of Dublin's sewer system. Nor is it the case that Marxist understandings of capitalism, modernity, and development are absent in the analyses of public utilities in literature that I perform in the following chapters. Particularly in chapters 3 and 4, I confront much more hostile reactions to the intrusions of public utilities into Irish life in the works of Denis Johnston and Flann O'Brien.

THE POSTCOLONIAL COMEDY OF DEVELOPMENT

My book parts company with those interested in the literature of the welfare states of Europe and the United States because I am primarily interested in the literature of the postcolonial state: a vast difference in terms of the experience of capitalism, modernity, and development. And the Irish state was and is, as David Lloyd has pointed out, an anomalous state.[14] On the one hand, Ireland was modernized under British rule with a merciless rapidity best exemplified by the mass deaths and mass emigrations that occurred during the Famine of the mid-nineteenth century.

And on the other, Ireland's trajectory in terms of economic development has since taken an almost miraculous turn toward European prosperity; its fate was not to be like that of Achille Mbembe's African postcolony.[15] But the experience of modernization in Ireland was nevertheless a colonial experience that produced a colonial reaction to modernity, a special version of the split between inner and outer life that Marshall Berman describes as "pervasive in European society" but at the same time as having "a special resonance in countries," like Ireland, that were "socially, economically, and politically 'underdeveloped.'"[16] Berman develops his idea of the split, as a function of what he calls the "underdeveloped identity," through a reading of Goethe's *Faust* that draws a clear line of continuity between the economic backwardness of Goethe's Germany and the conditions of underdeveloped nations in the late twentieth century: "German intellectuals in Goethe's age were the first to see their society this way when they compared it with England, with France, with expanding America. This 'underdeveloped' identity was sometimes a source of shame, at other times (as in German romantic conservatism) a source of pride, most often a volatile mixture of both. This mixture will next occur in nineteenth-century Russia. . . . In the twentieth century, intellectuals in the Third World, bearers of avant-garde cultures in backward societies, have experienced the Faustian split with a special intensity."[17] Now, this split, which takes a special form within the "underdeveloped identity" of romantic Germany (and colonial—or indeed postcolonial—Ireland, and much of the rest of the postcolonial world), gives birth to "one of the most original and fruitful ideas in Goethe's Faust . . . the idea of an affinity between the cultural ideal of self development and the real social movement toward economic development."[18] Berman is quick to distinguish here between modernization and capitalism; he concedes that "capitalism is one of the essential forces in Faust's development," but, he stipulates, "there are several Mephistophelean themes here that go beyond the scope of the capitalist economy."[19] He pits himself against Lukács's strict Marxist reading of Faust, suggesting that Lukács is "mistaken . . . in defining this context too narrowly, as a purely capitalist affair."[20] Berman thus decouples the problem of development in *Faust,* and in the "underdeveloped identity," from the problem of capitalism. This is a distinction that I borrow when I focus on public utilities, since, as we have already seen, public utilities emerge and exist in a problematic space between capitalist enterprise and the state.

It is also important to distinguish clearly between what Berman is describing as a split identity, caught between personal and economic development, and the affinity created, in the formal coherence of *Faust*, between personal and economic development. The identity split is manifest in Faust as a character until acts 4 and 5, when Faust undergoes a third and final metamorphosis into what Berman calls "the developer."[21] That metamorphosis is what merges personal and economic development and produces an imaginative solution to the split within the underdeveloped identity. Berman argues that Goethe's imaginative solution is the fulfillment of Faust's characterological development, an argument that contradicts the way "many nineteenth- and twentieth- century writers" saw it, as "a radical negation of the development of feeling," the ultimate failure of personal development.[22] Berman notes that "most interpretations and adaptations of Goethe's *Faust* come to an end with the end of Part One," as if the formal coherence that creates a unity between personal and economic development were rarely respected, and perhaps poorly understood.[23] Whether, in any case, the solution itself is a characterological fulfillment or a characterological failure, in Faust's case it proves to be tragic; Berman calls Goethe's *Faust* "the first, and still the best, tragedy of development."[24] I borrow the distinction between the split identity and its fictional, formal solution from Berman because I want to suggest that James Joyce's *Ulysses* and Patrick Chamoiseau's *Texaco*—the subjects of my chapters 2 and 5, respectively—are direct twentieth-century descendants of Goethe's *Faust*, at least as far as Berman's reading goes.

The key difference, however, is that both these twentieth-century novels should be considered, not as tragedies of development, but instead as postcolonial comedies of development. In both *Ulysses* and *Texaco*, the public utility offers an escape from the tragedy of development by holding out, precisely, that ambiguous but always hopeful distance from purely capitalist development and from the repressive aspects of the state. In the case of *Ulysses*, I locate this formal solution to the underdeveloped identity not in the novel as a whole but in the formal coherence of two of *Ulysses*'s episodes as discrete narrative units: "Wandering Rocks," centered on the sewer, and "Ithaca," centered on the waterworks. But I also argue that the arc of Joyce's fictional career from "The Dead" to *Ulysses* can be read in terms of finding a formal, fictional solution to the problem of the underdeveloped identity, a solution that, unlike Goethe's, will not end in tragedy. In that arc, Joyce reveals his wary, weak hope for the fledgling Irish Free State, which came into existence in the same year that *Ulysses* was published, 1922. To sketch this trajectory briefly, we can take *A Portrait of the Artist as a Young Man* as a midcareer example. From this way of looking, *A Portrait* is a classic Kunstlerroman exactly insofar as it is not a Bildungsroman, because in the end Stephen chooses art and aesthetics, not in combination with the acceptance of a social position, but rather as an alternative to social and political participation: the artist as exile. What is missing from the novel is *Faust*'s fourth and fifth acts, the metamorphosis into the developer. *Ulysses,* as I argue in chapter 2, supplies the rest: an imaginative solution to Berman's split identity in the image of the public utility. For Chamoiseau's *Texaco,* the formal solution resides in a teleological unity: from the protagonist's learning to read from a discarded electricity primer, then to her sentimental education in great works of literature (*Ulysses* prominent among them), and ending, with a formal nod to the beginning, with her lobbying for, and winning, electrical supply for the shantytown of Texaco. What all this suggests is that for the underdeveloped identity, and for the postcolonial writer, the teleological arc of personal development culminates in taking on—in metaphorical as well as more literal ways—the role of the developer, with all the Faustian risks and tragic potentialities that the role implies. In this dangerous endeavor Joyce and Chamoiseau conjure the public utility, in its idealized distance from capital and the state, as a fetishistic reminder of the postcolonial writer-developer's commitment, through and to her literary craft, to the development of the common good.

ALTERNATIVE MODERNITIES

In chapters 3 and 4, on O'Brien and Johnston, I carry the thread of this developmentalist argument through two examples of hostile literary reactions to modernization, both of which also thematize the public utility but for dissenting reasons. Both writers see in the public utility only the

Faustian tragedy of development. To some degree, however, their critiques of modernization tend to serve as an alibi for some other, veiled motivations. In O'Brien's case, his hostility to the public utility emanates from his position as a bureaucrat in a branch of the Irish Civil Service responsible for funding the waterworks, and from his position as a writer struggling to achieve recognition in Joyce's shadow; thus I read his novel *The Third Policeman* as a savage parody of Joyce's fetishization of the public utility in *Ulysses*. In Johnston's case, I argue that his hostility to the public utility in his *The Moon in the Yellow River* reveals mainly his dismay in the face of the transfer of power—from one power station to another, and from the Protestant Ascendancy to the Irish Catholic majority—that took place after the establishment of the Free State. But Johnston's play and O'Brien's novel also trade in devastating critiques of modernization that need to be acknowledged and accounted for, especially in a book like this one, where the general thrust is toward arguing for the postcolonial comedy of development.

Thus far I have anchored my claim for the special consideration of the public utility in literature first in the recent literary-critical focus on the welfare state and second in Berman's notion of the underdeveloped identity. My argument—that Irish modernism was largely a literary engagement with the problem of how to forge an Irish modernity after colonialism—speaks also to ongoing debates in postcolonial studies that usually unfold under the rubric of "alternative modernities." In a lecture titled "The Subaltern and the Popular: The Trajectory of the Subaltern in My Work," Gayatri Spivak looks back on her seminal essay from 1988, "Can the Subaltern Speak?" to assess its lasting legacy for postcolonial theory.[25] "The problems that emerged out of 'Can the Subaltern Speak?'" she says, "were a) the problem of subjectship and agency and b) the call to build infrastructure, in the colloquial not the Marxist sense, so that agency would emerge." What Spivak might mean by the colloquial sense of infrastructure becomes clearer later on in her talk:

> I teach at two ends of the spectrum: I teach and train teachers in those areas where there is no electricity, no running water, no toilets, no stores, no doors and windows, all that stuff—carefully—and I also teach English—not South Asia—I teach English to PhD stu-

dents at Columbia University in the state of New York. Two ends of
the spectrum. . . . But slowly I began to realize that this kind of work is
actually—needs to be done at both ends . . . the uncoercive rearrangement of desires, which is humanities teaching as such, very scary, because when teaching becomes kind of good, it becomes coercive, even
benevolently so. . . . that's the responsibility of the teacher, but at both
ends.[26]

Spivak always has her critical eye locked on to the international division
of labor and on the disparities of development that mark huge differences in class politics within, between, and across the first world and the
third. But if Spivak is illustrating a case of uneven development between
India and the West, she is also illustrating a problem for the concept of
uneven development by describing in India an infrastructure of teaching without an infrastructure of public utilities. In this latter sense her
village in India is unevenly developed not with respect to New York but
with respect to itself. In speaking of water, electricity, and toilets Spivak
speaks precisely in that colloquial sense of infrastructure that she first
mentioned. Who does not recognize, in exactly those terms, an absolutely
commonplace way of figuring the distance and the difference between
the developed and underdeveloped regions of the world: access to clean
water, hygienic waste disposal, and electrical light? Between public utilities and humanities teaching, which is the critical infrastructural form
most likely to make it possible for "agency to emerge"? Do both need to be
present? Does agency need to emerge before water and power can be won?
Is there a logical or teleological order to which their provision ought to
conform? These are not easy questions, and to answer them would require clarification of the nature of the relationship between public utilities and humanities education. One emotionally charged answer is given
by Balram Halwai, the protagonist of Aravind Adiga's 2008 novel *The
White Tiger*. Balram is born a peasant, becomes a servant and driver for a
local elite family, murders his master, and, with the money he steals, starts
up his own car service for outsourced call-center workers in Bangalore.
His story is a kind of noir version of the developer, with a thoroughly
capitalist, thoroughly globalized understanding of "development." "If I
were making a country," he says at one point after lamenting the absence

of public utilities in his village, "I'd get the sewage pipes first, then the democracy, then I'd go about giving pamphlets and statues of Gandhi to other people, but what do I know? I'm just a murderer!"[27] The charge, and the demand, is that there is an order to the development of democracy: certain infrastructural conditions must be met for democracy, and for a felt sense of citizenship, to flourish.

I don't want to pretend to answer fully the questions I've raised here. What I do want is to suggest that statements like Spivak's and like the fictional Balram's should be taken into consideration when speaking, as is popular in postcolonial theory today, of "alternative modernities." I also want to suggest that public utilities might stand as an ideal emblem for the crossroads ("carefully," is how Spivak reflects on those crossroads as she transitions from discussing water, gas and electricity to humanities education) between what Spivak calls "the uncoercive rearrangement of desires, which is Humanities teaching as such," and the violence of the imperialist mentality or the modernizing thrust of modern nation-states. As articulated by Dilip Parameshwar Gaonkar, the alternative modernities thesis is that "under the impact of modernity, all societies will undergo certain changes in both outlook and institutional arrangements. Some of those changes may be similar, but that does not amount to convergence. Different starting points ensure that new differences will emerge in response to relatively similar changes."[28] Gaonkar suggests that we must do away with teleological understandings of modernity because such understandings cannot account for the fact of the variety of convergences to and divergences from modernity—for which there is in any case no longer any normative definition to be had once the teleological schema is eliminated. This seems a welcome change from the modernization school of thought, until it is realized that if modernity has no normative standard, any kind of uneven development, and as a consequence any kind of deprivation, can be celebrated as "alternative." In fairness, this is hardly the purpose behind theories of alternative modernity. But it is a logical problem for their argument. For James Ferguson, "The application of a language of alternative modernities to the most impoverished regions of the globe has become a way of not talking about the non-serialized, detemporalized political economic statuses of our time—indeed, a way of turning away from the question of a radically worsening global inequality and its consequences."[29] Building on Ferguson's critique, Nirvana Tanoukhi locates the problem with alternative modernities in the paradigm's emergence just after the paradigm of development lost its power, which is also to say, just after the paradigm of development seemed permanently and hopelessly out of reach for many underdeveloped countries. In her view, the rise of alternative modernities can be understood in its most sinister aspect as simultaneous with the rise of, or rather as a sign of the acceptance of, the development of underdevelopment.

> Adopted as an analytical framework, "alternative modernity" has proved immensely fertile, producing a rich descriptive literature that demonstrates the versatility and creativity of "local" forms despite compromises with larger forces of homogenization. But the anachronism that belies this critical gesture is unmistakable. Is it really possible to borrow the cultural slogan of an era of economic optimism to describe the uneven world that emerged in its painful aftermath? This spirited body of work must neglect, as Jim Ferguson has observed, that the early postcolonial investment in cultural alterity lost currency when the prospect of economic progress became dim. That in fact, when economic convergence was no longer believed a historical inevitability, cultural alterity appeared more like the symptom (or even the cause) of permanent economic troubles. The language of alternative modernity thus disguises a real dissonance between an academic thesis that celebrates the periphery's specificity, and a local outlook that experiences "specificity" as a mark of inferiority. . . . If . . . the ethos of development is the historical condition that allowed the two terms "alternative" and "modernity" to be sensibly conjoined, what seems most troubling about the anachronistic redeployment of "alternative modernity" is that it should bear some trace of the actual decomposition that befell the paradigm of development, and which broke the once reassuring tie between cultural ascendance and economic progress. . . . How indeed does the theoretical framework of alternative modernity manage to do its work without bearing such a trace?[30]

It seems to me that public utilities—which, remember, are for Spivak a colloquial invocation of the kind of infrastructure that would support the emergence of agency—are in Tanoukhi's terms the trace of development that should be brought to bear on the study of alternative modernities. They are a normative standard of modernity: as Rynne defined them, "basic amenities." In the case of water and sewage, this is nearly too obvious to bear mentioning. But the point becomes interesting when the subject is electricity, because electricity bears an ambiguous relationship to the idea of "basic amenities." Water and waste disposal are basic necessities for life, but electricity is not. Thus the provision of electricity may be felt in any given context alternatively as a necessity, a modernizing imposition, a luxury, or a sign of the arrival of the "great society." In the last two chapters of this book, I take up this problem from two perspectives. In the Irish case, the Free State's scheme to provide electricity to the whole nation was met with some serious skepticism about what kinds of epistemic violence might be done by its introduction into traditional ways of life. But in the case of Chamoiseau's *Texaco*, the provision of electricity at the end of the novel is understood as "an unblemished joy" and signals a kind of political recognition, the bestowal of citizenship status on the residents of Texaco. In the very different fictional receptions of electricity from one end of the twentieth century to the other, we see the development of demands from below for amenities that pass beyond the level of necessity or, to put it slightly differently, that raise the bar on the definition of necessity. And this, I think, is what Spivak means when she makes infrastructure the handmaiden to agency. With this understanding in mind, it is possible to see how far public utilities can take us beyond the domain of utility.

THE HATRED OF UTILITY

In what follows I will be making the case for the presence, in the underdeveloped identity of the Irish colonial subject, of another split, related to Berman's split between personal and economic development, between the concepts of utility and the aesthetic. I contend that this "special resonance" in the underdeveloped identity of the Irish imagination—the opposition between utility and the aesthetic—is born of Ireland's early and traumatic experience of modernity and modernization. It was never that the Irish lacked modernity or development, but rather that they had too much of it, and without the protections of national sovereignty to soften its violent transformations. To see how this is true, we have only to look back to the Great Famine of the nineteenth century, from which, as I argue, we can see the underdeveloped identity developing its antipathy to utility. "No moment in Irish history," writes David Lloyd, "is more saturated with the consciousness of loss."[31] The Famine was "a colonial catastrophe" brought about in the name of modernization through "the deliberate use of famine relief projects, eviction, and emigration under duress to eradicate ways of life that had been recalcitrant to capitalism. . . . If not deliberately genocidal, British policy nonetheless sought to make of the Famine a means both to the clearance of what they regarded as a 'redundant' population and to the transformation and modernization of Irish agricultural processes."[32]

To understand the uses of the public works in Ireland as a "deliberate . . . means of clearance . . . and . . . transformation" is to see the depth and extent of the Irish antipathy to utility. If the Famine was "the last great subsistence crisis of its kind in Western Europe," then it may also be part of a continuous history of what Mike Davis describes as a string of "late Victorian holocausts" set in motion by imperial politics and policies: a colonial famine instead of—or as well as—a European one.[33] In a period of under ten years, roughly between 1845 and 1852, Ireland underwent "a process of enclosure that had taken place elsewhere in the British Isles over several centuries."[34] The Famine, for Joe Cleary, was an instance of colonial modernization, "a drastic reduction of population to market rather than expansion of market to population." It was an imperial act of "political modernization" that "meant [for the Irish] a diminishment rather than an extension of political sovereignty."[35] These factors—the temporal compression of those processes of modernization from "several centuries" to just several short years, and the diminishment of political sovereignty—define the difference in the underdeveloped identity between the colonial experience of modernization and the European experience. The "split" between personal and economic development in the underdeveloped identity threatens, in the Irish case, to erupt violently into a literal case of split personality. And indeed this happened, in the case of John Mitchel, to whom I will return at the end of this section.

My goal in outlining the antinomy between utility and the aesthetic in the Irish imagination is to lead us to James Joyce, whose writings, as I argue at length in the next chapter, sought to undo that antinomy. In showing how deeply that antinomy goes in the Irish context, I aim to impress the difficulty and courageousness of his undoing and its consequences for modernist and postcolonial literature. But it wasn't just the Irish context that influenced his thinking through of the problem of utility, and I will address Joyce's high modernist milieu to see how his contemporaries, Irish and otherwise, understood the relationship between utility and the aesthetic and how Joyce differentiated his work from theirs.

Public Works evolved inductively from my readings of certain passages in *Ulysses* that led me to the thinking and to the findings I present here. It is because of Joyce's overriding influence in shaping this book that I wish to frame my argument with one of his jokes, a joke that, as I will argue in what follows, holds the key to understanding the place of public works in the character of the Irish nation and in the Irish national character.[36] The joke comes from the "Aeolus" episode of *Ulysses,* where Professor Mac-Hugh is cracking wise at the lowly pragmatism of the old Roman Empire: "What was their civilization? Vast, I allow: but vile. Cloacae: sewers. The jews in the wilderness and on the mountaintop said: It is meet to be here. Let us build an altar to Jehovah. The Roman, like the Englishman who follows in his footsteps, brought to every new shore on which he set his foot (on our shore he never set it) only his cloacal obsession. He gazed about him in his toga and he said: It is meet to be here. Let us construct a watercloset."[37]

This is a joke that everyone within hearing understands because it plays perfectly on the stereotypical characterizations of the Englishman and the Irishman—or the Saxon and the Celt—nearly exactly as Matthew Arnold had characterized them in his lecture series "On the Study of Celtic Literature." The Romans here are really incidental to the import of the joke, since, as MacHugh notes, the Romans never set foot in Ireland. The thrust of the joke goes instead against British empire building, a way of insulting the entire mind-set of the Anglo-Saxon invaders, their practicality, ruthlessness, and self-control juxtaposed to the Irish national type—poetic, passionate, impractical—all delivered with scatological humor. The Irish, who as Arnold asserted were "always ready to react against the despotism of fact," don't build toilets; they build fictions, which are—following the logic behind MacHugh's humor—better, nobler things to build.[38] But the joke can play both ways. The Celt's refusal of the pragmatics of planning and building serves to justify the annexation of Ireland under the Act of Union of Great Britain and Ireland in 1800: "As in material civilisation he has been ineffectual," Arnold observes, "so has the Celt been ineffectual in politics."[39] The feminine Celt needs a master, and the masculine Saxon needs poetry; thus their political union can be justified as a species of harmonious and mutually beneficial marriage.

In her book *Haunted English: The Celtic Fringe, the British Empire, and De-Anglicization*, Laura O'Connor goes deeper into the racialized meaning and significance of MacHugh's joke about watercloset: "Ernest Renan's influential argument in *Poésie des Races Celtiques* (1854) that Celts' excessive 'poetic life' renders them unfit for politics has been widely contested by critics. Yet the anomalous use of literary genres as a racial category to divide Britons into 'prosaic' Anglo-Saxons and 'poetic' Celts goes unexamined, as does the notion that at the pinnacle of empire English is a utilitarian medium in need of a poetic Celtic infusion."[40]

O'Connor's explanation of the difference between contesting the racial categorization of Anglo-Saxons and Celts and examining that racial categorization applies perfectly to MacHugh's joke. The stereotypical difference between the Saxon and the Celt turns on the distinction between utility and the aesthetic. The joke works on the assumption that no one—except some travestied toilet-obsessed Englishman, not present—would ever imagine valuing utility over the aesthetic. Though MacHugh is Irish, and though the force of his contempt goes against the British, his joke does nothing to challenge or undo the stereotype. In fact, he reinforces it insofar as he clearly believes that it is better to have a refined aesthetic sensibility than to want to build, or to know how to build, or to have a characterological inclination to build, a toilet. The joke's humor is thoroughly structured by the pride, the shame, and the "often volatile mixture of both" that Berman identifies with the underdeveloped identity. Thus MacHugh goes some way, albeit unintentionally, toward explaining if not actually justifying Irish subjugation. The character traits that make it possible for the English to rule the Irish are, paradoxically, the very character traits that make them unworthy to rule over the Irish, whose refined sensibility deserves sovereignty without, again paradoxically, being able to assert it. This is a joke that is also a trap, for to whatever extent Mac-Hugh expresses contempt for his English masters, he also bows to the logic by which he is ruled, and eagerly so, because his belief in the superiority of the aesthetic over utility—or even, we might say, the absolute antagonism of utility and the aesthetic—is so strong. The only way out of this paradox is to give up on the opposition, to explore possible cognitive, categorical—and, following O'Connor, *literary* and *generic*—recombinations of utility and the aesthetic. This is what I argue that Joyce will eventually do, and to a lesser extent O'Brien and Johnston as well.

By using the watercloset as his example, I take MacHugh to be referencing a real advance over the outdoor privy: indoor plumbing, which on Bloomsday, June 16, 1904, was a far-from-universal convenience. The indoor watercloset was not, believably enough, an Irish invention. But the flushing toilet came to Ireland in a special configuration designed for Irish conditions. In 1855 John Grey proposed an institutional version of his toilet designs to the Royal Dublin Society, a system that he had experimented with at the North Dublin Union Workhouse:

> Not believing that domestics could be trusted to operate the device, Grey went on to design a "self-acting flusher," which he displayed before both the Physicians and Surgeons at their respective colleges. He designed a complete system for the workhouse, including a four-seater toilet, reporting how he had achieved by these means a "self-cleansing water-closet, that accommodates four visitors at a time, receives about 600 visits in the course of the day, and washes itself every ten minutes, while the drain pipe which receives ejecta of all these visitors is scoured out by a similarly self-acting mechanism once each day."[41]

If the Irish national character didn't have a toilet associated with it, then the character of the Irish nation did, insofar as the workhouse came to be one of the representative institutions of another Irish stereotype involving poverty, laziness, drunkenness, and ignorance. Slavoj Žižek has pointed out that ideology is at work in national differences of toilet design: "Each involves a certain ideological perception of how the subject should relate to excrement," so that "none of these versions can be accounted for in purely utilitarian terms."[42] The toilet Grey invented for the workhouse took its own utilitarian mandate so far that it actually reflected a national stereotype of Irish incompetence and barbarity. Like the workhouse itself, the workhouse toilet was an example of the everyday humiliations suffered by the poor Irish within the British institutional infrastructure: lack of privacy ("four visitors at a time") and an assumed lack of competency ("not believing that domestics could be trusted to operate the device"). The intensity of Grey's focus on efficiency of function belies a stunning insensitivity to the human conditions he was creating. There may be, I am suggesting, more to MacHugh's contempt for utility than simply excess love for the aesthetic. If the Irish experience of the application of utility in their country were always so humiliating, why would he have any reason to think otherwise?

In fact the Irish experience of the principle of utility in the nineteenth century was, almost invariably, not only humiliating but also grandly, historically traumatic. The overriding sense, even and especially among those at the helm of the social engineering projects undertaken at the time, was that Ireland was a brutal experimental testing ground for the most unpopular kinds of public works. As Patrick Carroll-Burke recounts, "As early as the 1830s, the political economist William Nassau Senior explained to Alexis de Tocqueville how, in Ireland, 'Experiments are made . . . on so large a scale, and pushed to their extreme consequences . . . that they give us results as precious as those of Majendie.'"[43]

Evoking Majendie, Nassau made it clear: vivisection was the only apt analogy for the policies being implemented. In 1831 in Ireland, the British opened the doors to the very first public national school system in the world. These schools taught in English, forbade the use of Irish, and tended to eviscerate attendance at the established hedge schools where Irish was taught but where students were required to pay.[44] Generally the public schools embodied, far from the humane promise of universal literacy, Foucault's disciplinarity at its most gothic or its most panoptic extremes, though (it should be added) with a solid dose of old-fashioned corporeal cruelty leavening the mix.[45] Again, however, the triumph of utility—or in this case, of utilitarian public works—was felt by the Irish as further humiliation.

The year 1831 also saw the foundation of the Irish Board of Works, which at first undertook relatively useful projects, mainly involving drainage schemes, that were vast and, for the most part, quite successful. But during the Great Famine, the board undertook all sorts of schemes that were to become well-known emblems of and monuments to the mistreatment of the Irish at British hands. This was the era of the famous "famine roads" that "began nowhere and ended nowhere," of "walls round nothing" and "piers where no boats could land."[46] The board was acting on strict orders that famine relief be contingent on work, even when there was no real work to be done. The episode marked a complete emptying out of the concept of utility, insisting that relief take the form of utility without the function, giving rise to the surreal existence of previously unimaginable human-made artifacts: an ornamental road, for example. The wages paid on the works were extremely low in order to discourage people from buying anything but food for subsistence; but because this wage could be earned only on the works, the Irish were prevented from reaping any harvest from their land—a vicious circle that exacerbated the effects of the Famine and added further proof to the Irish case against utility. The Irish historian Roy Foster recounts that demands from local authorities for a "dole" system "to keep people working on their farms" were met with a searing refusal from the assistant secretary of the Treasury, Sir Charles Trevelyan, who called the proposal a "masterpiece of that system of social economy according to which the machine of society should be worked backwards, and the government should be made to support the people, instead of the people the government."[47] Meanwhile, the works supported neither.

Foster considers that the absolute futility of the works may be exaggerated, asserting less forcefully that the works were "poignant metaphors for a policy that was neither consistent nor effective, but which expressed economic beliefs held by the governing classes of both countries."[48] Exactly so: their ineffectiveness contributed greatly to the Irish underdeveloped identity and to the popular and literary fictions that it produced. And if some of the stories about the works were exaggerated, the Irish prison system, another utilitarian institution that haunted the Irish particularly in the Famine years, did overwhelming justice to the absurdities of the situation. So catastrophic were the effects of the Famine, and so weak the efforts to relieve them, that the prison became a sanctuary from starvation, a supplement to the Board of Works' workhouses that ultimately surpassed them in desirability if not capacity; prison rations were known to be better and more generous than those of the workhouse. The situation in Limerick in 1849 was so dire that "it took a court only three days to deal with twelve hundred cases, because nearly all the defendants pleaded guilty in hopes of being held in prison."[49] Cormac Ó Gráda, attempting to characterize the state of affairs in Ireland during the Famine, has dubbed these absurdist aspects of the public works an "upside-down world," a world in which, again in County Limerick, "two defendants who were set free were recommitted the next day for 'an attempt to break into jail,'" where a meal and a bed were assured.[50]

IDENTITY CRISIS

MacHugh's joke, along with the history of utilitarian projects and modernizing efforts in Ireland, reveals a stereotypical Irish attitude toward utilitarianism and modernization. The implementation of large-scale public works in Ireland during the Famine in the nineteenth century seems to have had very little correlation with Smith's benevolent and idealistic definition of the public works in *The Wealth of Nations*. The Irish Board of Works served instead the goals of assimilation, land consolidation, and capitalist reterritorialization. The years of the Famine, and the attendant mockery made of progressive notions of modernization, utility, and utilitarianism, produced a revolutionary figure whose outlook seemed to come straight out of Berman's description of the underdeveloped identity. John Mitchel's story of identity crisis is worth dwelling on for a moment here because it offers a suggestive counterpoint to my argument about Joyce. If Joyce wrote the postcolonial comedy of development through an imaginative renovation of the public utility, Mitchel wrote, in 1848, a gothic drama about the splitting apart of his identity along the seams of personal and economic development; that split, as Mitchel represents it, is a result of the failure of the public works in the Famine years. Joyce's comedy of postcolonial development stands, more than seventy years later, as a response to, and an effect of, Mitchel's colonial tragedy of development.

Mitchel's brand of romantic Irish nationalism formed itself ideologically in opposition to the operating agenda of the public works in Famine Ireland; he reviled the state and state intervention, championing instead a "utopic dream of a pre-capitalist rural society of independent yeoman farmers."[51] In essence, he wanted the nation without the state. The Famine cemented—understatement is hard to avoid here—a profound distrust of the state and the state's rhetoric of improvement, benevolence, and the common good. Mitchel is widely recognized as the figure who popularized the interpretation of the Famine as part of a deliberate and genocidal policy of the British government to "take care of" the Irish problem, to get rid of a recalcitrant population that was in the way—physically and culturally—of a massive push toward agricultural modernization, rationalization, and land consolidation. Here is the most commonly quoted version of Mitchel's accusation of genocide against the British Empire: "In every one of those years, '46, '47, and '48, Ireland was exporting to England, food to the value of fifteen million pounds sterling, and had on her own soil at each harvest, good and ample provision for double her own population, notwithstanding the potato blight."[52]

The historical record does not bear out Mitchel's claims. But those claims' popular cultural hold, just like Foster's "exaggeration" of the futility of the works, indexes quite accurately the extent to which the Irish imagination suffered the split between personal and economic development. After repeatedly publishing such claims in his newspaper the *United Irishman,* after being convicted in 1848 of sedition and sentenced to fourteen years' "transportation," and after boarding the prison hulk that was to take him to his exile in Tasmania, Mitchel began writing daily in his *Jail Journal.*[53] What he wrote there, according to Lloyd, "articulate[d] the fixation of Irish nationalism on the question of individual and national identity."[54] One of his earliest entries records his anxiety that his identity might slip away from him while under transportation and his hope that writing about it might prevent it: "This book will help to remind me of what I was, and how I came down hither, and so preserve the continuity of my thoughts, or personal identity, which, there is sometimes reason to fear, might slip away from me."[55]

Eventually, it does slip away. A few months into his sentence, while anchored off Bermuda, Mitchel gets sick and is "unable to write."[56] The next entry in the *Journal,* dated two months after the last one, begins: "Last night, as my double-goer and I—for I go double—sat in my cell . . . the awful shade took occasion to expostulate with me."[57] What ensues is a political debate between Mitchel and his double-goer in which Mitchel's romantic and revolutionary nationalism finally triumphs, by assertion and vehemence, over the double-goer's liberal utilitarian arguments. A decisive moment in their debate occurs when, as the double-goer tries to evoke the "great society," the impressive spectacle of global markets and global development, Mitchel counters with a ghastly vision of the Famine.

> *Doppelganger.*—Suppose all this is true. I, at least, cannot think, without pain, of the inevitable destruction of all this teeming life and healthy, glowing action. It is a bright and stirring scene.

> *The Ego.*—But look well at the background of this fine scene; and lo! The reeky shanks and yellow chapless skulls of Skibbereen!—and the ghosts of starved Hindoos in dusky millions.[58]

Soon after this culminating moment, Doppelganger flies out the porthole, never to return. Mitchel resolves his split personality by banishing his Doppelganger, which is to say that he banishes from his identity, as a psychic measure to "preserve the continuity" of that identity, Doppelganger's desire to believe in the public works, or to look to them for anything more than the utter futility they offered in the context of the Irish Famine. The coherence of Mitchel's identity is constructed in the first place by two key fictions: on the one hand, his assertion that the Irish, left to their own devices, had plenty of food to feed themselves during the potato blight, and on the other, his conviction that the public works were nothing but an imperialist modernizing drive hostile to the needs of the population. The drama of the split personality he records in his *Journal* is a rehearsal, a psychic repetition, of those fictions, designed to maintain and reinforce the partition within the underdeveloped identity. And these complementary fictions are what make it possible, effectively and affectively, to banish any expectation of relief, help, support, or hope from the public works. Given such premises, the only hope left for personal development comes from the "utopic dream of a pre-capitalist rural society of independent yeoman farmers." I don't want to suggest that in Mitchel's case—he is writing, after all, from a prison ship—such a procedure is anything but imminently reasonable. But from within Mitchel's dilemma, in his ingenious solution to the split in the underdeveloped identity, we can see the origins of the hatred of utility, its peculiar strength and its "special intensity" arising from the trauma of the Irish experience during the Famine.

The hatred of utility that came out of the Famine era proved extraordinarily durable. For a revolutionary like Mitchel, it resulted in the ideal of an agricultural idyll. For Irish writers, it resulted in a valorization of the aesthetic at the expense of utility, the construction and fortification of a conceptual divide and a conceptual hierarchy. On the political front, that opposition was one of the first things that the 1922 Irish Free State would have to face up to, or face down. If, writing from the catastrophe of the Famine in 1848, it made perfect sense to construct an Irish identity in this way, by 1922 such an identity might have outlasted, to put it a little uncomfortably, its utility. And if we take Mitchel as a great exemplar of that identitarian construct, then we might think of James Joyce's *Ulysses* as its equally reasonable and necessary undoing, in the literary sphere, on the eve of the birth of the first Irish state.

THE USEFUL ARTS

Mitchel's identity crisis and his solution to that crisis stand in direct opposition, seventy years later, to Joyce's literary solution to the problem of the Irish underdeveloped identity. Mitchel reviled the public works because he was witness to—and victim of—the historical nadir of their deeply flawed attempts at managing the common good. Joyce renovated the image of utility in his work because he stood at a historical moment when an emergent Irish state, and thus an emergent Irish definition of the common good, that is to say, of Irish utility, was for the first time historically realizable. The project, given the Irish experience of modernization, would be enormously difficult; it would require tremendous imaginative resources and several successive revisions. I trace many of them in the next chapter. But Joyce faced more than just the opposition of the Irish underdeveloped identity. The high modernist establishment was not much more well disposed to utility than the Irish national imaginary. While the networked society and the advancements of town planning did make an impact on modernist thinking about the social and its relationship to high art, that thinking still worked fundamentally on the antinomy between the merely useful and the transcendently aesthetic.

Again, we return to the watercloset. Joyce was famous for introducing the toilet into high modernist literature. But he was not the first to introduce the toilet to high modernist art. In 1917 Marcel Duchamp displayed his Dadaist "readymades," one of which, entitled *Fountain,* was a porcelain urinal placed on a pedestal. One wonders how this would have struck Professor MacHugh, whose joke depends on the inviolable boundary between utility and the aesthetic. What happens when a utilitarian piece of material culture is ripped from its context, and in this case the connections that define its use and its nature, and rudely presented to the world of art? Stripped of utility, boldly defying its everyday relegation to the realm of the forgettable—the unthought known—the urinal obnoxiously and absurdly claims our full attention as an object of aesthetic contemplation and, whether ironically or not, of aesthetic appreciation. One is forcibly reminded here of the Famine "roads to nowhere," artifacts of the Board of Works whose existence confounded, like Duchamp's fountain, the boundary between utility and the aesthetic.

Not all modernists were up for this game of scatological—or utilitarian—show-and-tell. Virginia Woolf, who acknowledged the worth of *Ulysses* to the extent that she disavowed its potty humor and Joyce's Irishness, published a kind of response to *Ulysses* in 1925 with *Mrs. Dalloway,* in which the toilet was graciously excluded from representation: a refined version of the *Ulysses* conceits (stream of consciousness and the daylong duration) that shied away from *Ulysses*'s scatological sensationalism.[59] Of course Woolf's achievements in *Mrs. Dalloway* amounted to a great deal more than that, and Joyce's marginality in terms of his class and nationality, and his advantage in terms of gender, may have enabled him to do things with sex and plumbing in his writing that Woolf could not. But the watercloset was nevertheless closer to *Mrs. Dalloway* than we might suppose: "Woolf was thrilled," writes Victoria Rosner, "when the royalties from *Mrs. Dalloway* allowed her to provide her Sussex home, Monk's House, with its first indoor facilities in the form of

two lavatories and a bathroom."[60] Woolf's book, which purposefully set
out to show that one could, and should—contrary to Joyce's implicit rationale in *Ulysses*—write modern life without having to mention the un-
mentionable watercloset, ended up writing the watercloset into Woolf's
modern life.

Bruce Robbins has shown that Woolf was, in her other writings, engaged with and influenced by the expanding network of twentieth-century
public utilities and the discourse of town planning. She was very aware
of the potential for public utilities to transform daily life and to alleviate
some forms of human misery. But they did not form a part of her literary vision. Likewise, Ezra Pound conceded, although much more crankily
and grudgingly, that the networked society was a useful piece of technological progress: "Some one ought to be employed to look after our traffic
and sewage, one grants that. But a superintendence of traffic and sewage
is not the sole function of man. Certain stupid and honest people should,
doubtless, be delegated for the purpose. There politics ends [for] the enlightened man."[61] Such was the general tenor of the modernist attitude toward public utilities: useful, of course, but excluded from the artists' domain of modernist aesthetics.

The hierarchy of utility and the aesthetic within the modernism of
Woolf and Pound also characterized the literary modernism of the Irish
Revival. But as I have shown, the hierarchy was differently configured in
the Irish case; it had a "special resonance" and a "special intensity" owing
to Ireland's traumatic colonial experience of modernization during the
Famine. It is a hierarchy whose cognitive effects can still be felt in the
construction of the discipline of Irish studies, where, as Carroll-Burke
points out, the focus is almost always literary: "Books have been written
about 'Representing Ireland,' 'Writing Ireland,' and 'Inventing Ireland,' but
in every case the focus has been literary."[62] Andrew Kincaid, in his recent
book *Postcolonial Dublin,* has made a similar charge: "The field of Irish
Studies has long been dominated by a literary paradigm. Critical interpretations of Irish writing, most notably studies of the great modernists—
Yeats, Joyce, Beckett, and Synge—still make up the majority of books
published every year in the field. Even the current generation of leading
Irish critics, such as Declan Kiberd, Terry Eagleton, and Seamus Deane,
with their awareness of contemporary postcolonial theory and cultural

studies, have continued to focus almost exclusively on literature, poetry, and drama."[63]

Carroll-Burke and Kincaid are both right about the dominance in Irish studies of literary inquiry, although this is changing, and perhaps has already changed a great deal, in no small part because of their efforts. But while I agree with them I also think that the reason the field of Irish studies overemphasized the literary for so long is the same reason that Irish nationalists and Irish modernists struggled with the antinomy of utility and the aesthetic: the twin legacies of colonial modernization and the racialized discourse of the poetic Celt. Thus my project is an attempt to reread Irish modernism as an ambivalent and protracted struggle to forge an Irish modernity in defiance of the weight of both legacies. Though my work—which is centered on Joyce after all—might seem superficially to resemble the kind of literary studies that Carroll-Burke and Kincaid take to task for what they ignore, I intend a synthesis that places Ireland's material and engineering cultures in dialogue with Ireland's literary cultures. My book follows Joyce, O'Brien, Johnston, and Chamoiseau in seeking to trouble, and to find trouble in, the grounds of opposition between engineering and literary cultures. I wish to incorporate into my literary analysis Kincaid's and Carroll-Burke's insights about Ireland's "engineering cultures" and to show that Irish writers, especially those writing in and around the foundation of the Irish Free State, were charged to reformulate the relationship between their literature and the statecraft that was newly demanded of them. If the Irish literati were charged de facto with the task of imagining the nation through their writing, then what would be their role in imagining the new state? Such a task called for a rethinking of that old stereotyped opposition between utility and the aesthetic through literary and—following O'Connor's argument in *Haunted English*—specifically generic invention. For Joyce, and later in the larger postcolonial context for Chamoiseau, that rethinking took the form of a postcolonial comedy of development; for O'Brien, it took the form of an allegory of the nation-state; and for Denis Johnston, it took the form of what I call—after a Soviet joke—an electrifiction.

Reconfiguring the antinomy between utility and the aesthetic was one of the imperatives of Irish modernism. It was an imperative that arose distinctively from Ireland's colonial relationship to England. Joe Cleary makes

the point in the more familiar terms of modernization and modernism—
as opposed to utility and the aesthetic—when he suggests that the systematic underdevelopment of Ireland during colonial rule was a significant if partial cause of the astonishing innovation, impact, and even sheer
quantity of Irish modernist literary production. "The experimental thrust
of Irish modernism," he contends, "was essentially linguistic" and "con-
centrated in literature."[64] Emer Nolan corroborates Cleary's point when
she says that Ireland's modernism was "precocious by comparison with
developments elsewhere" and, curiously, "almost entirely confined to
literature."[65] That confinement was, according to Cleary, "partly . . . a response to a sense of linguistic alienation in English aggravated by the loss
of Gaelic Irish culture." But it was also

> partly due to the fact that literature is less immediately dependent
> on other large scale political and economic institutional supports and
> constraints than other art forms, such as architecture, sculpture or
> cinema, for example. But if its more artisan mode of production was
> one of the things that may have allowed Irish literary modernism to
> flourish, this also inevitably brought restrictions as well, since litera-
> ture cannot so immediately or spectacularly translate its visions into
> the everyday lifeworld of the masses as these other, more public media
> do. Because it was so confined to high literature, Irish modernism was
> inevitably, at a time when the bulk of the population had access only
> to primary education, largely a modernism of the intelligentsia and,
> as such, destined to remain rather detached from the everyday lives of
> the broader Irish public.[66]

Irish modernism distinguishes itself by two characteristics: its precocious-
ness, and its restriction to literature. Cleary offers two reasons for these
defining characteristics: linguistic alienation and the lack of political and
economic institutional supports. Cleary is certainly right to observe that
Irish modernism was "largely a modernism of the intelligentsia" and that
it might have been "destined to remain rather detached from the everyday lives of the broader Irish public." But I wish to add to Cleary's argument that the lack of access to certain kinds of infrastructure in Ireland—
capital-intensive and technologically determined modern media, along

with other "large scale political and economic institutional supports"—
led Irish modernists to examine in their work the humble, though of
course highly technological, capital-intensive, and imminently modern,
realm of the public utility and of infrastructure. In doing so they attempted, with however limited success, to create a vision of the "everyday lifeworld of the masses." Such a vision required linguistic and formal
innovation and lent its energy to the remarkable productions of Irish
literary modernism. The predicament is common to many colonial and
postcolonial literatures, and leads me to see—following Cleary and other
critics—Irish modernism in particular and even modernism in general
not as the exclusive product of metropolitan modernity but rather as "a
culture of incomplete modernization" produced from peripheral zones
of uneven development.[67]

The "special resonance" in Irish modernism of Berman's "underdeveloped identity" resides both in the loss of the Irish language as a result of
colonial modernization and in the restriction of Irish modernism to literary and linguistic outlets as a result of Ireland's uneven development.
It is easy to see Berman's "volatile mixture" of shame and pride at work
in the political posturing of key founders of the Irish Revival in the last
decade of the nineteenth century. At one extreme stood Douglas Hyde,
the founder of the language revival movement, whose thought, according to the historian Joseph Lee, was governed by an absolute "equation of
modernization with anglicisation."[68] "The whole infrastructure of modernization appalled him," Lee asserts, "and he assumed that the Irish could
not survive in a modernized world."[69] The combination of shame and
pride, and the consequent conceptual schism between Irish tradition and
English modernity, led Hyde to take up some absurd causes, among them
a campaign to rid Ireland of English trousers in favor of purportedly Irish
kneebreeches. "In his zeal for kneebreeches," Lee chides, "[Hyde] came
close to proclaiming 'down with trousers' as the battle cry of his brave new
Ireland."[70] In "failing to distinguish the specifically English from the generally modern," Hyde wedded Irishness to tradition and to antimoder-
nity, conforming, like the fictional MacHugh, to an Irish racial stereotype
whose origin lay, ironically, in British colonialism.[71]

Unlike Hyde, Patrick Pearse, writing in the years just before the 1916
Easter Rising he helped lead in Dublin, made a sharp distinction between

Anglicization and modernization. In his speeches and writings he encouraged armed rebellion and independence from Great Britain, and in a clear political departure from Hyde's ideas he called for a specifically Irish form of modernization through the establishment of a modern Irish state. Between June 1913 and February 1914 he wrote a series of articles entitled "From a Hermitage" for the newspaper of the Irish Republican Brotherhood, *Irish Freedom,* where he outlined his goals for political independence.

> A free Ireland would not, and could not, have hunger in her fertile vales and squalor in her cities. Ireland has resources to feed five times her population; a free Ireland will make those resources available. A free Ireland would drain the bogs, would harness the rivers, would plant the wastes, would nationalize the railways and the waterways, would improve agriculture, would protect fisheries, would foster industries, would promote commerce, would diminish extravagant expenditure (as on needless judges and policemen), would beautify the cities, would educate the workers, (and also the non-workers, who stand in dire need of it), would, in short, govern herself as no external power—nay, not even a government of angels and archangels—could govern her.[72]

In Pearse's assertion of Irish self-sufficiency ("Ireland has resources to feed five times her population") we hear an echo of John Mitchel's inflated accusation against the British Empire. But from that familiar romantic nationalist premise, Pearse nevertheless argues for a modern Irish state rather than an Irish rural idyll. His ideal, encompassing the "common good" of public works—drainage, education, reclamation of wastelands, town planning—was an imagining of Irish modernity and Irish utility that, in coupling Irishness and modernization, broke through the stereotype of Irish backwardness and its inverted nationalist image, a fantasy of archaic Irish tradition and rural simplicity. Pearse's was an "alternative modernity" that differentiates itself from our current theoretical conception of "alternative modernity" because it was, like Faust, deeply invested in the promise of development while at the same time insistent that such development need not capitulate to the modern state system.

Lee identifies Pearse as an unstable but "honest" thinker, "frequently more passionate than profound," who "failed to create a synthesis between his conflicting ideals" and whose "non-sequitors [sic] spring from logical confusion, not from ideological expediency."[73] However, Lee concludes, "part of Pearse's fascination in the broader context" resides in his attempt to synthesize modernization with romantic revolutionary nationalism,[74] whereas most Irish nationalists, like Mitchel and Hyde, treated modernization as merely another sinister aspect of Anglicization. But rather than analyzing the aporias that haunt their revolutionary thinking as a problem of individual intellectual eccentricity or even weakness, another way of looking would comprehend Mitchel's exaggerations, Hyde's war on trousers, and Pearse's non sequiturs as symptoms of the very same racial stereotype by which MacHugh traps himself, albeit humorously, in a false opposition between utility and the aesthetic.

It is to this legacy of Irish thinking about the (im)possibility of an Irish modernity that Joyce addresses himself in *Ulysses*, as I argue in chapter 2, and that leads him to the public utility as a lever for articulating a new relationship between utility and the aesthetic, and thus between modernization and modernism. But many other Irish modernists before and after Joyce would turn their attention to the public utility as an ambivalent emblem of the good society. Oscar Wilde's 1891 "The Soul of Man under Socialism" offers his social vision for the role of the public utility as a "slavery of the machine":

> Human slavery is wrong, insecure, and demoralising. On mechanical slavery, on the slavery of the machine, the future of the world depends. And when scientific men are no longer called upon to go down to a depressing East End and distribute bad cocoa and worse blankets to starving people, they will have delightful leisure in which to devise wonderful and marvellous things for their own joy and the joy of every one else. There will be great storages of force for every city, and for every house if required, and this force man will convert into heat, light, or motion, according to his needs. Is this Utopian? A map of the world that does not include Utopia is not worth even glancing at, for it leaves out the one country at which Humanity is always landing. And when Humanity lands there, it looks out, and, seeing a better country, sets sail. Progress is the realisation of Utopias.[75]

Wilde recognizes the revolutionary potential of "great storages of force for every city" but falls victim, like MacHugh's joke in *Ulysses* and Pound's rude dismissal in *The Egoist,* to the old opposition. These public utilities of which Wilde obliquely speaks are for him nothing more than slaves that, once put to work, are to be studiously ignored in the interest of cultivating the artistic genius of every individual. A forgone conclusion here is that the existence of such a revolutionary form of material culture would have absolutely no effect on the cultural production of such liberated subjects. Infrastructure and aesthetics remain utterly distinct, distant domains, the former subordinated to the latter. Wholly committed to the aestheticism of the Victorian decadent and the Irish writer, Wilde sees only human slaves replaced with mechanical ones. The indistinction, to go back to Adam Smith, between public works that anchor the great society (machines as slaves) and public works that define the greatness of the great society (works of art) is locked down and made absolutely distinct in the categorical hierarchy of utility and the aesthetic. The utopian potential that inheres in opening up that distinction to questioning—a potential that remains in Smith and that Joyce takes up later—is lost.

After Joyce, Samuel Beckett offered up his own, oblique version of MacHugh's watercloset joke in *Ulysses,* through the nameless narrator of his short story "First Love." Though written first in French in 1946, "First Love" is set in the Dublin of 1931, in the middle of the Free State era. Standing in his lover's apartment after she has invited him to stay there with her, the narrator makes some awkward attempts at conversation: "You have no current? I said. No she said, but I have running water and gas. Ha, I said, you have gas."[76] And with that witticism hovering awfully between them, he proceeds to barricade himself into her living room by throwing out all the furniture excepting the sofa, which he has turned toward the wall the better to isolate himself. "Do you know where the convenience is? She said. She was right. I was forgetting. To relieve oneself in bed is enjoyable at the time, but soon a source of discomfort. Give me a chamber-pot, I said."[77] Lulu's apartment does not have a bathroom. The conveniences must be down the hall, or up the stairs, but they are common to the building. The narrator riffs, here, on Joyce's *A Portrait of the Artist as a Young Man*: "When you wet the bed first it is warm then it gets cold."[78] And the passage sets up a string of punning associations with plumbing. One of them is a pun in the French that plays across French and English: "Se soulager dans son lit, cela fait plaisir sur le moment, mais après on est incommodé." *Incommodé:* uncomfortable, but also, if we translate to the English *commode,* "a chamber utensil; a close-stool." We arrive at the curious possibility of translating something like "To relieve oneself in bed is a source of not having a chamber pot." This seems a logically upside-down version of "Not having a chamber pot is a source of relieving oneself in bed," which actually makes some sense but goes against the strict chronological ordering of the French version, which puts being *incommodé* after, or *après,* relieving oneself in bed.

One thing we can say for certain is that Beckett is asking us to lift the public utility out of the realm of the unthought known and to think, perhaps excruciatingly, about what all this business about chamber pots and toilets means. And to the extent that *commode* can also be a colloquial English word for "toilet"—that is, a toilet in the sense of a fixture connected to the public utilities—we can conjecture that it is Beckett's narrator's pleasure to be without one, to be *incommodé,* as it were, una-commodated and, from the English version, un-convenienced. Which is to say that he rejects the provision of public utilities, recreating in Lulu's apartment his outdoor, vagabond existence as a self-imposed condition of indoor existential homelessness. The explanation for this resides in a complicated mixture of Beckett's modernism and of his background as part of the Protestant Dublin middle class. It has to do, as Seán Kennedy has observed, with the Protestant middle class's dismay and disdain for the avowedly Catholic Irish Free State, its actions and institutions, and the consequent disenfranchisement and marginalization of the Protestant minority.[79] The narrator is in this sense stateless and, as such, devolves into his own feral state: hence the reference to Stephen's predomesticated childhood bed-wetting in *A Portrait of the Artist as a Young Man.* The public utilities in Lulu's apartment and in her building are no longer his public utilities. The Free State had made him homeless, or, homeland-less, and he refuses the provision of public utilities because he feels excluded from what he understands as the state's definition of the common good. This understanding already adds some dimension to the narrator's initial aggressive outburst, "Ha! You have gas." Following Kennedy's argument that Beckett's vagabond characters are the imaginative result of Beckett's alienation from Ireland after the revolution, in "First Love" we can see one instance where that alienation takes the form of the narrator's refusal to avail himself of the new state's public works, a very primal kind of protest. In chapter 4, I elaborate this theme at length in the context of the state's nationalizing hydroelectric scheme and Denis Johnston's minority reaction—less primal than Beckett's but nevertheless directed precisely against the public utilities—to the transfer of power that the scheme entailed.

In 1928 Elizabeth Bowen published another, and entirely more genteel, protest against the Free State that directed itself at the public utilities. In an essay for the *Saturday Review of Literature* entitled "Modern Lighting," she perfectly recapitulated the split between utility and the aesthetic that haunted the Irish imaginary. "Living," she writes, "is less that affair of function we were forced to suspect, more an affair of aesthetics." She draws an example from the aesthetic arrangements of domestic lighting. "We can arrange our lighting. . . . The response from a light-switch, the bringing in of a candle is acute, personal as a perception."[80] Bowen's linkage of lighting with "an affair of aesthetics," and her assertion that "the response from a light switch . . . is . . . personal as perception," came a little less than a year before the Free State's Shannon Scheme went online and began supplying electricity for the first time. The media storm surrounding the Scheme, and the propaganda campaign the Electricity Supply Board mounted in support of it, were so ubiquitous a part of Irish cultural life in 1928 that it is almost unthinkable that Bowen was not aware of it. And I think it very likely that she had it in mind when she wrote "Modern Lighting," and that her essay was a response to it. Later in the essay, Bowen meditates on "Irish cities where we are naïve with dignity," and where "incandescence still blare[s] unchecked and electricity frowns boldly." Such meditations are directly opposed to her earlier notion of domestic lighting as "personal as perception." It is as if she means to defend the personal, the domestic, and the aesthetic from the harsh, blaring, frowning encroachments of the Catholic Irish masses, no longer figures of a dark premodern Irish past but now, in the time of the Free State, harbingers of a vulgar hypermodern future. As much as she poses the aesthetic against utility—her term is *function*— she poses the personal against modern development. And it is all figured and played out as the stakes of how one thinks about "modern lighting." The article is the first work of nonfiction that Bowen ever published, and Allan Hepburn points out that it is "somewhat overwritten."[81] As the whole thrust of the piece seems to be about protecting the personal and the aesthetic from the intrusions of development, it is overwritten for reasons that supersede her supposed inexperience and instead go deep into the Irish imaginary. The rest of Bowen's article explores the representation of light in literature, where she appreciates, among other things, the "recurrent crépuscule" that characterizes "the peculiar horror of Emma Bovary's fight for emotional survival." Twilight is indeed a fine figure for Ireland in 1928 as well, when the sun had already set on the Ascendancy and the Shannon Scheme had not quite yet begun to illuminate a new dispensation of power.

In Irish literary modernism, there is, as I have shown here, a limited but substantial engagement with and thematization of the public utility. That engagement resulted from the convergence of three factors: first, the burgeoning discourse of town planning, and the consequent proliferation of networked utilities that emerged at the turn of the twentieth century, whose nature and consequences were contested in part on the terrain of literary modernism generally; second, the special intensity of the Irish version of the underdeveloped identity, which raised particular objections to public works projects in light of their traumatic historical failures in nineteenth-century colonial Ireland; and third, the transfer of political power from the British imperial state to the Irish Free State, which resulted in a battle for political legitimacy that played out in large part through the provision of basic amenities. Thus the Irish modernists addressed themselves to the public utility, unevenly and with divergent ideas about how to relate them to their own work.

I see James Joyce in this context as a singular literary figure. Undoing the opposition between utility and the aesthetic allowed him to merge the otherwise incommensurable trajectories of personal and economic development and, despite his sincere and reasonable doubts, to hope weakly for the future of the Irish Free State. To borrow and to qualify a phrase from Berman, *Ulysses* may be the first postcolonial comedy of development. In Joyce public works and literary acts, while certainly not forged into an identity, enter into new relations with each other, unencumbered by their former opposition. Joyce liberated the public utility from its prison in the devalued discourse of utility by introducing the utility into literature and aesthetics. In *Ulysses* the public utilities are not treated as slaves as in Wilde, insulted as in Pound, mocked and boycotted as in Beckett, ignored as in Woolf, or snubbed as in Bowen. Joyce's public utilities are scenes of wonder in and for themselves, and they become occasions for remarkable experiments and innovations in narrative technique. If, as we saw, Wilde imagined that the public utilities would be the substitute slaves of turn of the century modernity, Joyce went further to imagine—through a renovation of the image of the public utility—a modernism without slaves.

PART I

WATER

CHAPTER

AQUACITY: PLUMBING
CONSCIOUSNESS IN JOYCE'S DUBLIN

TWO

*For the time being we have to settle for knowing less about
consciousness than novelists pretend to know.*
                                        —David Lodge, *Thinks . . .*

The sewer is the conscience of the city.
                                        —Victor Hugo, *Les Misérables*

In the introductory paragraph to his chapter on *Ulysses* in *Modern Epic:
The World-System from Goethe to García Márquez,* Franco Moretti in-
vokes Carol Reed's 1949 film *The Third Man* to set up his meditation on
the legacy and importance of the literary technique known as stream of
consciousness:[1]

> In a celebrated *film noir* from 1949, *The Third Man,* a middle-aged
> American writer finds himself unwillingly caught up in the mysteries
> of postwar Vienna. Amid vanishing witnesses, appointments on the

Prater Wheel, a semi-lynching, and shoot-outs in the sewers, something else happens to the protagonist: one evening, on returning to his
hotel, he is thrust into a large black limousine and borne at top speed,
through streets filled with sinister shadows, to a room full of people . . .
patiently waiting for his lecture on the modern novel. At the conclusion of a painful performance, a young man with an anguished expression raises his hand and asks the first question: "Tell us, Mr. Martin, do you believe in the 'stream of consciousness'?" It is clearly the
worst moment of the entire scene—Joseph Cotten is dumbstruck, the
director of the British Cultural Centre is acutely embarrassed, a number of ladies with grotesque hats get up and walk out—and bears witness to the aura of legend surrounding the stream of consciousness,
even outside avant-garde circles.[2]

In what follows, Moretti outlines a vision of the stream of consciousness in *Ulysses* as a product of life under commodity capitalism; as a dis-
tracted reaction to the constant stimulus of advertising in urban environments; and finally as a representation not so much of consciousness per
se as of what Freud calls the "preconscious." This is to think of stream of
consciousness and commodity capitalism as a very nearly seamless unity.
I want to argue, through an alternative reading of *The Third Man* here
and in an extended argument about Joyce in what follows, that there is
more to the story, something that escapes—if only to a limited extent—
the logic of capitalist modernity: public works.

Strictly speaking, Moretti is no doubt correct to call the young man's
question about the stream of consciousness "the worst moment of the
entire scene." But that is only because another and far worse moment actually goes unrepresented in the scene, since Martins's lecture poignantly
takes place off camera.[3] Instead, the action cuts to Popescu as he plans to
intercept Martins at the lecture. It is only through Martins's clear lack of
preparation at the beginning of the lecture, and through the visible discomfort and boredom of the audience at its end, that we are made to
understand that Holly Martins has prepared nothing to say about the
novel; does not want to give a lecture on the novel (he has, after all, better things to do, like solve murders and fight conspiracies); has in fact no
thoughts at all about the novel, despite being himself a novelist; and, as

a consequence, has delivered what must have been one of the worst lectures ever delivered on the subject of the novel. In a way, it would have been instructive and possibly even amusing to witness the worst lecture on the modern novel ever delivered. Perhaps Martins's lecture is simply too embarrassing, or too boring, to portray. Or perhaps the whole point of not showing Martins's lecture is to elevate it through absence to an unassailable exemplariness; no one may say, by way of personal experience of other, more terrible lectures, "I have seen worse," because there is simply no point of comparison. One can only imagine the stalling, the filler words and fidgeting and sweating and, above all, the awkward silences of that lecture. Nothing, in other words, could be more different from the stream of consciousness than a failed public lecture stymied by self-conscious doubt and embarrassment. In fact, there may be no better example of the exact opposite of the stream of consciousness. And for Holly Martins, there may be no better proof that his stream of consciousness doesn't exist, given the show-stopping embarrassment that causes him to have nothing at all to say. That is why the young man's question—"Do you believe, Mr. Martins, in the stream of consciousness?"—is significant in the way it is posed, because for Martins, in his position of extreme embarrassment, the experience of the moment is the experience of his mind's utter blankness. His answer, if he could think of it, would have to be "no," or at least "not anymore."

The heart of darkness that is Martins's lecture begs to be filled with narrative content; and it is, in the climactic chase scene through the sewers of Vienna. Running for his life through the sewer system, Martins's alter ego, Harry Lime, confronts, at a pivotal point in the final chase, a massive intersection of tunnels and pipes and spillways. He stops, confused and terrified. Sound is coming from everywhere and nowhere, amplified echoes of German words so distorted with repetition and reverb as to be incomprehensible, language subtracted of meaning but filled with paranoid fury, language as pure threat. At one point it is almost possible to believe we understand the word *hallucinate*—or is that itself a hallucination? This linguistic overload corresponds, I think, to the film's determined silence elsewhere, precisely, that is, the silence surrounding Holly Martins's missing lecture on the modern novel. If from Martins's lecture we might reasonably have expected some excursus on the stream of consciousness, instead the film gives us the stream of consciousness radically externalized in the sewer, no longer a subjective experience of one's own thoughts but rather the disembodied voices of others impinging on—and blocking—the thoughts of Harry Lime as he tries to think through his escape. The situation for Lime and for Martins is the same: the impossibility of thought and the consequent impossibility of real action (in Martins's case, speech; in Lime's, movement). Both of them are reduced to dumb, scared, cornered animals by situations that seem utterly different but are by the film's logic drawn into analogy, if not identity.

Such emptying out of thought might at first seem merely a confirmation of Moretti's argument concerning the stream of consciousness, in the sense that he understands it as always being in a presentist relation to external stimuli, especially advertising. But *The Third Man,* unlike Moretti, takes us into the sewer, and it is there that new dimensions of the stream of consciousness are revealed. We remember that in the film Lime conceals his underground movement in the sewer by entering through an advertising kiosk set over a manhole. He thus seems to have "disappeared" until Martins and Major Calloway discover the deception, not by reading the advertisements, but by moving the advertising kiosk out of the way. Advertising is a feint that protects Lime, and the sewer, from detection: a false lead. In the same way, the stream of consciousness eludes explanation if we focus too narrowly on advertising and on commodity culture; we have to look in the sewer, which is to say we have to look more to public works, for its sources. To consider the sewer as the antecedent for the stream of consciousness is, once one thinks of it, almost commonsensical, since to do so is really only to literalize the stream of consciousness for a modern urban setting, where there are few streams other than those in the sewer and where the sewer flows everywhere, underground and unseen. It is to see the extent to which the urban infrastructure impinges on the structures of urban subjectivity. The final question put to Martins by a member of the audience concerns James Joyce: "Mr. James Joyce, now, where would you put him? . . . In what category?" The answer is delivered for Martins—who can't answer—by the film's logic: in the sewer, in the waterways of the city's public works. In the reading of Joyce that follows, I will be concerned to show why, and how, that answer is borne out in Joyce's fictions.

FROM SMITHY TO SEWER

Quel peut être le rôle des chercheurs la-dedans? Celui de travailler
à une invention collective des structures collectives d'invention.
—Pierre Bourdieu, "Pour un savoir engagé"

This chapter argues that Joyce accorded special status to public works in his fictions. I give evidence from three of Joyce's texts: *Ulysses, A Portrait of the Artist as a Young Man,* and "The Dead." I approach these texts in reverse chronological order because I see Joyce's thinking about public works taking on a kind of maturity in *Ulysses,* and the emergent role of public works in his earlier texts is best explicated by looking back from that vantage point. Many critics have pointed to Joyce's fascination with modern technology. My aim is to bring together criticism concerned with issues of technology in Joyce and criticism concerned to excavate a "postcolonial Joyce," in order to show that Joyce's interest in technology was ultimately in the service of, in the well-known final lines of *A Portrait,* "forg[ing] in the smithy of [his] soul the uncreated conscience of [his] race."[4] The Joyce who wrote *Ulysses* finally discarded the metaphor of the smithy—and thus the implicit metaphor of the sword—in favor of public works. "Forging" national consciousness gives way after *A Portrait* to "engineering" national consciousness. This metaphorical movement reveals Joyce as not only modernist but also modernizing, a feature that distinguishes his work from that of many of his modernist peers, as well as his peers within the context of Irish national literature. As an Irish writer, however, Joyce was keenly aware of the complicity between colonialism and modernization. His version of modernization, therefore, much like his version of modernism, is eccentric and strains to find a way to reconcile the technological progress of modernity with a vision of the common good. Public works, I argue, are Joyce's answer to the depredations of modernity, as well as his affirmation of modernity's utopian promise. Because Joyce sought a position that could be anticolonial and at the same time modernizing, I read *Ulysses* as a distinctive generic variant of the novel that I called, in chapter 1, the postcolonial comedy of development.

In the introduction to their coedited volume *Semicolonial Joyce,* Marjorie Howes and Derek Attridge define the frontier not only for Joyce studies but for postcolonial theory in general by pointing to the impasses and repetitions that, in both fields, have amounted to a kind of stalemate. Perhaps the two most important problems they locate are, first, the limits of "resistance" as defined by postcolonial theory and, second, the culturalist bias of postcolonial theory itself, whose "home" tends to be the literature department as opposed, say, to the economics or political science departments. "[The] dangers [of] a certain fetishizing of 'resistance' [are that] recovery can become the reductive goal of every reading, a related and equally limiting dependence on an opposition between resistance and complicity, and a relative neglect of the massive material power and effects of imperial structures in favor of an overly textualist reading of their instabilities."[5] And as to the "culturalism of postcolonial studies," the field "tends to privilege culture (rather than, for example, economics or military force) as both an instrument of imperial domination and a vehicle of resistance to it," leading to "various forms of Irish exceptionalism."[6]

My intention here is to focus on the issue of public works in *Ulysses* as a way of responding to Howes and Attridge's critique of certain postcolonial reading practices. *Ulysses*'s consistent recourse to the theme of public works reveals Joyce making a stronger argument for the Irish state as a political structure than is usually asserted in the field of Joyce criticism. Joyce, we might say, is less a nationalist than a statist, and he has some very specific things to say about the state through his consideration of the social infrastructure of the city of Dublin. *Ulysses* posits a utopian vision, wholly distinct from Bloom's or Stephen's, that is rooted in the "material power" not so much of "imperial structures" as of state structures and infrastructures; to coin a clumsy paradox, we might call this Joyce's pragmatic utopianism, which is related to what I understand Pierre Bourdieu invoking in my epigraph: "the collective invention of collective structures of invention."[7] The crux of Bourdieu's formulation is that the utopian culturalist turn ("collective invention")—in order to be effective in the political sphere—*must* be grounded in realized social and political structures that must, in turn, be *re*invented. His imperative is emphatically not to invent utopias outside currently existing political structures but to imagine those utopias from within; attempts at political thinking outside these structures are doomed to ineffectiveness and damned to the limbo of the avant-garde of a putative "culture." Although *Ulysses* has always historically been understood as a leading member of such an avant-garde, we can see some clear signs that Joyce's novel is indeed a serious thinking-over of this idea of what constitutes a "collective structure of invention." Joyce's answer, his understanding of a collective structure of invention, may hinge first and foremost on his championing of cosmopolitan literary modernism as an institution.[8] But I want to point to another possibility: namely that for Joyce the project of culture and the project of engineering cultures come together in *Ulysses* at a moment in the text that has recently been rethought as a narrative crux.

COLLECTIVE STRUCTURES OF INVENTION

The nineteenth century: singular fusion of individualistic and collectivist tendencies. Unlike virtually every previous age, it labels all actions "individualistic" (ego, nation, art) while subterraneanly, in despised everyday domains, it necessarily furnishes, as in a delirium, the elements for a collective formation. . . . With this raw material, we must occupy ourselves. . . . In the nineteenth century, construction plays the role of the subconscious.

— Sigfried Giedion, *Building in France*

Now, postcolonial theory's focus on "resistance" may obscure its vision when it comes to something so seemingly boring—as Fredric Jameson calls it—as public utilities or pragmatic utopianism. And this myopia may go a long way to explaining why these things remain largely unexamined even as they are being noticed, which is why I want to begin my discussion at the point where at least two other prominent studies of *Ulysses* leave off, with a much-quoted passage from the "Ithaca" chapter:

What did Bloom do at the range?

He removed the saucepan to the left hob, rose and carried the iron kettle to the sink in order to tap the current by turning the faucet to let it flow.

Did it flow?

Yes. From Roundwood reservoir in county Wicklow of a cubic capacity of 2400 million gallons, percolating through a subterranean aqueduct of filter mains of single and double pipeage constructed at an initial plant cost of £5 per linear yard by way of the Dargle, Rathdown, Glen of the Downs and Callowhill to the 26 acre reservoir at Stillorgan, a distance of 22 statute miles, and thence, through a system of relieving tanks, by a gradient of 250 feet to the city boundary at Eustace bridge, upper Leeson street, though from prolonged summer drouth and daily supply of 12 1/2 million gallons the water had fallen below the sill of the overflow weir for which reason the borough surveyor and waterworks engineer, Mr Spencer Harty, C.E., on the instructions of the waterworks committee had prohibited the use of municipal water for purposes other than those of consumption (envisaging the possibility of recourse being had to the impotable water of the Grand and Royal canals as in 1893) particularly as the South Dublin Guardians, notwithstanding their ration of 15 gallons per day per pauper supplied through a 6 inch meter, had been convicted of a wastage of 20,000 gallons per night by a reading of their meter on the affirmation of the law agent of the corporation, Mr Ignatius Rice, solicitor, thereby acting to the detriment of another section of the public, selfsupporting taxpayers, solvent, sound.[9]

Fredric Jameson ends his "*Ulysses* in History" with this passage, though in truncated form; his quote ends on the fourth line above of the "answer" to the question "Did it flow?" ("£5 per linear yard . . .").[10] And Joep Leerssen ends his book *Remembrance and Imagination* here too, including more of the quote than Jameson but still not all of it, ending with "upper Leeson street . . . ."[11] Neither Jameson nor Leerssen offers an actual reading of the passage; for both critics the quote acts as a rhetorical flourish meant as a utopian gesture. This is what I meant when I said that these critics notice without fully examining the utopian gesture contained in the passage itself. And it is in there—but it is neither wholly contained nor fully articulated in the portion of the passage they quote.

For Jameson, the "yes" that answers the question "Did it flow?" represents an alternative to "the vitalist ideology of Molly's better known final affirmation."[12] This is because Jameson's focus on the social division of labor, and hence on alienation, is "invoked" by the passage and "by the most subterranean routes traced back . . . less to its origins in Nature, than to the transformation of Nature by human and collective praxis de-concealed."[13] His point is well taken: the passage takes the reader through a social infrastructure, the Dublin waterworks, that would ordinarily be considered "non-narrative" or "[un]recuperable for literature" in any more standardized or traditional aesthetic practice.[14] This is what he ear-lier refers to as "boredom"—in fact for him "Ithaca" is one of the "most boring chapters of *Ulysses*." But there is in this boredom "a productive use . . . which tells us something interesting about ourselves as well as about the world we live in today."[15]

Leerssen's point about this passage is related to Jameson's. What Jame-son calls boredom Leerssen calls "normalcy." For him, the passage repre-sents "an immense effort at normalizing and calibrating the position of Dublin in space and time, at showing how much part of the world it is, how it is synchronized with, and in proximity to, the rest of the world."[16] The point goes directly to Howes and Attridge's warning about the dan-gers of Irish exceptionalism. Leerssen is concerned to show that Joyce is critiquing such Irish exceptionalism through a focus, in "Ithaca," on the mundanity and minutiae of everyday life. "The great ingenuity of Joyce is that he dared to describe an Irish setting in terms of its *normalcy*—for that was precisely the quality which all earlier authors, whatever their persuasions and sympathies, had denied Ireland."[17]

As a counterexample to the celebratory way that Jameson and Leers-sen take up the waterworks passage—and as an indication of its curious gravitational pull for many readers and critics of *Ulysses*—Leo Bersani sees only the despair of alienated modernity.

It is the relentlessly tedious "Ithaca," with its nearly unreadable "scien-tific" expositions on such things as the many uses and virtues of water, and the recent restrictions on water consumption (when Bloom turns on the faucet), which, precisely because of the impersonality of its technique, becomes a kind of Pascalian meditation on the lack of con-nectedness not only between human beings but also between the human and the cosmos. . . . The anxiety which *Ulysses* massively, en-cyclopedically struggles to transcend—however we choose to under-stand its origins—is that of disconnectedness.[18]

To call "Ithaca" "relentlessly tedious" is not wrong—in fact, it is more or less in line with Jameson's and Leerssen's assessments. But it does nothing to account for the way that critics and readers have delighted in it without ever really opposing the idea that it is meant to approximate boredom or tedium; it does nothing to account for the reasons why one can agree that "Ithaca" has something to do with boredom without ever being bored by reading it. Bersani seems to be implying also that the waterworks passage fails to "transcend . . . disconnectedness" but does not say so outright. That it struggles—"massively," "encyclopedically"—to transcend disconnectedness is absolutely correct; that it fails or succeeds is exactly what is up for grabs. Jameson and Leerssen imply success, and in what follows, I will argue for it.

There is certainly something to Jameson's and Leerssen's points—in fact there must be a relation, given the echo between such similar terms as *boredom* and *normalcy*. But I will be concerned to show that the passage exceeds them. In the proliferation of details that is "Ithaca," there must be a reason why Jameson and Leerssen single out this passage; why it stands as a kind of crux for both critics; and why they do not consider it merely as an isolated example of what Rebecca Walkowitz calls the "trivial" in Joyce, "a tactic of heresy and insubordination" that privileges nothing and instead offers only an endless proliferation of fact after random fact.[19] We are left to ask why, in other words, this passage stands out among all passages as a singularly important instance of the boring or the normal or the trivial.

What Jameson describes as boredom I will describe as sublimity. And what Leerssen describes as normalcy I will describe as a *call* for normalcy, an important difference. All this will emerge from what both Jameson and Leerssen neglect to do with the passage and with the possibilities they eliminate from it when they selectively quote it. Put baldly, the passage needs close reading. This may seem a bit paradoxical, considering that "close reading" as a practice is so closely aligned with a certain "culturalism," or again with "overly textualist reading[s]" that seek "resistance" wherever it can be located. A close reading of this passage, however, offers crucial insights that pick up right from where Jameson and Leerssen so tantalizingly leave off.

First we notice the irony attending the one-word answer, "yes," to the question "Did it flow?" The period after "yes" indicates the contrary on the level of language; the tap may flow but the language used to convey that fact decidedly does not. Language comes to a stop after "yes" and then, unbidden, attempts a formal mimesis of the flow of the water with a very long and very ugly sentence describing the Dublin waterworks. Plagued by passive voicing, tortured syntax, and proliferating punctuation, the sentence appears to mock bureaucratic discourse, and from the point of view of poetic language it doesn't really flow at all; for Ariela Freedman, "It clearly does not flow but is deliberately clunky and digressive."[20] For all its ugliness, however, one thing it doesn't do is stop for nineteen lines. In other words, it does flow, not poetically but mimetically. The trick is that the sentence does not imitate the effortless natural flow of water; rather, it imitates the laborious flow of the waterworks: the whole complex of technology and labor for diverting water from its natural—"flowing"—course for utilitarian ends. In this sense the "flow" of the waterworks might usefully be contrasted with the "flow" of Molly's thoughts in "Penelope." There "flow" is mimetically attached both to the stream of consciousness and to Molly's menstrual cycle by means of the omission of punctuation and a (carefully crafted) parataxis. If Molly's soliloquy is a mimetic representation of the individual's stream of consciousness, the waterworks in "Ithaca" are a mimetic representation of the Dublin waterworks and a metonymic representation of the public works.

The "flow" of that long sentence completely overwhelms, even just in terms of textual space, the initial willful naïveté of the question, whose most immediate answer—"Yes."—is rendered inadequate by the detailed explanation that follows. The domestic scene of Bloom's house is dwarfed and trivialized by the sheer scale and scope of the "flow." The explanation after the answer seems to suggest its elaboration as a kind of necessary, but ordinarily suppressed, response both to the initial question *and* to the monosyllabic answer. It is not enough to answer the question "Did it flow?" with a negative or an affirmative. In fact, even an affirmative "yes" is here shown to be a negative in the sense that it truncates, or disavows, or closes off the "flow" by what it attempts to ignore: the vast public, political, and social machinery that enables it. And that repressed returns, fittingly, as an unstoppable flood stylistically rendered by the nineteen-line run-on sentence. The domestic tap *fails* to repress the "flow" in the bigger, metaphorical sense, and what I referred to in chapter 1 as the "unthought known" forces itself insistently on the reader's consciousness.

The explanation of Bloom's action is precise and importantly so: after sending him to the sink "to tap the current by turning the faucet to let it flow," Joyce reminds us that the faucet is never "off" but rather always "on," a continuous current that runs regardless of whether Bloom taps into it or not. If the faucet from a domestic point of view appears to possess the power to turn the water on and off, that is only the merest illusion, human hubris.

For at least three reasons this "flow" should be taken metaphorically as a stand-in for the social whole. First, the waterworks can be understood to reference civilization generally and the "urban revolution" specifically.[21] The first civic societies formed in the Near East more than six thousand years ago, specifically in desert zones, around the necessity of irrigation, a vast technological undertaking that required despotic centralization, capital, and an intricate division of labor.[22] Second, as Ariela Freedman contends, Joyce's waterworks have a "stylistic model and exalted precedent" in Sextus Julius Frontinus's *De aquis urbis Romae* (written during his tenure as Roman water commissioner between 95 and 100 AD), a work that "claims the Aqueducts of Rome as the most advanced products of an advanced civilization, and distinguishes between their monumental utility and other, lesser, purely aesthetic achievements."[23] It may be that Joyce had Frontinus's book in mind when writing the waterworks passage of "Ithaca" and that MacHugh's watercloset joke in "Aeolus"—which we saw in chapter 1—is a sarcastic and stereotypically Irish response to Frontinus's assertion of the superiority of utility over the aesthetic. Third— and this is the part that both Jameson and Leerssen leave out—we have a reference to "taxpayers," whose presence in the passage is precisely, as I'll argue, what needs most explaining.

The Vartry Waterworks Scheme, the system that Joyce traces in this passage, was the outcome of the Dublin Corporation Waterworks Act of 1861. It sought to answer Dublin's chronic water supply problems dating back to the late eighteenth century. There was not enough water from the Poddle River, the traditional source, to service even Dublin's slowly growing population, and the old mains system was heading toward total collapse. Remarkably, the Vartry Scheme was the most ambitious and most expensive of the various proposals submitted to the corporation at the time, and it came as a surprise when the royal commissioner chose it over other, cheaper ones. Various commercial interests, notably the canal companies, opposed the scheme, and the argument had to be taken to the House of Lords for decision.[24] When it was finished in 1868, it was "welcomed by all commentators."[25] One of them gushed, "No city in the kingdom is better supplied with this chiefest necessity of life. . . . Few cities have obtained so fine a supply [of water], delivered at high pressure, on such moderate terms."[26] The Vartry Waterworks became a utopian ideal and a high-profile success for the freshly minted discourses—and institutions—of public health and town planning, discourses whose power and legitimacy were rapidly growing at the turn of the century.[27] But the utopian and indeed radically democratic aims of the Vartry Scheme's architects—to eliminate differential class access to a source of clean, running water—were not to be realized. Those aims were thwarted by a rapid exodus of well-to-do Protestants from the inner city to suburban townships like Rathmines and Pembroke, leaving the municipal territory of Dublin city—circumscribed geographically by the two canals and the Circular Road—with a poor tax base. "The poor were abandoned to the city's beneficence," writes Jacinta Prunty, "and the city [was] denied the contribution, both financially and morally, which it could be expected the wealthiest would make."[28] In the poorest districts of Dublin proper, "the infrastructure to distribute the water . . . was very limited, so that ten years after [the scheme's] arrival . . . many residents were reliant for drinking water on water 'taken from the cistern intended to supply the water closet' resulting in typhoid."[29] An article in a contemporary journal advocated—in a dryly aloof tone of which the tail end of Joyce's passage is no doubt an indirect parody—for fountains of potable water to be placed in these affected districts, stating that "if some contrivance could be adopted whereby they would not, by waste of water, render the adjacent pavement sloppy, so much the better."[30]

These historical considerations reveal that, to whatever extent the passage can be understood as a "final affirmation" in Jameson's phrase, we need also to account for its evocation of the class politics and the ethnic segregation embedded in the city's infrastructural geography.[31] The contempt for the poor so palpable in the journal article quoted above is parodied in Joyce's passage through the free indirect discourse of Ignatius Rice, solicitor—and very likely a self-identified "taxpayer, solvent, sound"—who appears to represent the interests (whether as a matter of fact or as a matter of his own rationalization) of a whole like-minded and respectable body of "taxpayers, solvent, sound." Joyce's rendering, or even conjuring, of this one aspect of a broader social whole—the waterworks—finishes with a ventriloquized social commentary in the ironic mode. Ending with "selfsupporting taxpayers," the "flow" actually becomes a kind of free indirect discourse in which this personified entity, "selfsupporting taxpayers," reveals its ideological position, wherein charitable institutions like the South Dublin Guardians are understood as parasites who are cheating said taxpayers, who are themselves "solvent" and "sound." Again, even just the description of the taxpayers as "self-supporting" seems to go immediately against the grain of the passage, whose emphasis is on the vast public works that make running water possible in the first place. Someone somewhere is calculating how much water is needed and how to deal with unpredictable environmental conditions like drought; someone somewhere bought the piping, someone else laid the piping, and so forth. Collective thought, collective engineering, collective or public good, reduced in the end to a complaint about paupers using too much water: the bourgeoisie's delusory fantasy of self-reliance is thus rendered utterly absurd. The collective voice of the taxpayers, then, is the voice that would attempt to ignore all that came just before it: all the specialized labor and urban planning, the social infrastructure, the social scope and the social geography of the waterworks. If the tap fails to stem or control the flow, the taxpayers' sense of independence, of being "selfsupporting," closes the passage and puts an end to that overwhelming flood of information, that momentary awareness of all that goes into supporting and sustaining the unsung miracle of running water. But of course, that disavowal is not convincing here because the passage has already revealed far too much of the complexity of the system of running water. The taxpayers appear to be fooling only themselves.

This movement, from the seeming mundanity of the initial question "Did it flow?" to the sublimity of the long answer, and back again to the mundanity of the taxpayers' complaint, resembles very closely what Bruce Robbins has referred to as the "sweatshop sublime."[32] Robbins borrows from Kant's formulation of the sublime—defined as "a feeling of the inadequacy of [the] imagination for presenting the ideas of a whole,

wherein the imagination reaches its maximum, and, in striving to sur-
pass it, sinks back into itself, by which, however, a kind of emotional satisfaction is produced"—and converts it into a political category for understanding the global division of labor.[33] But if we change Robbins's concept
slightly, renaming it the social sublime as opposed to the sweatshop sublime, then we have a workable heuristic for understanding this passage
from "Ithaca": we can see that the taxpayers' complaint about paupers, and
their overdetermined and entirely false sense of their own independence,
turn on the same principle of a "sinking back" into themselves "by which
a certain emotional satisfaction is produced." That emotional satisfaction is shown up, however, by the structure of the passage, which makes it
clear just how false, in a way, that emotional satisfaction is. The taxpayers
not only do not contemplate the sublimity of the public waterworks and
their debt to it but instead invoke a different kind of indebtedness—the
ingratitude of mendicancy—in order to forget or ignore the social sublime that might otherwise hold them in thrall, in frozen awed contemplation, and that would reveal to them their indebtedness, their place within
a vast social whole, and their utter dependence upon this system of taxation and urban planning that provides their running water and, by extension, the innumerable other social services and institutions metaphorized
in the waterworks.

There is an excess in the phrase "selfsupporting taxpayers, solvent,
sound" that begs attention. On the one hand the repetition of roughly
synonymous adjectives—self-supporting, solvent, sound—sounds like
the almost ritualistic self-assurance of the taxpayers themselves, simply re-
peating words that might make them feel independent, healthy, without
debt. But in *solvent* we also ought to hear "water" again, the near-universal
chemical solvent, so that we are left with the paradox of the waterworks
dissolving into the taxpayers and the taxpayers dissolving into the waterworks. While the waterworks and the taxpayers are rendered as distinct
entities in the passage, the language works to make them far less distin-
guishable than their spatial separation—one opening the passage, the
other closing it—might otherwise suggest. And in *sound* we ought to
hear reference to a body of water, whether a "relatively narrow channel or
stretch of water," which would refer to the water's travels from Wicklow
to Eccles Street, or "a spring or pool of water," which would refer to the
Roundwood reservoir in Wicklow.[34]

The passage at first appears to "move" fairly logically through what Martin Heidegger marks as philosophy's "four causes" as applied to technology: beginning at the *causa finalis,* the end for which the works are created (Bloom's ability to draw water for making cocoa); moving through the *causa materialis,* the water itself, and the *causa formalis,* the shape and materials of the waterworks; and arriving finally at the *causa efficiens,* the taxpayers who pay for them.[35] But the solvency of the taxpayers leads us right back to water, so that the *causa efficiens* and the *causa materialis* become practically indistinguishable. Heidegger informs us, in fact, that all four causes belong "at once to each other," a fact that Joyce's double entendres also serve to reinforce. "The doctrine of the four causes," Heidegger goes on, "goes back to Aristotle. But everything that later ages seek in Greek thought under the conception and rubric 'causality,' in the realm of Greek thought and for Greek thought per se has simply nothing at all to do with bringing about and effecting. What we call cause *[Ursache]* and the Romans call *causa* is called *aition* by the Greeks, that to which something else is indebted *[das, was ein anderes verschuldet].* The four causes are the ways, all belonging at once to each other, of being responsible for something else."[36]

The passage in "Ithaca" answers questions unasked, questions about causation that not only make the initial answer seem woefully inadequate but force further questions about the causation of causation, leaving us with a Heideggerian injunction to think causation not as "bringing about" or "effecting" but as "being responsible for something else." If it is clear, then, that the passage distances itself from the point of view of the taxpayers with which it ends, then what might the passage, or the "flow" that seems to be speaking from this passage, be trying to say? What is this invocation of "selfsupporting taxpayers, solvent, sound" if not a call to responsibility—in the form of parodic free indirect discourse—for what we, following Robbins, are calling the social sublime? A call couched in the form of its own disavowal? A public conjured through its own self-abnegation? And not just any public either, but a specific "section of the public," taxpayers. This question of payment and of taxes, then, is crucially important because it brings us to the question of public debt, of the public's debt to the social whole, and of such a public's *difference* from the social whole.[37] A paradoxical axiom is revealed in the irony of the taxpayers' complaint: not only does the "public" as such constitute the social whole, but it has a responsibility to the social whole that is something *other* than a responsibility to itself. (Paupers don't pay taxes, for example, but they too are a "section of the public.") The responsibility of *this* public to *the* public is not self-identical, cannot be reduced to self-interest. Nor can the "public" be reduced to "taxpayers"; the latter are, as Joyce says, just "a section of the public."

This section of the public has its own group-think, its own common sense, its own habits of thought, a collective ideology that transcends or overrides any individual's opinion on the matter of charity or charitable institutions. "Don't get us started on where our taxes are going, we pay for *that?*"—such is the chitchat or gossip generated from within the role of "taxpayer," commonplaces whose enunciations vary individually but whose *énoncé* is always the same: this disavowal of indebtedness that seems to be a constitutive element of *being* a taxpayer. In some sense, those last two adjectives of the passage, *solvent* and *sound,* are the markers of that group-think; and we can imagine, too, that Bloom himself is implicated, since much of "Ithaca" exposes the reader, from an ironic distance, to Bloom's languid humanist fantasy life, what Jameson refers to wryly as his *bovarysme.* But what Joyce's passage insists on, by showing us how running water works and how taxpayers think, is that paying taxes is not the fulfillment of responsibility to the social whole but rather just the beginning of that responsibility. Payment, then, or at least the payment of taxes reveals itself not as *settling* a debt but as *instituting* one. This relation, this problem, is the central import of the passage, the social and political issue that shapes it.

Curious that, given his insistence on the alienation inherent in the modern capitalist division of labor, Jameson doesn't note the taxpayers in this passage; for they are modernity's answer to that alienation. Taxpayers may not understand the division of labor; they may not be able to comprehend the huge complexities of urban planning and development, of commerce and public works; but they pay their taxes and so they contribute, they pay their debt to the leviathan that supports them, that allows them to continue doing their small thing in some small corner of the division of labor, and they don't have to worry about how it works as long as they stay paid up. And apparently they are also entitled, or perhaps even coerced, into *feeling* little else but contempt for that division of labor, because they are still alienated from it in all senses but the financial. This brings us to the central question here: If Joyce is pointing to the limited and alienated consciousness of the taxpayer, then how can we see his evocation of the payment of taxes as in any sense utopian, or hopeful, or interesting beyond the level of parody?

The first reason that the mention of taxpayers in "Ithaca" is interesting is that it would be hard, in the temporal and geographical interstices of *Ulysses* and especially in the *writing* of *Ulysses,* to find anything resembling an actually existing constituency of taxpayers, whether in the petty-bourgeois, statist, or even national sense of the term. Taxpayers, as they are lampooned and stereotyped here in the passage, don't exist in the Dublin of 1904, and their existence in 1922 would be far more complicated than Joyce's parody suggests. One would imagine that taxes—which must have made the transformation from something like imperial tribute in 1904 to a source of deeply felt and lived national pride in 1922—would be, at the very least, a fraught category of experience and identity, one that would not, in this Irish historical context, lend itself to easy characterization, let alone satire. The "taxpayers" of "Ithaca" would actually have to be "taxpayers" in a standard, established (European) state, not the new taxpayers born of anticolonial struggle and postcolonial state formation. With "taxpayers," then, a whole range of scalar ambiguity is invoked without any gesture toward specificity or resolution: Are these British taxpayers, Irish taxpayers, Dublin taxpayers?

The second reason is also historical. The question of social infrastructure would not, after the British bombardments of 1916 in Dublin, be a boring one to Dubliners. As Enda Duffy has amply demonstrated, "In the very years that Dublin was being represented with an intense attention to detail in *Ulysses,* swathes of the real city center itself were being destroyed. . . . Rising in fiction, being destroyed in fact: this grim difference between the cityscapes described in *Ulysses* and the reality that had been wrought in the very years the book was being written bears witness to how history chases Joyce down in what might appear as the underpoliticized Dublin of the novel."[38]

Given these circumstances, the question "Did it flow?" that initiates the passage takes on a whole different significance. In a city subjected to partial military destruction, the question of whether the running water "works" or not is a practical question whose answer would not be a foregone conclusion. In the Dublin of 1904 the question *is* perhaps meaningless. In the Dublin of 1916 it is real and pragmatic. And in the Dublin of 1922, the question points most immediately to the political imaginary of the new Irish Free State, to the question of how to run and maintain a city, now a national capital—and from there back, finally, to this issue of taxes and taxpayers. To invoke Bourdieu a second time, in this historical interval "the collective invention of collective structures of invention" becomes a crucial issue for Ireland and, as I'm arguing, for *Ulysses* as well. And as our reading of "Ithaca" shows, Joyce deliberately addresses the issue not only on the level of aesthetics but all the way down to the level of taxation.

When Leerssen says that "the great ingenuity of Joyce is that he dared to describe an Irish setting in terms of its *normalcy*," he also misses the point.[39] Unless we take *normalcy* to mean the ways in which Ireland was subjected to the vicissitudes, disjunctures, and discontinuities of history, of capitalist modernization, imperial domination, and the struggle for independence—which would, actually, be something like "normal" historical experience for many peoples and many nations—then the term is misleading. Leerssen may intend to point to the fact that Joyce was willing to insist on the importance of such a normal or boring category of experience—taxes—as a site, however mundane, of utopian possibility and collective invention. Certainly *normalcy* cannot mean anything like continuity and peace. But in any case, if the word is to have any significance to the passage, it can only be in the sense that, perhaps, we can see the invocation of "taxpayers" as a kind of call to normalcy, or a call for a return to normalcy, from military insurrection "back" to everyday civic life, with "return" understood with all the complexity demanded by the idea behind the word, all the complexity necessary when talking about a postcolonial state: return, that is to say, as a form of revolution.

If taxation emerges from the passage as a "structure of collective invention" whose mundanity is transformed by history into utopian possibility, it is a weak utopia at best, as that voice of petty-bourgeois disavowal that closes the passage suggests. Nevertheless, we must insist on that weak messianic power because, as I'll show, Joyce insists on it; *Ulysses* insists on it.[40] The emphasis on taxation in the waterworks passage is generalized and diffused into multiple meditations, dispersed throughout *Ulysses,* on debt and mutual indebtedness. Debt becomes, from the first chapter of the novel, an alternative mode of imagined community that trumps ethnic identity, religion, Celtic Revivalism, and romantic nationalism. The milkwoman in the first chapter of *Ulysses,* "Telemachus," seems at first a parody of the *Sean-Bhean Bhocht,* that overdetermined sign and symbol of authentic Irish identity, since it is immediately revealed that she neither speaks nor even recognizes the Irish language.[41] "Is it French you are talking, sir?" she asks when Haines, the English amateur anthropologist, says a few Irish words to her (1.425). And when she learns that he speaks Irish, she makes the same mistake he does with her, assuming he is from the west of Ireland. Haines thinks that because she is Irish the milkwoman speaks Irish; the milkwoman thinks that because he speaks Irish Haines is Irish—the tautological identity politics that equate geography and culture are thrown into question by the misunderstanding that results. There is nowhere to go with this—it is a dead-end conversation. So they raise the issue of the bill, as if to have done with each other. But instead of a final reckoning, Buck and Stephen come up short of cash.

> Buck Mulligan brought up a florin, twisted it round in his fingers and cried:
> —A miracle!
> He passed it along the table towards the old woman, saying:
> —*Ask nothing more of me, sweet.*
> *All I can give you I give.*
> Stephen laid the coin in her uneager hand.
> —We'll owe twopence, he said.
> —Time enough, sir, she said, taking the coin. Time enough. Good morning, sir. (1.451–60)

The milkwoman's repetitive, ritualistic formula—"Time enough, sir. . . . Time enough"—resuscitates nationality through a far more mundane understanding of what it means to live with others. It conjures a volunteerist bond through time. It assures or even creates a future time by deferring any final reckoning of the bill indefinitely. Cultural identity is marginalized as a nationalist "cause" in favor of obligation, a "being responsible for." Haines's Irish speech is not quoted in the passage, as if the content of the language were unimportant to the solidarity forged between the Irish characters. Bound together through time by debt, Buck and Stephen and the milkwoman (Haines does not pay the milkwoman and does not touch the coin as Stephen does) *do* share something like Irishness, alternatively conceived not as a cultural inheritance but as mutual indebtedness. Oddly, perhaps even in a troubling way, the milkwoman *does* represent Ireland after all — it's just that one myth of nationhood is here replaced with another. If this first invocation of what we might call the nationalist debt is premodern insofar as Buck and Stephen and the milkwoman all interact face to face, then the novel's last invocation of the national community — the waterworks passage in "Ithaca" — is thoroughly modern insofar as the paupers and the taxpayers interact only via the mediation of the waterworks and the taxes that fund them: an imagined community in Benedict Anderson's sense of the term, with the qualification that the waterworks also links them, infrastructurally and concretely, in a relationship of material connection and interdependence.

The great counterexample that brings the point home is Mr. Deasy's boast to Stephen in "Nestor": "Do you know what is the proudest word *[sic]* you will ever hear from an Englishman's mouth? . . . *I paid my way. . . . I never borrowed a shilling in my life.* Can you feel that? *I owe nothing.* Can you?" (2.244–54). Nothing could better highlight the difference in conception of personal and national sovereignty between the two men. Deasy's "one word" turns out to be at least four (if we are counting conservatively), a telling mistake that drives home the absurd overestimation of his — and his ideal Englishman's — self-sufficiency. Deasy wants to pin his identity to "one word" — presumably a talisman that would eliminate the need for other words — such that by his own standards his statement appears positively logorrheic. Stephen, of all people, cannot "feel that"; his thoughts turn straightaway to his own debts. "Mulligan, nine pounds, three pairs of socks, one pair brogues, ties. Curran, ten guineas. McCann, one guinea. Fred Ryan, two shillings. . . . The lump I have is useless" (2.255–59). Stephen defines himself through his debts. Later, in "Scylla and Charybdis," Stephen's telegram to Mulligan makes a similar point: "*The sentimentalist is he who would enjoy without incurring the immense debtorship for a thing done.* Signed: Dedalus" (9.550–51). Applied to the waterworks passage of "Ithaca," this declaration makes the case against the one-word answer to the question "Did it flow?" as mere sentiment; it makes the case against Deasy's mysterious and unutterable "proudest word" as a fantasy; and finally, it makes the case against the taxpayers' belief in their own self-sufficiency as a delusion. *Ulysses* itself is a kind of testimony against Deasy's thinking, a novel whose principle of inclusiveness always seems to verge on the universal, and thus seems without principle. In terms of debt processed through Joycean wordplay, we could say, without much exaggeration, that *Ulysses* is—in a way entirely opposed to Deasy's emphasis on solvency and independence—all interest and no principle.

Even the most fundamental principle of *Ulysses*—the Homeric parallel—is a principle based on borrowing. And Joyce's "borrowing" from Homer is often cavalierly undisciplined. So it might seem at first unpromising to try to find a Homeric parallel for the waterworks passage. On a thematic level, Freedman points out that on his return to Ithaca, Homer's Odysseus "pauses at the city's fountain and enters into a brief description of its appearance and origin," a narrative detour imitated in Joyce's "Ithaca."[42] There is a formal parallel too, in the notion of Homeric digression that Erich Auerbach explores in the opening chapter of *Mimesis*. There Auerbach describes an episode in the *Odyssey* in which Odysseus's nurse Euryclea recognizes him, though he has not yet revealed his identity, from a scar on his thigh as she is washing his feet. At the moment of her recognition, seventy verses interrupt the present action to describe the origin of the scar, an interruption of the narrative that resembles the wildly digressive rhythm of Joyce's "Ithaca." Homer's "basic impulse," according to Auerbach's analysis of the scene, is "to represent phenomena in a fully externalized form, visible and palpable in all their parts, and completely fixed in their spatial and temporal relations."[43] And a little further: "The Homeric style knows only a foreground, only a uniformly illuminated, uniformly objective present." There is no "subjectivistic-perspectivistic procedure."[44] The story of the scar remains syntactically unsubordinated to the main storyline, in effect independent of it and without any linguistic indication that it is less important than the main storyline of Odysseus's return to Ithaca. This kind of insubordination, as it were, is evident in Joyce's passage about the Dublin waterworks. The travels of the water take up more textual space than the narrative of Bloom's actions. "Did it flow?" is a yes-or-no question. What follows after the answer "yes" defies the discipline of the structure: the question wants results, while the answer gives, instead, explanation and description, creating an effect something like a child asking "Why?" after every adult answer. There is no indication that the path of the water is anywhere in Bloom's conscious thought, just as Odysseus himself never remembers the story of how he got his scar; these are not subjective digressions but literally objective ones in which "a newly appearing object or implement, though it be in the thick of battle, is described as to its nature and origin."[45] We might call this the insubordination of things in texts, things that take up textual space, that have their own stories to tell, and that (or who) won't shut up and let us get on with the story. Of course, Bloom is not in "the thick of battle" but rather is busying himself making cocoa for his guest; but he is, like Odysseus, lately returned home, so that the slaughter of the suitors that marks the homecoming of Odysseus to Ithaca is precisely the parallel structure. To whatever extent Joyce modeled "Ithaca" on the catechism in form, in content it is—or at least, the waterworks passage is—modeled on Homeric digression.

Yet again, however, we are forced to ask why we should privilege the waterworks passage over innumerable other digressive passages in "Ithaca," other than simply because Jameson and Leerssen privilege it. The digression of the scar in Homer is a digression concerned with the lineage of the mark or proof of identity (the scar proves it is Odysseus), of individuality (there can only be one with such a scar), and of sovereignty (the mark of the king). Joyce's digression on water could be considered similar in almost every respect, once the terms of sovereignty are shifted from classical monarchy to the modern state form. One of the effects of the waterworks digression is to remind us that many people have the *same* experience at the tap throughout the course of a day and even simultaneously. It reminds us of the authority of the state, of the institutions that guarantee that the water flows so reliably into 7 Eccles Street that under normal narrative circumstances no one would bother to ask, "Did it flow?" Under such normal narrative circumstances we might never be treated to the explanation of how, from where, by whose authority, with what financial resources, and to what satisfactions and dissatisfactions it flowed. The waterworks are the consequence of a corporate authority, a collective one, which is to say, paradoxically, an incorporeal one, one that cannot by definition have a speaking voice as a character in a novel, at least, again, under normal narrative circumstances. The body of the king or sovereign dissolved into the broad division of labor that characterizes modern authority; the individual turned into many; sovereignty divided into multiples and placed, finally, nowhere in particular but everywhere, in every home—all this sounds very much like what Auerbach is saying at the end of the last chapter of *Mimesis,* "The Brown Stocking," in reference to Virginia Woolf's *To the Lighthouse*:

> It is precisely the random moment which is comparatively independent of the controversial and unstable orders over which men fight and despair; it passes unaffected by them, as daily life. The more it is exploited, the more the elementary things which our lives have in common come to light. The more numerous, varied, and simple the people are who appear as subjects of such random moments, the more effectively must what they have in common shine forth. In this unprejudiced and exploratory type of representation we cannot but see to what an extent—below the surface conflicts—the differences between men's ways of life and forms of thought have already lessened. The strata of societies and their different ways of life have become inextricably mingled. There are no longer even exotic peoples. . . . It is still a long way to a common life of mankind on earth, but the goal begins to be visible. And it is most concretely visible now in the unprejudiced, precise, interior and exterior representation of the random moment in the lives of different people. So the complicated process of dissolution which led to fragmentation of the exterior action, to reflection of consciousness, and to stratification of time seems to be tending toward a very simple solution.[46]

Joyce's waterworks put forward the public utility as a crucial social fact for modernist literature, as an often overlooked "elementary thing . . . which our lives have in common," one of the modalities through which "the differences between men's ways of life and forms of thought have already lessened." If Auerbach is, rather surprisingly, seemingly positive about "a common life of mankind on earth," surely his optimism cannot be about the process of commodification; surely not about standardization under the Fordist mode of production; surely not about the extensions and retreats of various despotisms across the globe. But perhaps it could be about the public utilities that bind us together into groups that rely on the same networks of water pipes, gas lines, power grids, and—though this is beyond the scope of the present work—communication networks.

PLUMBING CONSCIOUSNESS

Such are *Ulysses*'s hopes for the utopian promise of technology. If the waterworks can hijack the narrative flow of Joyce's fiction with its own, and if the collective voice of that fourfold causal force can be "heard," in some sense, in the passage—if, that is to say, the taxpayers' dissolution in the waterworks and the waterworks' resolution in the taxpayers can be said to produce a kind of subjectivity not merely of the imagined community but of the communion between an imagined community and its built environment—then we can say with some conviction that the waterworks "speak" in "Ithaca." To put it another way: Joyce gives epistemological teeth to the critical commonplace that the city is also a character in the novel. *Ulysses* literalizes that cliché, makes it mean something by concretizing it in public works. The idea is at work, for example, in this passage from "Aeolus," in which Bloom imagines the noise of the printing press as a kind of speech: "Sllt. The nethermost deck of the first machine jogged forward its flyboard with sllt the first batch of quirefolded papers. Sllt. Almost human the way it sllt to call attention. Doing its level best to speak. That door too sllt creaking, asking to be shut. Everything speaks in its own way. Sllt" (7.174–77).

Declan Kiberd, in his *Irish Classics,* has isolated this passage to demonstrate Joyce's "utopian view of technology."[47] Joyce, Kiberd argues, "was writing at a time when the sociologists of the Frankfurt School had not yet depressed themselves about the way in which technology could be used to flatten individuality and manufacture consensus, and so his treatment of mass media is more celebratory than critical. . . . The suggestion is that every single object has its own history and consciousness, albeit mute, and that it will yield a meaning if accorded the sort of loving attention that Bloom gives to things."[48]

I have suggested that the waterworks themselves might be considered the narrating consciousness of "Ithaca," and this suggestion bears itself out in "Wandering Rocks" with even more force. "Wandering Rocks," more than any other episode of *Ulysses,* stages simultaneity; the chapter's nineteen sections narrate several distinct moments as told from different focalized characters. Its perspective is presumably that of the omniscient narrator, though this narrator has a sense of irony in tone and style that defies traditional omniscient narration. "The mind of the city" in "Wandering Rocks," as Clive Hart puts it, "is both mechanical and maliciously ironic."[49] As characters intersect each other, many of their movements are repeated, interrupted, and re-presented without any of the syntactic cues that would normally allow the reader to switch from one perspective to another. The viceregal cavalcade that gets full treatment in the final section begins its procession at Phoenix Park and, in its path through the city, greets and is greeted by the characters treated earlier in the chapter: "Mr Thomas Kernan . . . greet[s] [the viceroy] vainly from afar" (10.1183–84); the cavalcade goes "unsaluted by Mr Dudley White, B.L., M.A." (10.1185–86); "Mr Simon Dedalus . . . st[ands] still in midstreet and br[ings] his hat low" (10.1199–1200). Amid this list of characters, the Poddle River appears where it merges with the Liffey and offers its salute as well. "From its sluice in Wood quay wall under Tom Devan's office Poddle river hung out in fealty a tongue of liquid sewage" (10.1196–97). That "tongue," I want to suggest, is—barring the improbability of talking sewage—a plausible narrating voice for "Wandering Rocks" as a whole.

The ironic tone of the chapter might easily be summed up in the description of the Poddle's tongue of liquid sewage: the river gives a raspberry to the cavalcade, announcing its subversive "fealty," and, not content to stop at mocking authority, mocks throughout nearly every character it encounters. As Hart again points out, the Poddle empties into the Liffey at Wellington Quay, not Wood Quay, as this line from "Wandering Rocks" would have it (Wellington Quay is about a half-kilometer downriver of

Wood Quay; both run along the south bank of the Liffey, with Essex Quay separating them). Hart interprets the geographical imprecision of the line as one of Joyce's few factual feints in *Ulysses*. The viceregal cavalcade around which "Wandering Rocks" is organized, for example, actually took place on May 31, 1904, not June 16. While this is easily explicable as the author's need to "change some of the facts to accommodate his fiction," other factual changes, like moving the Poddle's mouth from Wellington to Wood Quay, have less to do with plot and more to do with symbolism.[50] Because the Dublin Corporation Cleansing Department Offices were located at 15–16 Wood Quay, Hart suggests, it makes sense to have the sewage emerge from just underneath the building; it produces "a more powerful image of unified sewage."[51]

More than an image of "unified sewage," however, the relocation of the Poddle's sluice gate to Wood Quay is one more way of rendering Dublin, in Michael Seidel's words, "as a city of traps, a city of irresolution, *cul de sacs*, accidents, missed connections and missed streetcars, misread signs, wrong turns, indignities, and sheer labyrinthine terror, a Minoan as much as a Greek adventure."[52] And it is true that the characters in "Wandering Rocks" seem as confused by Dublin's geography as the reader may be, as if Dublin suffered in both fiction and fact from a certain unreality. The Poddle, we remember, was the source of much of Dublin's drinking water before the Dublin Corporation Waterworks Act of 1861. That a source of potable water should be, by 1904, reduced to "a tongue of liquid sewage" adds another indignity to Seidel's list and makes a complete mockery of the name of the institution dedicated to its maintenance, The Dublin Corporation Cleansing Department. Joyce's fictional relocation of the Poddle's mouth creates not only an image of unified sewage but, as it evokes the Poddle's civic role through a long history, a tragicomic image of urban ecological degradation through time.

Under the sign of unified sewage emerges also a powerful image of the urban totality. Wood Quay was the site of the very first Viking settlement in Dublin in 841 AD, just east of the point where the Poddle met the Liffey. Those early Norse settlers docked their ships in a body of stagnant water at the rivers' intersection that they called "Black Pool," a phrase taken from the Irish "Dubh Linn," which was borrowed from the Irish Christian monastery they conquered when they settled there. For Joyce to relocate the "tongue of liquid sewage" to this historical site of *nomos* is to give that tongue something rather specific, if maybe a little disappointing, to say: "Dubh Linn," or "Dublin."[53] Joyce is just as interested in relocating the rivers' confluence in time as he is in relocating it in space, marking the beginning of the history of a place called Dublin in a real but long gone "black pool" that has since metempsychosed into a black pool of liquid sewage.[54] The tongue speaks the etymology of the Hiberno-English word Dublin; it speaks the ontology of the vital entity known as Dublin; likewise, it speaks a whole history of conquest (from the Celts to the Vikings to the Normans) and relativizes what appears, in such a long historical perspective, as the pompousness, the ignorance, and above all the fleetingness of the authority represented in the viceregal cavalcade. Dublin speaks itself and its defiance from the river's mouth, mocking the cavalcade with sly civility.[55] Liquid sewage grants being to the city of Dublin, naming an organism but also giving it a voice.[56]

The Poddle was and is a small river, so small that it was bricked over in 1800, so small that it could almost be called a stream. The Poddle's tongue asks us to make a big conceptual-metaphorical leap by way of simple word association from river to tongue to stream to "stream of consciousness" to "sewer of consciousness." If the stream of consciousness was overburdened by an almost involuntary association with a kind of natural idyll—a stream in some pristine Alpine setting surrounded by firs, or some such—then Joyce in a fashion typical of his scatological thinking replaces that association with a stream of liquefied human excrement, which is really only to say that he literally humanizes it.[57] The networks of rivers, sewers, and canals that make up Dublin's circulatory system, when taken as a whole, present a plausible "point of view" from which the narrating voice of the chapter gains its multiple and simultaneous perspectives, and they explain why "Wandering Rocks" can jump from one section to another without syntactic connection. The infrastructure of the city "lives" each geographical point simultaneously, it *is* everywhere at once; it doesn't need syntactic connection because it has infrastructural connection.

If the stream of consciousness is confusingly merged here with omniscient narration, that is only because the sewer's point of view is not humanly possible and thus appears improbably synoptic; it is, however, bounded by its human-built limits, its engineered corporality. The narrating voice of "Wandering Rocks" is not omniscient at all—it simply remains within the limited geographical scope of the networks of rivers and sewers that define the municipal boundaries of the city of Dublin. The impression of omniscience is not superhuman but rather nonhuman; it is, moreover, not even omniscience so much as the "stream of consciousness" of the sewer, its "thought," so to speak. To borrow a suggestive term from D. A. Miller's *The Novel and the Police*, "Wandering Rocks" may be said to operate on a principle of panoptical narration.[58] Of course, unlike Jeremy Bentham's panopticon, the sewer is not a machine for seeing, but it is descended from the utilitarian ideal of governmentality, and as an ubiquitous urban infrastructure it inadvertently offers a "point of view" that is no longer rooted in human subjectivity. As Ann Banfield points out, "Point of view in language in the sense of a spatial position is not a grammatical notion, but a pragmatic one. In language, it has been axiomatically taken as located in a speaker." But in Joyce's literary experiment in "Wandering Rocks" (and elsewhere in *Ulysses*), "Point of view becomes a concept which can be independent of the speaker's role in communication."[59] The narrator of the chapter is "not objective, centreless," but rather "subjective but subjectless . . . representing the perspective of no one."[60] In this experiment it is possible to see a kinship between Joyce's modernism and Walter Benjamin's phantasmagorias of modernity, dreamworlds in which, to borrow from Jürgen Habermas, "even things encounter us in the structures of frail intersubjectivity"[61] and where, for Martin Jay, "objects [are] metamorphosed into subjectivities."[62]

"The sewer," wrote Victor Hugo in *Les Misérables* in 1862, "is the conscience of the city," a sentence I borrowed as an epigraph for this chapter.[63] The line comes from a chapter in the novel called "The Intestine of Leviathan," which momentarily suspends the plot structure of the novel, pausing instead to make a lengthy digression into the history of the Parisian sewer system. Digressions like these were a feature of the nineteenth-century epic novel—one thinks, for example, of certain sections of Melville's *Moby Dick* as well. But here, in *Ulysses,* the sewer as conscience of the city is not merely asserted but performed through narrative technique.

It is one of the signal differences between the nineteenth-century realist novel and Joyce's twentieth-century avant-garde modernism that the former should declare the sewer as the conscience of the city—in French *conscience* serves ambiguously for both the English words *conscience* and *consciousness*—while the latter should enact the sewer as the consciousness of the city by ventriloquizing it, personifying it, and endowing it with fictional being.

The represented thought of the sewer is the product of a *tekhne* that is both an engineering marvel and a literary innovation: *tekhne,* that is to say, as inseparable from *episteme.* "At the beginning of its history," argues Bernard Stiegler, "philosophy separates *tekhne* from *episteme,* a distinction that had not yet been made in Homeric times." From Plato onwards a conflict arose in Greek philosophical discourse: "The philosophical *episteme* is pitched against the sophistic *tekhne,* whereby all technical knowledge is devalued." As a result, "The analysis of technics is made in terms of ends and means, which implies necessarily that no dynamic proper belongs to technical beings."[64] In Stiegler's account of the classical split between *tekhne* and *episteme* we find another way in which *Ulysses* can be considered deeply Homeric, in the sense of being pre-Socratic, because the technical objects that appear in *Ulysses* are not at all represented "in terms of ends and means." In the case of the Poddle's tongue, in fact, technical objects are granted being, if not human-being, and even the potential for speech. *Ulysses* thus "locates" narrative authority—what I've been calling panoptical narration—in the *tekhne* of public works in "Wandering Rocks" just as in "Ithaca." This panoptical narration is also a mechanical form of stream of consciousness because it is a representation of how a machine—the public works—endowed with being might think. The novel locates the imagined urban community of Dublin in the simultaneous connection of the city's inhabitants through infrastructure, and it threads that connection through the deep temporality of the city's *nomos,* Dubh Linn. In doing so, *Ulysses* forges "another relationship to technics," to borrow again from Stiegler, "one that rethinks the bond originally formed by, and between, humanity, technics, and language."[65]

The thorny question of being for technological objects is taken up directly in the thirteenth section of "Wandering Rocks," close to the center of the chapter, when Stephen improbably addresses his thoughts to an electrical power station in Fleet Street: "The whirr of flapping leathern bands and hum of dynamos from the powerhouse urged Stephen to be on. Beingless beings. Stop! Throb always without you and the throb always within. Your heart you sing of. I between them. Where? Between two roaring worlds where they swirl, I. Shatter them, one and both. But stun myself too in the blow. Shatter me you who can. Bawd and butcher were the words. I say! Not yet awhile. A look around" (10.821–27).[66] Stephen's trepidation around the throb and hum of the powerhouse bears a striking resemblance to Joyce's famous fear of thunder and thunderstorms. "The thunderstorm as a vehicle of divine power and wrath," Richard Ellmann writes, "moved Joyce's imagination so profoundly that to the end of his life he trembled at the sound."[67] "Beingless beings" may be a reference to divine creative power, and since Stephen places himself "between two roaring worlds," we might imagine that he is thinking about his identity as an artist, as someone trying to access the divine in order to create something transcendent in the human world. Stephen conceives of himself, that is to say, as a mediator between the human and the divine, or the profane and the sacred.[68] The problem with this is that the power station is a thunderstorm created by humans, god's power usurped by the Dublin Corporation Electric Light Station.[69] In other words, the power station is, in some sense, the artist's competition. This, perhaps more than anything else, is the source of Stephen's ambivalence, characterized by both an urge to "be on" and a vocation to sing the machine's "heart." (Figure 1 is a photograph of the inner workings of the Fleet Street Station, a machinic, industrial, technological "heart" whose conventional ugliness contrasts sharply with Stephen's aesthetic visions.) Here is a moment when the familiar Celtic hatred of utility combines uneasily with an acknowledgment of genuine competition between utility and the aesthetic: a confrontation that ends in Stephen's turning away from it in fear and confusion.

That the power station could be the throbbing heart of "Wandering Rocks" and the sewer its municipal circulatory system bears witness to the fact that Joyce, unlike Stephen, did eventually find a way to sing the machine's heart: by using the basic technologies of the urban *polis* as epistemic engines of his fiction. The generating station that Stephen confronts

Figure 1. Dublin City Power Station at Fleet Street, about 1900. Reproduced by kind permission of ESB Archives.

on Fleet Street in "Wandering Rocks" had been around since 1892. It generated "electric light on a small scale" in the city center. The Pigeon House plant in Ringsend, which went into service in 1903, was much bigger and "facilitated the introduction of electric trams and the more widespread use of electric lighting," though "crucially, the power was not sufficient for a 24-hour supply."[70] The distinctive smokestacks of the Pigeon House were, and still are, some of the tallest structures in Dublin; they were strikingly visible from points all over the city and especially from Sandymount Strand, where Stephen walks on the beach in "Proteus," meditating on the "ineluctable modality of the visible" (3.1). Throughout *Ulysses,* Joyce presents the progress and promise of electricity as a preoccupation for Dubliners. In "Telemachus," Mulligan jokingly asks Stephen to "switch off the current, will you?" (1.28–29), though there is no electrical current in the Martello Tower; Bloom muses on "electric dishscrubbers" in "Circe" (15.1691); Bloom and Stephen worry about the negative effect of gas and electric light on "paraheliotropic" plant life in "Ithaca" (17.45);[71] the Cyclops hurls at Bloom a Jacob's Biscuits tin whose report is likened to an earthquake (Jacob's Biscuits was one of the first industrial clients for Dublin Corporation's electricity in the 1880s) (12.1853–1918).

Another, more direct example from "Cyclops" is a joke disparaging the public utilities—not unlike MacHugh's watercloset joke—voiced through the spirit of the lately buried Paddy Dignam. Speaking from the dead and enumerating the advantages of the afterlife, Dignam offers a satiric paean to the public utility:

> In reply to a question as to his first sensations in the great divide beyond he stated that previously he had seen as in a glass darkly but that those who had passed over had summit possibilities of atmic development opened up to them. Interrogated as to whether life there resembled our experience in the flesh he stated that he had heard from more favoured beings now in the spirit that their abodes were equipped with every modern home comfort such as tālāfānā, ālāvātār, hātākāldā, watāklāsāt and that the highest adepts were steeped in waves of volupcy of the very purest nature. (12.347–55)

The utopian hopes of the public works here run into the incongruity between the divine world and the seemingly petty earthly luxuries of all modern conveniences. The result is a joke that, by mockingly inserting the modern conveniences of watercloset and telephone into a sacred rhetoric and an exotic typography, makes "all mod cons" appear as the absolute poverty of the utopian imagination. The joke implies that under modernity technology has become an end rather than a means and that as a result man's ends become mean, and stupid. It would be a mistake, however, to allow this passage the last word in *Ulysses*, a novel that, as I've argued, tries very hard to rethink the Socratic understanding of technology beyond the standard terms of ends and means.[72] It is, instead, a joking index of the extent to which utopias—even utopias of the afterlife— cannot but be imagined in terms of the actual, in terms, that is to say, of the "collective invention of collective structures of invention."

ART AND UTILITY:
A PORTRAIT OF THE ARTIST AS A YOUNG MAN

Ulysses meets its most powerful resistance to that rethinking of technology in the figure of Stephen, Joyce's fictional, ironically distanced surrogate. The artist who writes *Ulysses* and the artist represented in *Ulysses* are separated by the imaginative act of writing *Ulysses*. The novel is the material evidence of how much Joyce's understanding of the relationship between modern technology and modern literature had changed since he had inhabited Stephen's point of view. Stephen's ambivalence about electricity in "Wandering Rocks" shows his contempt for and competition with the public works, while, on the other hand, the sewer's prominent role in the chapter belies a wholly different writing sensibility for the postcolonial comedy of development. One of the most telling differences between *Ulysses*'s author and Stephen-as-author reveals itself in Stephen's notorious adversity to bathing, his dislike, as "Ithaca" tells us, of "the aqueous substances of glass and crystal," his distrust of "aquacities of thought and language," and, furthermore, his belief in "the incompatibility of aquacity with the erratic originality of genius" (17.239–40, 247). The aquacity of the narrator's language betrays Stephen even while expressing his opinion, for if we take seriously the waterworks passage of "Ithaca" and the Poddle's voice in "Wandering Rocks" as narrative expressions of the urban totality, we are left precisely with "aquacity" as both a valorized principle of literary art (as wordplay, pun, *portmanteau*) and a literal expression of Dublin's urban essence: Dublin as a true aqua-city, defined and expressed through its waterworks and—by metonymic extension—its public works.[73]

Consider, for example, an important scene in the final chapter of *A Portrait of the Artist as a Young Man,* in which Stephen is sitting in at a University College Dublin lecture about electricity, and during which he is bantering with his classmates rather than paying attention. Stephen's boredom is expressed as an electrical metaphor. "The droning voice of the professor continued to wind itself slowly round and round the coils it spoke of, doubling, trebling, quadrupling its somnolent energy as the coil multiplied its ohms of resistance" (210). Two things are striking about this sentence. First, its accurate and exact use of electrical terminology to describe Stephen's "resistance" (something more telling than simple boredom) forces the realization either that Stephen is paying more attention to the lecture than he pretends to be or that the narrator at least has paid more attention to electricity than Stephen has. Second, the metaphor is as absolutely counterintuitive as it is absolutely accurate. The standard or clichéd use of electricity as a metaphor usually signifies the polar opposite of boredom: excitement, discovery, a sudden illumination or revelation. The narrator corrects the lazy use of electricity as a metaphor by using it precisely, thereby demonstrating the dangers of an "aquacity of thought and language" of which Stephen is just becoming anxiously aware.

Resistance to electricity, not indifference: this, as we've seen, is the secondary import of the metaphor. It is a resistance born of the artist's hatred of utility, based on the (defensive) conviction of the absolute autonomy of the work of art. Art should never be useful, should never serve as a means to an end. Technological things that do serve in such a way are subordinate to art, beneath it, contemptible, boring. Such a distinction is part and parcel of Stephen's aesthetic education by way of Aquinas and Aristotle. By contrast, before his education, when Stephen is a small child, he finds wonder and terror in simple things like indoor plumbing. His childish interest mirrors Stiegler's call for "another relationship to technics . . . that rethinks the bond originally formed by, and between, humanity, technics, and language." In this case that other relationship is to be found in the innocence of the child before he learns to separate humanity, technics, and language.

Suck was a queer word. The fellow called Simon Moonan that name because Simon Moonan used to tie the prefect's false sleeves behind his back and the prefect used to let on to be angry. But the sound was ugly. Once he had washed his hands in the lavatory of the Wicklow Hotel and his father pulled the stopper up by the chain after and the dirty water went down through the hole in the basin. And when it had all gone down slowly the hole in the basin had made a sound like that: suck. Only louder.

To remember that and the white look of the lavatory made him feel cold and then hot. There were two cocks that you turned and water came out: cold and hot. He felt cold and then a little hot: and he could see the names printed on the cocks. That was a very queer thing.

And the air in the corridor chilled him too. It was queer and wet-tish. But soon the gas would be lit and in burning it made a light noise like a little song. Always the same: and when the fellows stopped talk-ing in the playroom you could hear it. (8)

Stephen is struck in the Wicklow Hotel by the onomatopoeic correspon-dence between the sound "suck" and the word *suck*. But the word *suck* is "queer" because it can also signify something else: ass-kissing, in refer-ence to Moonan's behavior with the prefect, which causes an unspoken association, no doubt, between the anus, the "hole in the basin," and the sound "suck." Sexual anxiety and social taboo vie here with the child's polymorphous perversity because he cannot control—and is only be-ginning to learn to repress—the associations he is making. The result is fear over the power—and in particular the *aquacity*—of language, a fear that arises right at the site of water's entry and exit into the hotel bath-room, as if the orifices of the building were directly analogous to the ori-fices of the child's body.

Next he is at the bath in the Conglowes lavatory wondering at the power of the printed cocks. The words *hot* and *cold* have the power to make Stephen feel hot or cold as he contemplates them, and because the words are printed on the cocks, their association with the lavatory fix-tures is indelible. Stephen does not know if the cocks make him feel hot and cold or if the words make him feel hot and cold. The key here is that childish conjunction "and," as in "and he could see the names," a para-taxis that makes it impossible for Stephen to distinguish between the words as cause and the cocks as cause. Note, too, that water is entirely absent in this scene; its power to make Stephen feel hot or cold he does not con-sider. For him it is a contest only between public works and language. As to the question of what it is that causes Stephen's later hydrophobia, we can say with some confidence that his worry about the "aquacity" of language finds its source in the Wicklow lavatory, in the conjunction ("and") of architectural and bodily orifices, in the contiguity between the sound of words and their meaning, in the confusion of phonetic same-ness ("suck"), and in semantic difference (a sucking sound down the drain versus sucking up to someone). All this remains undifferentiated for Ste-phen, who can only call it "queer," a term whose vagueness combines with its connotations of sexual impropriety to sum up quite efficiently the feeling generated by Stephen's excitement, wonder, and confusion.

A little later, Stephen calls on the certainties of religious faith to hold at bay the terrifying arbitrariness of the signifier: "Though there were different names for God in all the different languages in the world and God understood what all the people who prayed said in their different languages still God remained always the same God and God's real name was God" (13). But as he loses his belief in the catholic god, his terror of aquacity increases, and the arbitrariness of the signifier is buried under the strictures of Stephen's Aristotelian aesthetic theory. Hydrophobia is the symptom of that repression. If the watercocks offered Stephen a kind of Saussurean linguistic lesson about how language works, then the gas jet in the last paragraph of the quoted passage offers him an early intimation of what language can do beyond signifying and communicating. It can sing, adding the musical and poetic dimension to what will later be Stephen's vocation as a writer of literature. It can offer rapturous sensations, as the synesthetic description of the gas jet suggests. It is "light noise," figuratively airy, literally the sound of light: sight, sound, and touch all engaged in what is an understated description of aesthetic experience. If Stephen's introduction to language as a signifying system occurs via the taps and drains of the lavatory, his introduction to language as art comes through the gasworks. That these experiences of the power of language should be welded so firmly to public works reveals a very different conception of public works than merely as a means to an end. Here technology is not the means to art but the child's first experience of art itself, in the classical sense of *tekhne*. This is the position that the author of *Ulysses* takes up in the writing of *Ulysses*, a position far closer to Stephen as a child than Stephen as a young man.

If, as Jameson suggests, the waterworks are the real "final affirmation" of *Ulysses*, then that passage may serve also as a correction to Stephen's final affirmation in *A Portrait*, where he vows to "forge in the smithy of [his] soul the uncreated conscience of [his] race." The metaphor of the smith and (presumably) the sword gives way in *Ulysses* to the engineer and the public works as the defining force—beyond ethnicity, beyond religion, and beyond culture in the narrow sense laid out by the Irish Revival—of Irish national consciousness. Donald Theall has shown the extent to which Joyce thought of himself as an engineer and his texts as machines. Theall notes that Frank Budgen, who had spent time with Joyce while he was working on "Wandering Rocks," described Joyce's method as something like "an engineer at work with compass and slide-rule."[74] At some point even before finishing *A Portrait of the Artist as a Young Man*, then, Joyce had already discarded the forge as his principal metaphor for both artistic composition and national consciousness, in favor of the public works. In "The Dead," the final short story of *Dubliners*, we can see the origins of the shift.

IN THE WORKS: "THE DEAD"

Even the twilight which illuminates our private and intimate lives is ultimately derived from the much harsher light of the public realm.
—Hannah Arendt, *The Human Condition*

"The Dead," Joyce confided to his brother Stanislaus, is "a ghost story."[75] The statement is false to the extent that the story remains within the boundaries of the expectations for realist fiction: no ghosts appear, though characters often feel "haunted." The statement is true to the extent that Joyce modeled the story on gothic fiction and ghost stories and emulated the mood that those stories evoked. He accomplishes this through a trick of the light; reading the role of gaslight in "The Dead" is the key to understanding how. The public works haunt "The Dead" in the form of the gasworks. Michael Furey is described as "a boy in the gasworks."[76] If Furey is the obvious "ghost" in the story, it is his medium and not his spirit that is the message. And in the word *medium*, we should hear a reference both to the Aristotelian philosophical concept and to the Yeatsian (or perhaps Madame Blavatskian) mystical concept. As Luke Gibbons has argued,

> Despite all Joyce's skepticism towards the occult and spiritualism [developed in contradistinction to and with a certain contempt for Yeats and the Irish Revivalists], he retained an interest in key theosophical

concerns such as cyclical history and the pursuit of arcane, hermetic knowledge. One particular aspect that held an enduring fascination was the possibility of world memory, an "akasic" medium, as described in *Ulysses,* that records "all that ever anywhere wherever was." . . . For while the shade of Michael Furey is clearly lodged, at one level, in Gretta Conroy's unconscious, it also has a "trans-subjective" element, impinging on Gabriel's consciousness as if it had an (after)life of its own.[77]

Furey is indeed "impinging on Gabriel's consciousness" and in a "trans-subjective" way, but the "akasic medium" is hardly mysterious here: it is gaslight, in particular the gas-fueled streetlight outside the window of Gabriel and Gretta's room in the Gresham Hotel. Joyce's "skepticism towards the occult and spiritualism" plays out in the way he sets up Michael Furey's haunting as rooted in a very material, even mundane, source, wholly explicable without any recourse to the supernatural. It is Joyce's way of undermining the occultism of the Revival while at the same time writing a ghost story that participates in the Revival's tradition. Remaining within the tradition while subtly undermining its mysticism, Joyce can thus offer an alternative model of national community via the medium of public works. He writes a gothic story about Irish nationality that turns on a very modern technology, the gasworks, instead of some other supernatural source by which to explain the occulted experience of his protagonists. The "shade of Michael Furey" "imping[es]" on Gabriel's consciousness" because Furey's ghost is conveyed via the "akasic" medium of the gaslight streaming into Gabriel and Gretta's hotel room. Mysticism is no longer opposed to modernity, as it was for the Revivalists; instead, Joyce suggests that modernity contains its own modes of mysticism and, along with them, its own modes of community.

The moment "The Dead" shades into the genre of the gothic or the ghost story—the moment, that is, when the ghost of Michael Furey enters the scene—occurs as a hotel porter guides Gretta and Gabriel into their room at the Gresham Hotel.

The porter pointed to the tap of the electric-light and began a muttered apology but Gabriel cut him short.

—We don't want any light. We have light enough from the street. And I say, he added, pointing to the candle, you might remove that handsome article, like a good man.

The porter took up his candle again, but slowly for he was surprised by such a novel idea. Then he mumbled good-night and went out. Gabriel shot the lock to.

A ghostly light from the street lamp lay in a long shaft from one window to the door. (216)

Gabriel insists that the street lamp light the scene because he thinks he is creating a romantic setting in which to seduce his wife. But the street lamp—which was at the time of the story's setting gas fueled—powerfully insinuates Michael Furey into their room, creating a morbid three-way intimacy instead. The passage, however, is meaningfully ambiguous about the kind of lamplight coming in from the street, characterizing it only as from a "street lamp," failing twice to specify the source. This appears as a kind of sly refusal made up of two dissimulating answers. What kind of lamp lights the street? A "street lamp," of course. All right, but what kind of light comes out of the street lamp? "Ghostly light." Okay, but what kind of ghostly light? Would it have been too obvious to say "gaslight"? Is there a meaning to the text's refusal to name the quality of the light by its material source, relying instead on ambient description?

Luke Gibbons confirms that the street lamp outside the hotel is indeed a gas lamp: in 1904 Dublin was making its first transitions to electrical street lighting, but at that time it was mostly in commercial use and, as we saw in our discussion of "Wandering Rocks," there was not a twenty-four-hour supply.[78] Joyce surely knew this without saying so, because otherwise Michael Furey's ghostly presence in the Conroys' hotel room makes a lot less sense. The lamp, by the logic of the story, has to be gaslit in order to create, to borrow a phrase from Hart, "a unified vision of" the gasworks. Certainly we can hear "gaslight" in the weak rhyme Joyce evokes with "ghostly light" or even, in one of the more telling misprints in early versions of "The Dead," "ghastly light."[79] The light's ghostliness, however, may refer not only to the ghost of Michael Furey that inhabits it but also to its own soon-to-be-realized obsolescence and replacement by electrical light, whose qualities of harshness, brightness, and much-increased visibility would banish both the gasworks and the ghost in them to the dustbin of history. "As early as 1888," reports Colin Rynne, "Dublin Corporation had already decided to create a municipal electricity service, under its direct control, and to dispense with the services of gas for public lighting purposes." Following up that resolution in 1892, the corporation opened the Fleet Street Electrical Station, the same one Stephen confronts in "Wandering Rocks."[80] The gas lamp outside the Gresham is already, in 1904, a remnant. How would a story about a boy in the gasworks be told without gaslight? In what way would his story remain haunting at all?

Within a few moments of entering the room, Gretta tells Gabriel about Michael Furey. She describes him as a boy who "was in the gasworks" (219). "He was in the gasworks" is an Irish colloquialism denoting the fact that Michael Furey worked in the Galway gasworks, no different from saying "He was in the civil service" to mean "He worked in the civil service." But the phrase is doing more work here than just providing authentic vernacular dialogue. It does so first by abstracting us from the notion of an individual's "work" to the notion of the gasworks, an institutional brand of work; second by abstracting us from the Galway gasworks in particular to gasworks in general, pointing to the way in which every modern city or town will have a gasworks, such that it is not necessary to signal in speech any more specificity than "the gasworks" once we know that she is talking about Galway; and third by decorporealizing Furey, rendering him ambiently present in the gasworks rather than assigning him a place and definite set of activities or tasks. To say that Furey is "in the gasworks" is not a very precise kind of localization and should forcefully recall Aunt Julia's earlier usage of another colloquialism, which she utters in reference to Mr. Browne: "Browne is everywhere. . . . He has been laid on here like the gas" (207). Where do the gasworks end anyway? At the place where gas is produced, or much further on, at the ends of the gas mains through which gas is piped into streetlights, commercial buildings, government offices, and private homes—all the places, in other words, where the gas is "laid on"? The latter is, of course, the implication of the story: Furey is, it turns out, everywhere that gaslight is. This is to say that he is everywhere the story takes place, everywhere it is possible to see anything, every place about which a story of a dark night and human interaction and movement through space and time can be told.

He encompasses the entire visual field of the story from beginning to end, with the one exception of the hotel porter's candle. The only real inaccuracy in Gretta's description of what Furey "was" rests in her use of the past tense. Furey *is* in the gasworks. Of course, her choice of words is over-determined by Gabriel's hostile question "What was he?" which embodies not the reality of Furey's pastness but Gabriel's determined wish for it, as well as a dismissive objectification—not "Who was he?" but "What was he?" Gabriel attempts with the question both to dehumanize Furey and at the same time to initiate a social comparison by which he, Gabriel, seems more appealing. Was he a cosmopolitan bourgeois writer like myself? Do you not prefer me to a boy who, because he worked in the gasworks, had no real hope for the social mobility you have achieved through your marriage to me?[81] In the larger Joycean context, however, of the way that Stephen in *A Portrait* responds to the electricity lecture; of his hydrophobia in response to his early aesthetic experiences in the lavatory; and of his nervous—I am arguing, jealous—response in *Ulysses* to the Fleet Street electrical plant, can we not see in Gabriel's reaction to Michael Furey more than the surface story of sexual jealousy? Gabriel seizes Furey as a sexual rival, but actually he feels his humiliation most keenly as inflicted not by Furey in particular but by "a boy in the gasworks," which may be to say the gasworks themselves. Again we see the anxious comparison and competition between the writer—this time Gabriel—and the public works, the same anxiety we saw in Stephen in *A Portrait* and in *Ulysses,* and for which the drama of sexual jealousy between Gabriel and Michael is, in part at least, a cover story.[82]

The gasworks, then, are the medium by which the ghost of Michael Furey haunts the characters in "The Dead" "trans-subjectively," as Gibbons puts it. It is remarkable how well such trans-subjectivity can stand as a version of the imagined community of the nation. And it is equally remarkable that, when critics take up the last paragraph of "The Dead" as an instantiation of the imagined national community, the snow—and not the gasworks—stands as the metaphor for that community. The snow, however, is really a trick of the light. Snow reflects light; it doesn't produce it. And if it is snowing, there is cloud cover, which is to say that there is no natural light in "The Dead," which begins around ten o'clock and ends before sunrise—no moon, no stars, and no sun. What does snow look like in pitch darkness? It doesn't look like anything, because it, like everything else, is not visible in pitch darkness. The image, then, of the snow falling generally all over Ireland forces the reader to imagine snow visually, which is impossible unless we are to imagine a light source where, precisely, there is no natural light source. We are in a world lit only by gas, and Furey is thus "in" the works—the fictional works, so to speak—in ways so fundamental that we have to consider him, and gaslight too, as something more than merely a theme of the story, or the point of the story, or the subject of the story. Gaslight and Furey are even more embedded in the narrative apparatus than that: in fact, they might be said to *be* the narrative apparatus in some important sense, or at least an indispensable part of it. In other words, "The Dead" stages a confrontation between two historically antagonistic modes of writing or representing Ireland: literary culture versus engineering culture. This is to see gaslight not as an *akasic* medium but rather as a medium in the classical Aristotelian sense of the word. For Aristotle, according to Kevis Goodman, a medium is "a necessary condition of sense perception, although not a sufficient one (. . . [media] are part of a complex relationship that includes the accessibility of the object and the development of the faculty of sense)." "As in the example of the ether," Goodman further suggests, such media "can easily escape notice, lurking somewhere beneath conscious perception."[83] Joyce, mobilizing gaslight as a trope, illuminates the medium by which perception is possible and, because gaslight is pointedly technological—as opposed to natural—casts as a narrative medium that which is in fact an infrastructural medium.

The snow is immaterial to the imagined community; it is not a medium in the Aristotelian sense; and it is in any case a natural phenomenon that does not and cannot respect national boundaries. The opposition between a modernity embodied by Gabriel and a traditional or authentic Irishness embodied by Michael Furey is also false. The very existence of the Galway gasworks—as immediately comparable to the Dublin gasworks—renders, instead, a modernity always already inscribed in every character and every location in "The Dead." The gasworks are an entirely modern institution with no links to any rural idyll or traditional culture. The transition to electricity in Dublin is, far from being an indication of the difference between the modern East and the traditional West, rather a proof of the relentless pace of change within an all-encompassing modernity. "Here," Kevin Whelan suggests, "lay Joyce's most profound

insight: the Irish in this condition were not deprived of modernity—
they literally embodied it."[84] Michael Furey in this sense both embodies
the gasworks and is embodied by them.

The real stakes in "The Dead" are between the newspapers (which are
the public organs that report the snow to be "general all over Ireland")
and the gasworks (which are the public works that allow us to visualize
the snow as "general all over Ireland" [225]). Michael and Gabriel are the
opposing poles of nation building, two competing versions of Bourdieu's
"collective structures of invention": the culture of the word versus engineering culture, their antagonism exemplified in Gabriel's sexual jealousy. The narrating voice of "The Dead" is the synthetic dissolution of the
opposition between the two. Joyce marries them, realizing in the process
the meaning of public works as both literary and infrastructural or, in
Stiegler's or Heidegger's terms, technological. A "queer" marriage, to be
sure, an eccentric one: but it is exactly this to which—in no small part—
Joyce's unique place in the modernist canon is to be attributed.

"FOR POSSIBLE, CIRCUITOUS OR DIRECT, RETURN": *ULYSSES*, AGAIN

To show how such a union—of literary and engineering cultures via the
concept of public works—should be in some sense utopian in Joyce's
work, we return once again to the taxpayers in *Ulysses.* One of the things
Ulysses is best known for is its dogged and meticulous mapping of the geography of the Dublin cityscape as it was in 1904. As Enda Duffy demonstrates, that cityscape was under erasure by British bombardment in 1916,
just as Joyce was writing some of the most geographically detailed chapters of *Ulysses.* Joyce started writing "Ithaca" in earnest in late February
or early March of 1921, though he had already done extensive notetaking
for the chapter.[85] Between the conflagration of 1916, when large parts of
Dublin were destroyed, and the signing of the Anglo-Irish Treaty in December 1921, when the southern counties became a Free State, the imagined national community was in a zone of epistemological uncertainty.
In this period, as Duffy emphasizes, "knowledge of the physical city and
its features shared by the citizens assume[d] greater importance in fos-
tering anything approximating an 'imagined community.'" Thus he ac-

counts in some part for Joyce's fixations on waterworks and sewers. And yet, Duffy continues, "without the existence of some viable civic communal relations, the link that the ethnologist claims to discern between the built environment and the community relations it memorializes . . . can scarcely exist either."[86]

It is to the idea of "some viable civic communal relations" that the taxpayers in "Ithaca" speak, however recalcitrantly. With the destruction of the physical city, the sphere of civic finance makes its phantom appearance as that other mode of imagined community. Although the question of the *desire* for such a mode of imagined community is wholly buried under the disavowal of indebtedness that we saw in the waterworks passage, it emerges boldly elsewhere in "Ithaca":

> What rendered problematic for Bloom the realisation of these mutually selfexcluding propositions?
>
> The irreparability of the past: once at a performance of Albert Hengler's circus in the Rotunda, Rutland Square, Dublin, an intuitive particoloured clown in quest of paternity had penetrated from the ring to a place in the auditorium where Bloom, solitary, was seated and had publicly declared to an exhilarated audience that he (Bloom) was his (the clown's) papa. The imprevidibility of the future: once in the summer of 1898 he (Bloom) had marked a florin (2/-) with three notches on the milled edge and tendered it in payment of an account due to and received by J. and T. Davy, family grocers, 1 Charlemont Mall, Grand Canal, for circulation on the waters of civic finance, for possible, circuitous or direct, return.
>
> Was the clown Bloom's son?
>
> No.
>
> Had Bloom's coin returned?
>
> Never.
>
> Why would a recurrent frustration the more depress him?
>
> Because at the critical turningpoint of human existence he desired to amend many social conditions, the product of inequality and avarice and international animosity. (17.973–92)[87]

Desire announces itself in this passage in two ways. Most obviously, it announces itself when Bloom marks the coin. The pathos of this gesture is its commonality—we have all either done this, or received in routine exchange and with at least mild curiosity someone else's attempt to do this. The act "marks" the desire for a *return of the same* in a money economy whose circulating medium is by definition indifferent to such a desire. It doesn't matter, technically, if Bloom ever sees his florin again. He will see many such florins, each of them with the exact same exchange value as the one he marked. We might understand this as a gesture of de-alienation in the sense that Bloom is fighting abstract equivalence with physical particularity, the singularity of "his" florin. We might understand this as an attempt to reimagine civic finance as an imagined community, reflecting not alienation but personalized integration, a state structure that could somehow recognize difference, perhaps even, we might dare say, a reimagination of the state that could somehow recognize and respect subalterity—again, a weak utopian gesture at best, the sheer bathos of which is staged by the other episode involving, of all things, a circus, a clown, and public humiliation.

But the episode with the clown, with which the episode of the coin is critically paired, signals the obverse side of such a desire for particularity and difference. Desire in this episode is not "marked" by Bloom's intent but rather, by the humiliating revelation of his fantasy of return through the antics of a circus clown. The episode is especially embarrassing not only because Bloom is singled out from the crowd but, more poignantly, because Bloom does in fact want his son Rudy back, and because we know that he has spent a good deal of time fantasizing about adopting Stephen Dedalus into that role. The recollection of the episode with the clown highlights the bathos of Bloom's motivations for inviting Stephen to stay the night at 7 Eccles Street. In a reversal of roles, it is now Bloom declaring paternity for Stephen rather than a clown declaring Bloom's paternity. What the episode reveals is Bloom's desire for the return of his son Rudy as in some sense less particular than it may at first have seemed—as the desire for the return of *a* son. The question that initiates the answer is driven by the previous passage, in which Bloom and Stephen are discussing future meetings, with Bloom already fantasizing a father-son relationship between the two of them. Desire is, here, the desire for a structural relation, father-son or better, "Bloom & Son," and not a relation between particularized individuals (Bloom-Rudy). The sadness of Bloom's

desire is rendered ridiculous not only by the fact that he attaches the desire to a clown but also by the publicness of the spectacle of misrecogni-
tion and, finally, by the apposition of floating a marked coin on "the waters of civic finance, for possible, circuitous or direct, return."

The strange apposition of these two episodes reveals the ambivalences
that structure the imagined community of the city. It is categorically mistaken to wish, as Bloom does, for limitless exchangeability in the sphere
of familial relations, just as it is categorically mistaken to wish for absolute difference or singularity in the sphere of civic finance. The sphere
of civic finance is defined by limitless exchange, the sphere of the family,
by particularity. At least, this would seem to be the implication of the results: "Was the clown Bloom's son? / No. / Had Bloom's coin returned? /
Never." Yet both of those wishes, however impossible, exist as one of the
constitutive ambivalences of modern citizenship. It is not so important
to recognize the impossibility of realizing these desires as it is to recognize that these very contrary desires structure the division between the
economic and the domestic, equivalence and singularity, the impersonal
and the personal, affiliation and filiation, and structure the traffic across
the boundary between the two. Less important than the impossibility of
the desire is the utopian wish that its very existence affirms: an imagined
community that bridges the gap between them. Bloom's desire is for a
city that is more like a family, but also for a family that is more like a city.

Such a desire is not the same as analogizing the city to the family, of
merely wishing that the city were more like a family. On the contrary, the
passage shows the extent to which the city, metaphorized as civic finance,
is its own model of community, however alienated, and that that urban
model of community can serve equally to remodel how one understands
the family. Jameson is not wrong to argue that the archetypal patterns
of father-son relationships in *Ulysses* reveal nothing but "break-down
products and . . . defense mechanisms against the loss of the knowable
community," or "the impoverishment of human relations which results
from the destruction of the older forms of the collective."[88] But what is
missing in his argument is the extent to which these new and "alienated"
models of the collective are, in spite of their alienation, just that: new
models of the collective. Further, his argument does not address the re-
ciprocal consequence of modern urban life on the family: How does it

affect family life, other than rendering it "residual"? The fantasies that arise from phenomena as impossible to hold in one's head as the urban social whole contain a utopian element that Jameson is unwilling to grant. "How can a vision of liberation," asks Emer Nolan, "be distinguished from a fantasy of it?"[89] Although nothing so grand as liberation might have been realized in Irish independence—and particularly in paying Irish taxes—that is no reason not to see in the "structure of collective invention" of taxation, or of civic finance generally, the seeds of a project of liberation, or a potential site of liberation: "For *Ulysses* is grounded in real states, in real possibilities, real outcomes, even though it recognizes how subtly these are interwoven with dreams of possibilities that have not been and may never be realized."[90] Bloom's marked coin is one of those "dreams of possibilities," one that is oddly foreclosed on and at the same time left with some weak messianic power. For, if the syntax and the verb tense of the last question and answer are broken down, we can see the possibility in the answer "Never": "Bloom's coin *had* never returned," or has never *yet* returned. *Never*, here, does not mean never. To borrow Nolan's construction, it is simply that it "has not been and *may* never be realized." Given the "imprevidibility of the future," the return of Bloom's coin is not, finally, impossible—it has a certain promise still, a faint hope.

Bloom's florin recapitulates, on the level of "the whole dead grid of the object-world," the Ulysses narrative.[91] Bloom's desirous act of marking the coin, of wishing for its return, amounts to a fetishization that endows it with its own subjecthood. Sailing the waters of civic finance, the coin attempts to make its way back to its Penelope, Bloom. Since the coin "had" never come back, it seems safe to say that if it returns at all it will be a "circuitous return" as opposed to a direct return, fraught with adventure and suspense. Jameson has a very poetic way of saying just this, although he does not talk about this particular passage: in pointing to the ways in which Bloom's fantasies are "inextricably bound up with objects," Jameson argues that Bloom's fantasies are "falsely subjective fantasies" and that finally, "here, in reality [the reality of 'Ithaca'], commodities are dreaming about themselves through us."[92] This is a provocative figuration whose import is borne out almost to the letter by the coin-as-Ulysses scenario, except that it is not commodities that are dreaming about themselves through us but money that is dreaming about itself through us. It is an important distinction, too, because to say commodities is to focus too narrowly on the commercial world, whereas to say money is to focus more broadly on *civic* finance, on the city and the modes of imagining its own phantasmal totality that the city enables and requires. To say *money* is not necessarily to invoke the commodity—in this case, I'm arguing, it is to invoke taxes and taxpayers, as in the first passage examined here. To imagine this marked coin as it makes its way around the city, passing through the hands of vendors, workers, government employees, municipal employees, all the while gaining that intricate and intimate knowledge of the city so prized by Duffy's eponymous colonial-metropolitan *flâneurs,* is to see the extent to which civic finance is the phantom appearance or trace of the imagined community, whose spatial and architectural orientation—whose sense of itself—was so roughly shaken by the conflagration of 1916. The coin's point of view, its special function as circulating medium, allows it privileged access to the mysteries of the social division of labor, mysteries inaccessible to the citizens alienated by that division of labor. And that is why Bloom releases it and desires its return, so that it may come back and disclose to him the humanly indescribable secrets of the urban totality.

Because the passage recapitulates minutely and spectrally the *Ulysses* conceit, there is also here at least a speculative answer to the question of who or what *narrates* "Ithaca," or at least the two passages examined here. Is it not possible—once we have described the narrating voice of the waterworks passage as a 'flow,' and once we have established that what is being described there is the movement of water through the city—that the "voice" of *Ithaca* is actually the chorus of those "waters of civic finance," reified, fetishized, and subjectivized, which, like Bloom's coin, are "dreaming about themselves through us," with "us" understood now as us "selfsupporting taxpayers, solvent, sound"? And if this were credible, then it means that the taxpayers' disavowal of indebtedness is powerfully rejected, overridden, or exposed by the dreams—utopian and communal—of those civic waters. When Bloom marks his coin, then, he moves beyond that petty-bourgeois disavowal, allowing the dream being dreamed through him to possess him fully, if momentarily. This is a kind of fetishism, to be sure; but again, to add a further corrective to Jameson, to say "fetishism" is not to say "commodity fetishism." It is simply that spectrality, or magic, or ghostliness upon which the whole concept of fetishism, from its origins in the prehistory of anthropology, derives itself as a so-called "scientific" concept created to explain so-called "primitive" societies.[93] This would have to be something like fetishism unbound from the commodity—to be blunt, something like a "good" fetishism. This is what Jameson's interpretation doesn't see, at least not fully. And it is this kind of imagining, this kind of magic, evoked by Jameson but not quite unfolded, that holds together the imagined community of Dublin through the historical transition and trauma of the years between 1904 and 1922.

At the very least, we can suppose a powerful sub- or unconscious connective flow that creates the imagined community in *Ulysses,* quite apart from and perhaps even in spite of the more conscious and directed versions of such communal relations: cultural-nationalist revivals, armed resistances, and so on. And thanks to Joyce, we are lucky enough not to have to abandon this other imagined community to the abstracted realm of mystifications like the "collective unconscious" or an "akasic medium"; in this case, we see magic and blunt economic materialism side by side or, as it were, in the same figure: the public works. If there is a community to be found in the alienation of the modern division of labor, from the anomie of urban anonymity, it is here in Bloom's coin, or rather, in the desire that Bloom's coin represents and articulates. Rather than see only the destruction of the erstwhile face-to-face communities of the precapitalist and the premodern, as Jameson does, Joyce actually presents us in "Ithaca" and "Wandering Rocks" with a reimagining of the urban community that, while still shot through with the sense of loss and alienation that Jameson highlights, is nevertheless a powerful, hopeful, and original imagining of the urban community. Meanwhile, Bloom's coin is still out there, adventuring its way home. His hope—and ours— for its return is the promise of the community-to-come, suspended somewhere between "not yet" and "time enough, sir. . . . Time enough."

A FOUNTAIN OF NATIONALITY: HAUNTED INFRASTRUCTURE IN FLANN O'BRIEN'S *THE THIRD POLICEMAN*

THREE

There are things of which I may not speak
How strange things happen to a man.
He dabbles in something and does
Not realize that it is his life.
　　—Patrick Kavanagh, "Self-Portrait"

In this chapter I interpret Flann O'Brien's novel *The Third Policeman* not only as a general response to Joyce's *Ulysses* but also, and most importantly, as a largely hostile critique of *Ulysses*'s experimentation with the public utility as a liberating, utopian, metonymic representation of the common good. The result of O'Brien's hostility, however, is not a dismissal of the public utility as an appropriate literary theme but, on the contrary, an obsessive debunking that in its sheer repetition undermines its own aims, making the public utility into a central trope of O'Brien's fiction. Compounding the problem for O'Brien was his employment in the financial office of water and sewage in the Free State's civil service and the fact that he was a native Irish speaker and a bilingual author. Embodying the state's cultural ideal of Irish national identity on the one hand and employed in engineering the state's modernized institutions on the other, O'Brien lived and wrote in a zone of what I call, following Benedict Anderson, an "unstable negativity." From this perspective I interpret *The Third Policeman* as a special kind of national allegory—what I call an allegory of the nation-state—that focuses its anxious attention on the hyphen between the two terms.[1]

THE WATERWORKS AND THE REVIVAL

On November 25, 1892, Douglas Hyde delivered his famous speech to the Irish National Literary Society in Dublin, "The Necessity for De-Anglicising Ireland." There he exhorted his audience "at once [to] arrest the decay of the [Irish] language."[2] Hyde's speech launched the Irish Revival, a forty-year-long period of Irish cultural and linguistic self-assertion that, according to Laura O'Connor in her book *Haunted English,* "set in motion what were to become two major political and philosophical developments in twentieth-century literature: the emergence of language and literature as a medium of decolonization; and the emphasis on the primacy of 'language as such' in European cultural modernism."[3]

The "political and philosophical development" of "language and literature as a medium of decolonization" took place in Ireland as a deep rupture between intellectuals who championed language as a medium of decolonization and those who championed literature. On December 17, 1892, less than a month after Hyde's watershed speech, the newspaper *United Ireland* published in its letters to the editor section William Butler Yeats's response to Hyde, which he rather disingenuously titled "The De-Anglicising of Ireland," and which argued almost exactly the opposite of what Hyde had argued in "The Necessity for De-Anglicising Ireland." It was, Yeats agreed sophistically, necessary to de-Anglicize Ireland, but it was not necessary to restore the Irish language to the status of the national language. "Can we not keep the continuity of the nation's life," he asked, "not by trying to do what Dr. Hyde has practically pronounced impossible, but by translating or retelling in English, which shall have an indefinable Irish quality of rhythm and style, all that is best of the ancient literature?"[4] He compares the Irish situation to that of the United States, that "parvenue among nations," where the national literature is "as much different from English literature as . . . the literature of France . . . and yet America [sic] was once an English colony."[5] A national literary tradition was for Yeats indifferent to the language in which it was written. As long as Irish myths, Irish ways, and Irish inflections were a part of Irish literature in English, Irish literature in English would always be distinctly Irish. Concluding his letter to the editor, he pleads: "Let us by all means prevent the decay of that tongue where we can, and preserve it always among us as a learned language to be a fountain of nationality in our midst, but do not let us base upon it our hopes of nationhood."[6]

Despite Yeats's gesture toward the preservation of the language as a "learned language" like Latin, there is no mistaking the morbid gesture in the "fountain of nationality"; Yeats meant to ensure the place of the English language by giving the Irish language an elegy and a monument. The fountain was a tombstone, the Irish language the dearly departed whose cherished memory would live on as long as it was remembered in Irish national literature. At the time, using the figure of the "fountain of nationality" might have been a gesture innocent of special resonances. But in time, the figure would fairly vibrate with them. In 1965 Chinua Achebe, famed author of the 1958 novel *Things Fall Apart*—the title was of course a tribute to Yeats's "The Second Coming"—used a similar figure when arguing for the inevitable utility of the colonizers' language in African literature: "[African] languages will just have to develop as tributaries to feed the one central language enjoying nationwide currency."[7]

Depending on how we understand the word *fountain* in Yeats's formulation, Achebe's "tributary" may be a faithful figure. A fountain, however, can be a naturally occurring phenomenon or a wholly constructed technical affair—a decorative granite fountain in the middle of a city, for example, or a drinking fountain—or anything in between.[8] The waterworks in *Ulysses*: Are they not a fountain of sorts too, a purely technical, utilitarian fountain supplying the municipality of Dublin with water? Can we not, if we are going to speak of fountains of nationality, also speak of fountains of the state? Joyce's waterworks took Yeats's fountain of nationality in the direction of the state, of a collectivity defined—through the geographical limits of its political boundaries—by its public works,

rather than through shared ethnicity or cultural tradition. The point of
the episode in "Telemachus" involving Stephen, Mulligan, Haines, and the
milkwoman was that "Irishness" could be redefined, no longer as the link
of shared culture and language, but as a relationship of paying and owing,
of partaking and provisioning, of giving and taking. If the episode with
the milkwoman—"time enough, time enough"—exemplified that process through an indefinite space of time (duration), then the waterworks
passage exemplified it through a definite history of space (infrastructure),
and the figure of the taxpayer synthesized both into a unified, though
alienated, image of modern political being. Joyce thus formulated his
definition of the common good of an Irish state—hypothetical in 1904,
real in 1922—not only through a synchronic image of the public works
as a static network but also, like Adam Smith in *The Wealth of Nations,*
through a diachronic image of their funding, construction, and upkeep.

The ideological distance between Yeats's image of the fountain and
Joyce's image of the waterworks could not demarcate any more starkly
the difference between cultural nationalism and modern statism. In Irish
politics as in aesthetic theory the two writers were usually at opposite
ends of the spectrum. When they met for the first and only time in a Dublin café in October of 1902, Yeats was taken aback by Joyce's youthful
arrogance. Joyce, Yeats recounts, "began to explain all his objections to
everything I had ever done." His parting words to Yeats were "I have met
you too late. You are too old."[9] Yeats responded encouragingly, nevertheless, by letter: "You have a very delicate talent. . . . I cannot say more than
this. Remember what Dr. Johnson said about somebody[,] 'let us wait
until we find out whether he is a fountain or a cistern.'"[10] Again, ten years
later, he offered up—through Johnson—the trusty fountain, this time
as a figure for Joyce's literary talent and as an exhortation to Joyce to use
that talent as a fountain of Irish nationality. Joyce chose, with a combination of comic perversity and deadly seriousness, to be the cistern. Indeed, the trope, and the choice, runs straight through Joyce's oeuvre from
his very first collection of poems in 1907, punningly titled *Chamber Music.*
To Yeats's cultural Celtic Twilight Joyce counterposed his own infrastructural Celtic Toilet, not merely as an insult, but—through his literary ele-
vation of the public utility—as a genuine political and aesthetic theory.

Once the Irish Free State established itself in 1922, the stewardship of
the Irish language became a state-supported function, as much a part of

the public works in the cultural sphere as the waterworks were in the sphere of infrastructure. From that point forward, it would be harder to tell the difference between the domain of the nation and the domain of the state: a difference that was, under British colonialism, much more reliable of both detection and demarcation. The lines of battle drawn by Hyde, Yeats, and Joyce would have to be redrawn along the tense hyphen that separated and conjoined the nation and the state. And any understanding of public works would now have to grapple with a newly complicated relationship between the causes of the great society and its effects.

WORKING IN THE WORKS

Enter Flann O'Brien, whose literary career is generally understood to have been stifled in advance by two hard burdens: coming after James Joyce, and living in — and working for — the Irish Free State. When on July 29, 1935, O'Brien (as Brian Nolan) started his first day at his new job in the Irish Civil Service, he unwittingly became a crucial but absent character in *Ulysses*. The social coordinates at which he found himself match all too perfectly with Joyce's utopian cartography of the waterworks in the "Ithaca" chapter of *Ulysses*. Considered in this light, O'Brien's new office job becomes rather astonishing for its fidelity to the Joycean text: "He was assigned to that section of the Department which supervised the waterworks and sewerage undertaken by Local Authorities and provided for the financing of these undertakings by way of loans and grants."[11] O'Brien, in other words, managed the cash that kept Ireland's fountains flowing. It was precisely at that intersection of taxation, finance, and urban infrastructure that Joyce in *Ulysses* made his plea for a new Irish state. Flann O'Brien stepped into this representational hall of mirrors as the real embodiment of Joyce's fictionalized hope.

O'Brien was also born and raised speaking Irish, an increasing rarity in Ireland after the Famine, when as a result of the mass deaths from starvation and the hemorrhage of emigration, the language went into a steep decline: the same decline that Hyde sought to reverse and that Yeats tried to declare a fait accompli. In the years of the Free State, despite all the measures taken to foster the Irish language, there was little indication that things were getting any better. "There were two hundred thousand

Irish speakers in 1922," reports Clair Wills; "by 1939, the number had been cut in half."[12] O'Brien's linguistic rarity also made him a top candidate for the job he won in the civil service; the Free State offered preferential employment to Irish speakers. Thus O'Brien's situation traced the contours of the split in the postcolonial underdeveloped identity between economic and personal development, between utility and the aesthetic, and between the state and the nation. In his *person* he literally embodied the possibility—held out by the postcolonial state—of the affinity between personal and economic development: as a bilingual writer and as a functionary in the water-and-sewage department of the Office of Public Works. In O'Brien's case as a bilingual writer, however, the split between personal and economic development fractured once more along another critical fault line, between Hyde's Irish language and Yeats's Irish literature. In other words, although he never wrote a postcolonial comedy of development, O'Brien appears in his actual historical reality as if he were a Faustian character in one.

Understandably, he was uncomfortable in this role, and, as I will be arguing throughout this chapter, he was excruciatingly aware of his forced representativeness in terms both of the postcolonial state's hopes for the revival of the Irish language (and the institution of an Irish literature) and of the postcolonial state's duties to erect and maintain a national infrastructure of public works and public utilities. O'Brien felt charged to do the work, at one time and in one person, of the traditional culture and of the modernizing state of Ireland. Adding literary poignancy to these already painfully overdetermined expectations, O'Brien was equally keenly aware of the special connection—via the waterworks passage in *Ulysses,* as well as in a more general sense—between himself and James Joyce: the Irish literary giant that he, like so many of his generation, struggled with as an inspiration and an antagonist during the whole of his literary career. Even the building where he worked, the Dublin Custom House, seemed to collude in creating an altogether uncanny, Kafkaesque environment for Ireland's newest civil servant. He was given a desk in one of hundreds of "oak-panelled rooms opening off long, seemingly endless, identical corridors."[13] He was made to sign "the Official Secrets Act and also documents on 'The Use of Influence by Civil Servants' and 'Civil Servants and Politics,'" which together effectively forbade O'Brien from engaging publicly or in print the politics of the state while using his real name.[14] From that first day the bureaucratic machine began a many-month-long process of breaking O'Brien of his famous college-boy ir-reverence for institutional authority and of disciplining him in the art of the office memo and the official report. As his immediate superior John Garvin would recall, "It took some time to channel [O'Brien's] rich lin-guistic flow within the bounds of objectivity and exactitude and to make him realize that official letters were not an appropriate medium for ex-pressing his personality."[15] This was not a personal reproach; Garvin liked O'Brien very much, and—in a crowning irony, as if O'Brien's literary-Oedipal dilemma were not already pronounced enough—he was also a literary critic who would eventually write a scholarly book on Joyce's *Finnegans Wake*.[16]

These multiple pressures on O'Brien's identity produced a rather spec-tacular version of Marshall Berman's split in the underdeveloped iden-tity. Combining Berman's split with the language question produced what I call, following Benedict Anderson, an "unstable negativity" set off by linguistic ambivalence. O'Brien did not split himself in two (like John Mitchel, for example) but fragmented himself into many. The imposi-tion of writing-discipline in the office demanded not a simple repression but rather a kind of partitioning, and O'Brien channeled his "personality" elsewhere, most notably to the *Irish Times,* where his "Cruiskeen Lawn" column appeared regularly between 1940 and 1945 under the pseudo-nym Myles na gCopaleen. O'Brien's column testifies to his gift for per-verting the bureaucratic idiom he was forced to practice in the office for radically different ends—usually in the form of savage parody. Essen-tially, O'Brien divided himself into multiple selves with multiple pseu-donyms in order to enable himself to do his job and to follow his literary vocation. At least one pseudonym was necessary by law, as it was illegal to speak publicly about politics if employed by the civil service. But O'Brien had many names: Brian Nolan, Brian O'Nolan, Brian O'Nualláin, Brian Ua Nualláin, Myles na gCopaleen, Myles na Gopaleen, Flann O'Brien. I refer to him throughout as Flann O'Brien, first because it is the literary work he signed with that name that primarily concerns me, and second because it is the only one of his names that did not tend toward alpha-betic mutation. It is clear in any case that there are three distinct identities

here—Brian, Myles, and Flann—and that there are variations of Brian
and Myles that fluctuate according to the place and emphasis on the language question.

O'Brien's first language was Irish. By the logic of cultural nationalism and linguistic preservationism, hiring preference was given to Irish
speakers in the civil service. O'Brien was a shoo-in because, for the most
part, Dubliners of his generation grew up speaking English and learning
Irish as a second language. As a result, the bureaucratic structures of the
state ended up speaking and writing their own distinctive version of Irish,
a state Irish that varied considerably from any other kind. Perhaps for
this reason, although the facts are unclear, O'Brien was officially known
as "B. Nolan" in civil service documents referring to him. O'Brien was
irritated by this and made it known in a letter of complaint that reveals
the cracks in the walls separating his multiple selves:

> During my recent absence from the office, I received two letters ad-
> dressed to B. Nolan. This is not the name under which I entered the
> Civil Service, nor is it the English transliteration in use by my family.
> My own name is one of the few subjects upon which I claim to be an
> authority and notwithstanding any colloquialism countenanced for
> the sake of convenience in the office, I would be glad if my own predi-
> lection in the matter be accepted in official correspondence in future.
> I also desire that my name be correctly entered in any future edition
> of the telephone guide or any similar circular.[17]

The tone of this missive is deeply ironic—false humility ("one of the few
subjects upon which I claim to be an authority," "I would be glad if . . .")
mixed with an unconditional demand to have his authority restored to
him. This is one of those official documents in which O'Brien allowed his
"personality" to show itself. But O'Brien is evoking, not the authority of
his proper name, but rather his authority *over* his proper name. He does
not say, "You have my name wrong. It is properly this and not that." He
says, "I claim my authority to name myself—not according to tradition or
according to some other ancient or sacred textual source, but according to
my will." It is a demand that, if sustained, would wholly subvert the state's
authority. But subversion is not exactly his goal; instead, he presents the

moment of his contract with the state as the evidence of his will *and*, importantly, as evidence of his submission to the state: "the name under which I entered the Civil Service," which, otherwise stated, also means "the *terms* under which I agreed to join the Civil Service." A few months later, after his two-year probation as a junior civil servant, O'Brien became an established civil servant under the name Brian Ó Nualláin.

To complicate the matter, it is entirely possible that O'Brien did in fact originally sign his paperwork as B. Nolan. This is, according to O'Brien's biographer Anthony Cronin, the most likely case, even though Irish names were encouraged in the civil service. Other applicants used their Irish names as a badge of qualification, or, if they did not have Irish names, they Gaelicized them for the purpose, assuming that the more Irish their name, the more likely they were to be hired. Yet O'Brien had registered for the service's Irish language exam as B. Nolan, so it is possible, even probable, that he did similarly for the service. In other words, not only is the tone of O'Brien's letter ironic, but the whole affair looks almost like a prank; he accused the state of getting his name wrong by Anglicizing it, when in fact the state was far more likely to do the reverse, ever ready as it was to Gaelicize anything and everything that it could. Out of carelessness or malice or ambivalence or all three, O'Brien signed his deal with the state with his Anglicized name. Despite the relative smallness of the whole episode, it brings into relief some much bigger issues: the co-optation of the Irish language for state purposes, which a native speaker like O'Brien would be in a unique position to feel as an affront to his personal history with the language; the ambivalence of the Irish state itself— a modern institution for the most part modeled on, and inheriting the institutional culture of, the British state—which was attempting to valorize and integrate into itself a language born of wholly different and even contradictory political forms; and finally, the importance of naming and the control of names for state power, as well as O'Brien's wily awareness of what was at stake in the game. Though his resistance usually took more literary forms, it is also here in this letter. O'Brien keeps the state guessing, and in doing so retains a kind of authority. He asserts sovereignty over his identity without asserting a sovereign identity, and he does so in the dialectic of submission and empowerment that characterizes the individual's relation to the modern state. If the Irish state was in some sense

founded on the notion of protecting, cultivating, and institutionaliz-
ing Irish difference, O'Brien was in the business of repeatedly pointing
out that such a mission would, paradoxically and in the same gesture, be
blinded to Irish *differences.* The sheer number of names he accepted as his
own would attest to this.[18]

In the difference between a reliance on the proper name for authority
and the assertion of the authority to change the proper name lay the dilemma of the Irish Free State. Declan Kiberd puts it succinctly: "Ownership of the state, and not its very nature, seemed in retrospect to have been
the primary point of contention between the Irish and the British."[19] Thus
a parliament became a Dáil, and a prime minister, a Taoiseach; the office
did not change, only the name.[20] This is not to say that changing a name
does not in some fundamental way change an office—in fact it was precisely this linguistic logic that motivated the name changes in the first
place. But it is to suggest that the transformative power of translation cannot, or at least in this case did not, prove transformative *enough,* and that
is what concerned O'Brien. It is also a way to understand the distance
between Joyce's utopian state normalcy and the grim realities of Irish independence.

Those grim realities were the result of a deep economic recession beginning in the late 1920s; the inherent fiscal and institutional conservatism of the new Irish government; and the economic war with England in
the 1930s that cut Ireland off from formerly lucrative British markets.[21]
Along with these historical obstacles came the social-psychological trauma
of years of revolution and civil war, the exhaustion of revolutionary ener-
gies, and the return to the often sordid pragmatics of survival and everyday life. Again, Kiberd synthesizes a series of historical data into a phrase
that conveys the postrevolutionary Irish sensibility as that of a "post-
heroic society: a people who had once asserted revolution or death now
has to cope with the death of the revolution."[22] Or as Terence Brown has it,
"There was a general sense that the heroic age had passed."[23] And after the
heroic age, we might say, comes the bureaucratic age. The state became an
end in itself, "the be-all and end-all of the new elites. They worked to defend it rather than reshape it to the needs of the people. Many of those
people—landless labourers, women, Protestants, Gaeltacht dwellers—
were still so estranged from the official apparatus that they behaved like

members of an underground movement in their own country."[24] This was also true of the intellectuals, though at the same time they were the ones in control of the state, with privileged access to political power. The intellectuals' double bind consisted, first, of "being a beneficiary of a nationalist revolution which you had largely come to despise" while at the same time "it was unthinkable that you could regret the passing of British rule" and, second, of being "a passive or active upholder of a faith [Catholicism] which you often found abhorrent either in its beliefs or, at the very least, its public attitudes." These factors led such intellectuals-cum-bureaucrats into "a curious kind of latter-day aestheticism," in which "you were in an ambiguous, not to say dishonest position, morally, socially and intellectually. You were a conformist among other conformists in terms of the most important social or philosophical questions you could face. But yet you knew about modern art and literature. You had read most of the great moderns and, above all, you had read James Joyce. That was what marked you out as different, the joke you shared against the rabblement of which you were otherwise a part."[25] For Cronin, it is "impossible to exaggerate the importance of Joyce in their view of things."[26]

Re-enter, then, James Joyce, or rather, Joyce's deeply felt absence, Elijah presiding, from his empty chair at the table, over the state's proceedings, stalking the "long, seemingly endless, identical corridors" of the Custom House. John Garvin, O'Brien's boss in the civil service, authored, under the pseudonym Andrew Cass, a political-allegorical reading of *Finnegans Wake* in which Shem the Penman figured Joyce and Shaun the Post figured Éamon de Valera. Such an interpretation may not have been a particularly good reading of the *Wake*, but it was probably an accurate temperature-taking of the state—if not from the point of view of the state's subjects, then at least from the point of view of many of its functionaries. Perhaps the measure of Joyce's influence in the civil service can be taken simply by pointing to the fact that in just one division, there was one civil servant, Garvin, writing books about James Joyce and another, O'Brien, writing books like James Joyce's. Garvin and O'Brien, like many other civil servants, would have absorbed Joyce's worldly vision and then found themselves constrained to the provinciality of the state's conservatism and isolationism, thus engendering their split personality and their multiply lettered lives of civil pseudonymity.

In this context O'Brien was the self-styled and self-conscious heir, as I pointed out at the beginning of this chapter, to Joyce's literary vision and to his hopes for the Irish Free State. Between 1935, when he entered the service, and 1939 he wrote and published a novel about a man writing a novel whose characters rebel against him and plot to kill him. The metafictional conceit of *At Swim-Two-Birds* is all-too-readily recognizable as O'Brien's problems with and reaction to the anxiety of influence. But when we consider, too, the rather fantastic idea that O'Brien was scripted into *Ulysses,* that *Ulysses* anticipated him, and that it anticipated him in his role as civil servant as opposed to his literary self, then we begin to see that the problem is not so simple—is not, that is to say, simply or wholly a question of the literary anxiety of influence, but has something to do also with the state, the nation, and the public works. Joyce was a literary figure who haunted the Irish political world as much as he haunted the Irish literary world, in part because the literati populated the state institutions and in part because his books had something to say about the state. O'Brien found himself at the center of this haunting, and his work should be read in this light.

THE THIRD CIVIL SERVANT

There he is, says I, in his gloryhole, with his cruiskeen lawn and his load of papers, working for the cause.

—James Joyce, *Ulysses*

The Third Policeman was the novel O'Brien wrote just after *At Swim-Two-Birds*: its dark double, its failed unpublished twin. It stayed unpublished until shortly after his death in 1966, when his widow Evelyn found the manuscript among his things and sent it out for publication. Twice in 1940 O'Brien tried to publish *The Third Policeman*. After the London publisher Longman's rejected it as "too fantastic,"[27] however, O'Brien hid it away, told anyone who asked that he had "lost" it, and decided to begin writing in Irish. The result was the successful *An Béal Bocht,* or in English *The Poor Mouth,* which, as Clair Wills argues, followed O'Brien's original formula for using Irish forms—Irish legend in *At Swim-Two-Birds* and the Gaeltacht autobiography in *An Béal Bocht*—in a way that the interim novel *The Third Policeman* seems to have abandoned.[28] O'Brien's turn back to Irish form, this time combined with a turn to the Irish language, occurred at roughly the same time that Samuel Beckett, a few years earlier, gave up writing in English and dedicated himself to French.[29] English, it appears, was no longer a viable language of literary expression for either of the two modernists. The formal and linguistic break between *The Third Policeman* and *An Béal Bocht* is a big part of what makes deciphering the obscurity of the former novel so pressing, and so interesting. If it is divorced from the novels that preceded and followed it in form, then what form does *The Third Policeman* take? And was there anything in the writing of *The Third Policeman*—some impasse other than the failure to publish—whose solution O'Brien sought in the switch back to Irish afterwards?

The rest of this chapter reads *The Third Policeman* as an allegory of the nation-state structured around the concepts of utility and the public works. Between his send-ups of Irish legend in *At Swim-Two-Birds* and the Gaeltacht autobiography in *An Béal Bocht*, O'Brien tried to interarticulate the nation and the state in *The Third Policeman*. The novel is an instructive, understudied, and flawed experiment in generic invention that moreover grapples with the public works, imagining them as the critical hinge between the nation and the state. My reading reveals in the novel an imaginative mapping of the nation-state that is much more than a parody, if much less than a utopia.

The first and primary proof of the book's status as an allegory of the nation-state is in its setting. When O'Brien tried for the second time to publish the book, he changed the title from *The Third Policeman* to *Hell Goes Round and Round*; the setting was therefore inferred by many, including O'Brien's biographer Anthony Cronin, to be hell itself. But this hell, as Cronin dryly puts it, "is situated somewhere near Tullamore," in the Irish midlands, where O'Brien "spent a good part of his boyhood, apparently enjoying an idyll."[30] Cronin reads the novel's vision of hell as a revelation of O'Brien's usually dormant Catholicism and his belief in the Manichean struggle between good and evil that was engendered by it.[31] Similarly but more secularly, Anne Clissmann reads the novel as "a picture of dislocated reality" that parodies "all speculation on the nature of life and death."[32] O'Brien, in his own description—and plot synopsis—of the book, would seem at first glance to endorse both of these interpretations:

> When you get to the end of this book you realise that my hero or main character (he's a heel and a killer) had been dead throughout the book and that all the queer things which have been happening to him are happening in a sort of hell which he earned for the killing. Towards the end of the book (before you know he's dead) he manages to get back to his own house where he used to live with another man who helped in the original murder. Although he's been away three days, this other fellow is twenty years older and dies of fright when he sees the other lad standing in the door. Then the two of them walk back along the road to the hell place and start thro' all the same terrible adventures again, the first fellow being surprised and frightened at everything just as he was the first time and as if he'd never been through it before. It is made clear that this sort of thing goes on for ever—and there you are. It is supposed to be very funny but I don't know about that either. . . . I think the idea of a man being dead all the time is pretty new.[33]

When O'Brien calls the world of the novel a "sort of hell," it is as if he says it for lack of a better term: not hell, "a sort of hell," an Irish sort of hell that looks "sort of" like Tullamore. What is being laid out, however, is not a Catholic hell but a national hell. The hell of *The Third Policeman* is the landscape of the national imaginary incorporated into the state's modern grid, resulting in sublime horror and comic farce. When Cronin jokes that "hell is situated somewhere near Tullamore," he dismisses the import of the joke's content, which is that O'Brien had in his novel effectively transformed his "boyhood idyll" into an existential nightmare. The question that looms up from this but that is wholly eclipsed by the joke is why O'Brien would want to do that.

Finding the "why" goes back to the language question insofar as it is wrapped up in the national question. In *The Spectre of Comparisons*, Benedict Anderson points to the ways in which, in Lord Acton's words, "exile is the nursery of nationality."[34] Exile, however, is not to be understood in purely geographical terms but also and especially in linguistic terms. Speaking of the results of the twin currents of the rise of the centralized, bureaucratic, modern state and "the spread of a centralized, standardized, steeply hierarchical system of public education," Anderson explains that "the social and political hierarchy of vernaculars and dialects . . . was increasingly linked to employment possibilities and opportunities for social mobility."[35] In this environment, it was

> small wonder that people were becoming ever more self-conscious about their linguistic practices and the consequences of those practices. *Quite often the effect was a kind of exile.* The more a standardized vernacular ceased to be merely the internal language of officials and became the official language of a propagandizing state, the more likely became the emergence in Old Europe of something reminiscent of the creole or native: the not-really-German German, the not-quite-Italian Italian, the non-Spanish Spaniard. As in the Americas, *a kind of unstable negativity appeared.* Nothing, therefore, is less surprising than that the nationalist movements which transformed the map of Europe after 1919 were so often led by young bilinguals, a pattern to be followed after 1919 in Asia and Africa. How could a boy who learned Czech from his mother and German from his schooling unlearn a Czech that had left no contaminating traces on his German-speaking classmates? How could he not see his Czech as though in exile, through the inverted telescope of his German?[36]

Anderson's description needs modification in order to adapt it to the Irish case generally and to O'Brien specifically, but it is in its essentials already evocative of O'Brien's situation and of his book; he felt himself in a kind of exile, hence the destruction of his childhood idyll and its recreation in *The Third Policeman* as "a kind of unstable negativity." The problem for O'Brien is the obverse of the one posed by Anderson here. The twist on Anderson is that O'Brien felt this way because his Irish was *not* inflected with English in the way it was for most. His was a "pure" Irish, an ideal Irish. O'Brien learned Irish from his mother and English from his schooling. He left Tullamore when, after the treaty was signed and the Irish Free State established in 1922, his father took a post in the Irish Civil Service as a taxman and moved the family to Dublin. The language revival had at that time reached its peak of enthusiasm. Irish was now, officially, the national language. Yet few in Dublin could speak it, and fewer still could speak it like O'Brien. In his angry letter to the civil service in which he demanded that his name be changed from Nolan to Ó Nualláin, one can now see the twisted pathos that must have motivated him and the utter incomprehension of the authority to which he addressed himself. Celebrated as an authentic exemplar of Irish national identity, O'Brien felt himself to be an outsider in the culture of Dublin and the culture of the civil service. The state authority would have been all too happy simply to change his name in their records to one that it would have preferred him to carry in the first place. O'Brien did not want to hear this, or he did not like the sound of it when he was forced to listen. The encroachment on his personal history and his mother tongue, the making public and the making idyllic of it, must have triggered an "unstable negativity" much like that of Anderson's intra-European creoles created by the national schools. O'Brien was, in his own mind, a not-quite-Irish Irishman, and he experienced this with a vivid intensity. Yet when O'Brien tried to get this across in the confused and confusing letter about his name, the state was not able properly to interpret his hostility.

When Anderson uses the example of "a boy who learned Czech from his mother and German from his schooling," he may have some "young bilingual" Czech nationalist in mind. But the example that must come to mind for modernist literary scholars is Franz Kafka.[37] O'Brien's work bears a striking resemblance to Kafka's, a resemblance that is telling of the extent to which they shared Anderson's exile and "unstable negativity," along with their relationship to large, alienating bureaucratic structures. I suggest here that O'Brien's English in *The Third Policeman* needs to be read, in a modified version of Anderson, "through the inverted telescope of [Kafka's] German."[38] Though written in English, *The Third Policeman* "often reads like a translation from the Irish, but it is not the poeticized version of Irish syntax given by Lady Gregory and John Synge which had become known as 'Kiltartan.'" Instead, Cronin continues, "its very meticulousness, a sort of painstaking clarity and flatness, [gives] the impression that English [is] being written as if it were a dead language."[39] In other words, we might think of *The Third Policeman* as having been written in English as a *second* language, similar to the way Beckett used French, for example. O'Brien's creole dialect is something like the Irish language's revenge on the English language. He writes a low-cultural "Irish" idiom into the English language and in doing so insults English, high-nationalist Irish and most of all the ideals inscribed in the foundation of the state. His unstable negativity resides precisely in the fact that he feels he must attack those ideals that, ironically, most favored him. In the state's Irish O'Brien could not recognize, or did not want to recognize, his own; his assault on English was designed to render it as strange to the state as the state had rendered Irish to him.

THE THIRD POLICEMAN

And then he starts with his jawbreakers about phenomenon and
science and this phenomenon and the other phenomenon. . . .
Didn't I tell you? As true as I'm drinking this porter if he was
at his last gasp he'd try to downface you that dying was living.
*—*James Joyce, *Ulysses*

O'Brien's novel opens in what, knowing what is to come, we might call a realist mode. The narrator has let himself be convinced by a man named Divney to rob and kill another man, Mathers, who "had spent a long life of fifty years in the cattle trade and now lived in retirement in a big house three miles away. He still did large business through agents and the people said that he carried no less than three thousand pounds with him every time he hobbled to the village to lodge his money."[40] The words "cattle trade" and "big house," while they seem merely descriptive here, are inescapably evocative of the Anglo-Irish landlord's Big House, and thus the plot hatched by Divney is obliquely linked to a long history of Irish agrarian violence. While Divney persuades the narrator to act as his accomplice through constant complaints against the Jews and Freemasons, and through appeals to the narrator's scholarly ambitions, his most telling argument is also, for the narrator anyway, just as unconvincing as the rest: "Once he said something about 'social justice' but it was plain to me that he did not properly understand the term" (15).

The opening of the novel thus alludes, in a way that is practically sub-liminal in its understatement and merciless in its demystification, to a national narrative of British oppression and Irish agrarian uprising that underpins the mythology of Irish independence. Rewritten here as a tale of petty greed and prejudice, that narrative has already begun to devolve into an unstable negativity: a "not-quite-Irish" Irish national tale. Div-ney and the narrator carry out the murder but do not collect Mathers's money. Instead Divney hides it from the narrator with the rationale that they must wait for their criminal trail to become cold. They wait for three years, in which time the narrator never leaves Divney's side for fear of being betrayed. As it turns out, Divney has hidden the money in a "black box" in Mathers's own house, and once they make their way there, he sends the narrator inside by himself to fetch it. At this point, space and time begin to lose their connection to reality. As the narrator crosses the threshold of the window he has forced open, he finds himself "not at once in a room, but crawling along the deepest window-ledge I have ever seen. When I reached the floor and jumped noisily down upon it, the open window seemed very far away and much too small to have admit-ted me" (22). When the narrator is about to grasp the box, which Divney has supposedly hidden under the floorboards, "something happened." At the end of the book, the reader discovers that Divney has planted a bomb in the black box, which has gone off at this precise moment. But the narrator's experience of his sudden violent death is wholly different than what we might expect. "It was some change which came upon me or upon the room, indescribably subtle, yet momentous, ineffable. . . . The fingers of my right hand, thrust into the opening in the floor, had closed mechanically, found nothing at all and came up again empty. The box was gone!" (23).

What ensues is a fantastic narrative of some netherworld that never-theless remains faithful to the notion of a transformation that is both in-describably subtle and yet momentous. To characterize this place, we will have to bear in mind both the allegory of the nation-state at the center of its production and another reference to Joyce. Our narrator is never named, but after his death he becomes aware of a voice in his head that he decides to call "Joe." This is very close to the structure of the "Cyclops" chapter of *Ulysses,* where a nameless narrator relays the action to his friend Joe. The structural similarity, aside from identifying what is almost certainly a direct reference, helps to understand where the narrator of *The Third Policeman* finds himself after his death. At one point in "Cyclops" the narrator excuses himself from the pub to urinate with the words, "Goodbye Ireland I'm going to Gort."[41] Marjorie Howes has pointed out that this is a deliberate misquotation of the colloquialism "Goodbye Dublin I'm going to Gort," producing the nonsensical implication that Gort, while in Ireland, is somehow *not* in Ireland.[42] This impossible national space—inside and outside the nation—is where the narrator of *The Third Policeman* finds himself just after he is blown to bits by Divney's bomb.

If it is true that because he is dead he is now somewhere outside of Ireland, it is also true that his surroundings are still Irish, that to all appearances the narrator is still in Ireland, and that inexplicably, the narrator still *is.* In death the narrator carries on as if nothing had happened. He is more determined than ever to find the black box. The payoff gets bigger and bigger in his mind as he wanders further and further away from his life, back out of Mathers's big house, where he lost it: "I crept out of old Mathers' house nine hours afterwards. . . . My heart was happy and full of zest for high adventure. I did not know my name or where I had come from but the black box was practically in my grasp. . . . Ten thousand pounds' [previously, it was three thousand] worth of negotiable securities would be a conservative estimate of what was in it. As I walked down the road I was pleased enough with everything" (37).

The landscape he passes through upon leaving Mathers's house can best be described as uncanny. It is in all respects normal for the Tullamore region, yet there is some excess, some insistent difference, that the narrator cannot help but notice.

There was nothing familiar about the good-looking countryside which stretched away from me at every view. I was now but two days from home—not more than three hours' walking—and yet I seemed to have reached regions which I had never seen before and of which I had never even heard. I could not understand this because although my life had been spent mostly among my books and papers, I had thought that there was no road in the district I had not travelled, no road whose destination was not well-known to me. There was another thing. My surroundings had a strangeness of a peculiar kind, entirely separate

from the mere strangeness of a country where one has never been before. Everything seemed almost too pleasant, too perfect, too finely
made. Each thing the eye could see was unmistakable and unambigu-
ous, incapable of merging with any other thing or of being confused
with it. The colour of the bogs was beautiful and the greenness of the
green fields supernal. Trees were arranged here and there with far-from-
usual consideration for the fastidious eye. The senses took keen pleasure from merely breathing the air and discharged their functions with
delight. I was clearly in a strange country but all the doubts and per-
plexities which strewed my mind could not stop me from feeling happy
and heart-light and full of an appetite for going about my business
and finding the hiding-place of the black box. (39)

This is a description of an uncanny landscape: close to home yet far
away, familiar but persistently strange. The narrator says confusingly that
he is "two days from home," but "not more than three hours' walking";
time and space are out of joint. The feeling of strangeness governing the
scene is muted by the pleasant impressions of the landscape: green fields,
beautiful bogs, "trees . . . arranged . . . with far-from-usual consideration
for the fastidious eye." While he walks, the narrator, otherwise so preoc-
cupied with his quest for the black box, allows himself to daydream
about revisiting "this mysterious townland upon [his] bicycle and prob-
[ing] at [his] leisure the reasons for all its strangenesses" (39). But that
pleasantness seems at every moment just about to tip over into menace,
threatening to become "too pleasant, too perfect, too finely made." It is
thus because of its suspicious idyllic perfection that the landscape ac-
quires its strangeness, not because of its unfamiliarity. In the end, however, the strangeness of the scene derives primarily from its obvious contrivance, from the trees "arranged" with "far-from-usual consideration
for the fastidious eye," to the scenery "too finely made." The suspicion
of some unknown but powerful arranging agency is highlighted again in
this passage: "I found it hard to think of a time when there was no road
there because the trees and the tall hills and the fine views of bogland had
been arranged by wise hands for the pleasing picture they made when
looked at from the road. Without a road to have them looked at from they
would have a somewhat aimless if not a futile aspect" (37). The road here

gives a clue as to the arranging agency. If the surroundings arrange them-selves to maximize their visual splendor from the road, then it would make sense that whoever built the road arranged the scenery. There is uncertainty here about which came first, the road or the landscape. In the first sentence, however, the scenery presupposes the road, as if the road were the only natural element involved in the landscape, the rest of it having been planned. In the second sentence, the road presupposes the scenery, or rather, the road grants meaning and beauty to an otherwise wild and futile landscape (in the imperial vocabulary, a wasteland). This is, I think, to pose the question of the relation between the nation and the state: the beautiful, elegiac landscape evokes the nation, whereas the road evokes the roadworks, the public works, and thereby, the state. That is why both landscape and road are represented as the product of some kind of *work*. The landscape is not a natural phenomenon insofar as it is an Irish landscape, which, as such, is the product of the work of the na-tional imaginary. Likewise the road is the product of the (more tangible, more recognizable) work of the state. The excess or surplus of beauty in the landscape, as the product of imaginative work, combines with the in-frastructural work of the road to make the narrator uncomfortable. In this strange world, the work of the national imaginary—like the work of the state in the "real" world—is manifest in his natural surroundings: lit-eralized nation building, with nature as the building blocks and the road as foundation.

This bizarre landscape may, moreover, have a historical precedent in the Great Famine of the nineteenth century. Let us consider for a mo-ment that what the narrator is describing is a famine road, one of those commissioned by the Board of Works that, as we saw in chapter 1, "began nowhere and ended nowhere." In the phrase "if not a futile aspect," we are given the ambiguous possibilities of utility on the one hand and aes-thetic "aimlessness" on the other. Or alternatively, his description of the landscape as having "a futile aspect" might be understood as a willful transposition of that futility from the road to the landscape. This trans-position is necessary, in a way, because if the narrator is traveling on the road its utility cannot realistically be questioned by him, at least not without throwing him back into an unstable negativity. He thinks, after all, that he knows where he is going—to find the black box—and that the road leads there. But the absence of utility—always about to strike the narrator's consciousness but never quite getting there, having been transposed from the road to the scenery—manifests itself as a surplus of aesthetic stimuli, the "pleasing picture." On the road to nowhere, even art is anxious, overbearing. The scene thus appears saturated with the pathos of the Famine works, with the concept of utility emptied of its purpose and function, and the aesthetic impression is thereby made uncanny. The narrator's account of his pleasant walk closely resembles one of John Mitchel's contemporary accounts of Famine Ireland: "A calm still horror was over the land. Go where you would, in the heart of the town or in the suburb, or the mountainside or on the level plain, there was the stillness and heavy pall-like feel of the chamber of death. You stood in the presence of a dread, silent, vast dissolution. An unseen ruin was creeping around you. You saw no war of classes, no open Janissary war of foreigners, no human agency of destruction."[43] The narrator of *The Third Policeman* seems just on the other side of noticing the horror behind the "pleasing picture," in which, as in Mitchel's description, there are no other people, and no sign of their recent passage. Even the road does not signify, in the narrator's description, a present human agency. The narrator's drive to obtain the black box deadens his senses to the "vast dissolution" and keeps him from confronting the "unseen ruin" that is everywhere around him. The feeling of uncanniness, however—of a scene "almost too pleasant, too perfect, too finely made"—registers a repressed knowledge that the narrator is indeed on a road to nowhere, surrounded by death.

To whatever extent we can understand the scene as a characterization of the Irish nation-state, we should also be reading the palimpsestic impression of the states that came before. The failures of the British public works during the Famine haunt O'Brien's understanding of the public works within the Free State. The legacy of the old Board of Works, and the uncertain legacy of the Free State's renamed Office of the Public Works, are the transparent overlays that threaten to transform the narrator's idyll into a nightmare, and the only thing standing between the narrator's uneasy pleasure in the scene and the scene's nightmarish reality is the quest for the black box. The uncanniness of this landscape is the product of mapping "the long, seemingly endless corridors" of the state on top of the rural landscape of the Irish midlands, the palimp-

sest of bureaucratic, statist ideology that makes O'Brien's childhood landscape into a kind of hell—a deliberate and imaginative conflation of nation and state.[44] That anxiety over the distinction in turn produces the
overall incapacity for enjoyment, the unstable negativity governing the
scene. Though the words *Irish* and *Ireland* are not mentioned here,
the scene has certain similarities to Anderson's understanding of nationalism in England in the nineteenth century. "It was beginning to become possible to see 'English fields' in England—from the window of a
railway carriage," or, in this case, it was beginning to become possible to
see Irish fields from an Irish road, but in a rather uncomfortable way for
the narrator.[45] He seems to be witnessing this transformation, of "mere"
landscape into "Irish" landscape, in the very moment of its "becoming
possible." And the result, in the Irish case and in the way O'Brien depicts
it here, is more ghastly than anything Anderson imagines; "something
happened," says the narrator as he crosses over Mathers's window-ledge,
that was "indescribably subtle, yet momentous, ineffable."

Anderson stipulates a precondition for the becoming-possible of the
national narrative: amnesia. "This [new national] consciousness, embedded in homogeneous, empty time, create[s] amnesias and estrangements
exactly parallel to the forgetting of childhood brought on by puberty. . . .
At this juncture emerge[s] the narrative of the nation."[46] Indeed, it may be
telling that while the Famine goes unmentioned in *The Third Policeman,*
it surfaces as a trace in the narrator's description of the strange country
in which he finds himself—another amnesic symptom. Stepping into the
phantasmagoria of homogenous, empty time, and stepping into the literalized grid of the nation-state, the narrator—always unnamed for the
reader—forgets his own name and, moreover, often forgets to care that
he has forgotten his name, as the black box completely replaces such a
concern. The "becoming possible" of the national narrative—"Irish"
landscape from an Irish road—goes hand in hand with the narrator's
amnesia. The narrator's death marks his ascent to the national public
sphere, his transformation into a public subject: "In the bourgeois [read
also *national*] public sphere . . . a principle of negativity [is] axiomatic:
the validity of what you say in public bears a negative relation to your
person. What you say will carry force not because of who you are but despite who you are. Implicit in this principle is a utopian universality that
would allow people to transcend the given realities of their bodies and

their status."[47] As Michael Warner argues, a "principle of negativity" governs the "utopian universality" of the bourgeois public sphere. This principle of negativity, so central to the public sphere created by print media like newspapers, and thus also central to the imagined community of the nation, is at the same time the utopian universality that characterizes the black box motivating the narrator's quest; this is what the narrator refers to when he mentions "negotiable securities." More or less another way of saying "money," saying "negotiable securities" lays emphasis on the fact that such instruments can be exchanged without proof of ownership or identity. Negotiable securities circulate "not because of who you are but despite who you are." Their guarantee is with the state or with a bank, not with the economic agent wielding them, and their ownership springs not from a signature or a title but from possession. The narrator of *The Third Policeman* forgets who he is but never forgets what he is after; he literalizes the principle of negativity in his death, and he figures utopian universality in his amnesic fixation on the black box. Later in *The Third Policeman*, Sergeant Pluck refers to the narrator's death as "a piece of negative nullity," reinforcing the point that the principle of negativity is as much a part of the narrator's death as is his "real" death. In death, the narrator embodies the principle of negativity that defines the citizen-subject through Anderson's "amnesia," the public citizen-subject through Warner's negativity, and utopian universality through the "negotiable securities" the narrator supposes to be the contents of the black box.[48]

But anonymity has its limits, and its anxieties. As Mathers asks the narrator in their posthumous conversation, "How could I tell you where the black box was if you could not sign a receipt? That would be most irregular. I might as well give it to the west wind or the smoke from a pipe. How could you execute an important Bank document?" (31). And later, when Sergeant Pluck decides to hang the narrator for murder for no particular reason, his rationale leverages the narrator's namelessness against him:

> Anything you do is a lie and nothing that happens to you is true. . . . For that reason alone . . . we can take you and hang the life out of you and you are not hanged at all and there is no entry to be made in the death papers. The particular death you die is not even a death (which is an inferior phenomenon at the best) only an insanitary abstraction

in the backyard, a piece of negative nullity neutralised and rendered void by asphyxiation and the fracture of the spinal string. If it is not a lie to say that you have been given the final hammer behind the barrack, equally it is true to say that nothing has happened to you. (102)

Betrayed by what seemed previously to be his best protection against the law, his namelessness, the narrator attempts to take refuge in an alternative concept of identity that, until now, has appeared nowhere in the cold, absurdist logic of the novel: "I began to feel intensely every fragment of my equal humanity" (102). "Equal humanity" may be no less a "piece of negative nullity" than the negativity of the citizen-subject, but it has the virtue of breaking the strictly national frame of reference from which the novel is, until this moment, constrained. Yet it is not spoken; it never becomes part of the terms of debate between the narrator and Sergeant Pluck. It is a weak gesture toward a weak concept and cannot, in the end, break free of the national imaginary that silences it—it is not even possible, in this place, to say it out loud. If indeed the world of the novel is the national imaginary delinked from any other reality, or any other epistemological regime, then this makes perfect sense. Here, there is no other frame of reference than the nation-state: not nature, and certainly not humanity.

Unable to avoid execution by invoking his citizenship, and unable even to utter the only other invocation, humanity, available to him, the narrator tearfully accepts his fate. In the event he escapes execution only to run headlong into repetition, the bad infinity that characterizes the world in which he finds himself: homogeneous, empty time. The narrator is doomed to relive his little war of independence, his encounter with, struggle against, and escape from the policemen, over and over. To the extent that *The Third Policeman* is an allegory of the nation-state, then it accuses the nation-state of what, according to the novel, would be its epic failure.

"THE MOST WATER-PIPED EDIFICE IN THE WORLD"

If O'Brien pronounced the Free State an epic failure in *The Third Policeman,* we should remember that his novel about the failure of the state was also itself a failure; O'Brien never sent it out to publishers again after it was rejected by Longman's. But the target for O'Brien's satirical attacks in the novel is not only the Irish Free State but also James Joyce. The most direct of those attacks appears in O'Brien's novel indirectly, as a footnote, a humorous aside. But it is nevertheless centrally significant, because it is the only moment in the book where we can see clearly the convergence between Flann O'Brien's fiction and his reality, between his literary work and his work on the Irish waterworks. It was a convergence that made him profoundly uncomfortable: hence the footnote, hence the unpublished novel. The footnote in *The Third Policeman* is an eruptive device that in this case takes up almost as much room on the page as the main text. It interrupts the narrative plot of the novel at a decisive moment when the narrator is about to be sentenced to hang. It is also a moment in which the carefulness of O'Brien's reading of *Ulysses* becomes apparent through parody. In the footnote, the nameless narrator of *The Third Policeman* offers an anecdote concerning his scholarly obsession with the eccentric genius de Selby, a comical narrative thread that runs parallel to the main plot of the novel throughout.[49] All the anecdotes about de Selby are written in high parodic mode against academic and/or official, bureaucratic discourse. De Selby is presented as a lunatic who does not in any way merit the long scholarly debates that his scribblings have generated and that so obsess the narrator. But in his last pseudoscientific experiments with water, de Selby's activities intersect both with Joyce's waterworks passage and with O'Brien's civil service job.

De Selby, the narrator tells us, was obsessed with water. "He praises the equilibrium of water, its circumambiency, equiponderance and equitableness, and declares that water, 'if not abused' can achieve 'absolute superiority'" (146). (Already, there are strong echoes of the "Ithaca" chapter of *Ulysses*, from the passage immediately following the waterworks passage, where Bloom is musing on the "universality" of water, "its democratic equality and constancy to its nature in seeking its own level . . . its climatic and commercial significance . . . its vast circumterrestrial ahorizontal curve" [17.185–208]). The narrator of *The Third Policeman* then begins to describe the interior of de Selby's house, where all of his experiments with water took place. The house is a kind of monument to de Selby's achievement (or lack thereof), since little else "remains save the record of his obscure and unwitnessed experiments" (146).

Hatchjaw [another scholar of de Selby] (in his invaluable *Conspectus of the de Selby Dialetic*) has described the house as "the most water-piped edifice in the world." Even in the living-rooms there were upwards of ten rough farmyard taps, some with zinc troughs and some (as those projecting from the ceiling and from converted gas-brackets near the fireplace) directed at the unprotected floor. Even on the stairs a three-inch main may still be seen nailed along the rail of the balustrade with a tap at intervals of one foot, while under the stairs and in every conceivable hiding-place there were elaborate arrangements of cisterns and storage-tanks. Even the gas pipes were connected up with this water system and would gush strongly at any attempt to provide the light. (148)

All of this piping, the narrator tells us, and the voluminous amounts of water that went through it, did not fail to attract the attention of the authorities.

The story is one of a long succession of prosecutions for water wastage at the suit of the local authority. At one hearing it was shown that he had used 9,000 gallons in one day and on another occasion almost 80,000 gallons in the course of a week. The word "used" in this context is the important one. The local officials, having checked the volume of water entering the house daily from the street connection, had sufficient curiosity to watch the outlet sewer and made the astonishing discovery that *none of the vast quantity of water drawn in ever left the house.* The commentators have seized avidly on this statistic but are, as usual, divided in their interpretations. In Bassett's view the water was treated in the patent water-box and diluted to a degree that made it invisible—in the guise of water, at all events—to the untutored watchers at the sewer. Hatchjaw's theory in this regard is more acceptable. He tends to the view that the water was boiled and converted, probably through the water-box, into tiny jets of steam which were projected through an upper window into the night in an endeavour to wash the black "volcanic" stains from the "skins" or "air-bladders" of the atmosphere and thus dissipate the hated and "insanitary" night. . . . On another occasion he had to face the curious charge of hoarding water, the police testifying that every vessel in his house, from the bath down to a

set of three ornamental egg-cups, was brimming with the liquid. Again
a trumped-up charge of attempted suicide was preferred merely because the savant had accidentally half-drowned himself in a quest for
some vital statistic of celestial aquatics. . . . Virtually all that remains of
de Selby's work in this regard is his house where his countless taps are
still as he left them, though a newer generation of more delicate mind
has had the water turned off at the main. (146–48)

First, the house: Is it not simply Joyce's waterworks turned inside out,
the public waterworks recreated in the privacy of de Selby's home? Water
here is revealed as the fetishistic fantasy of the social—what de Selby is
really interested in is the workings of the social world. And he attempts
to recreate it in miniature in his house, by mimicking the vast complexity of the waterworks infrastructure through the metaphor of water. He
even converts his gas pipes into water pipes (for the sake of consistency,
easier conceptual hold?) for the purpose. The "trumped-up charge of suicide" is perhaps not as off the mark as it seems, since de Selby is in fact
looking for the join to the public subject-citizen, the principle of negativity that would propel him into the public sphere and into the pure
realm of the social, into the dis- or unembodied phantasmagoria of the
nation-state. In another footnote the narrator quotes de Selby directly
from a statement he made during one of the "numerous petty litigations
in which [he was] involved." When the Bench asks "why the defendant
did not avail himself of the metered industrial rate if 'bathing is to be
persisted in so immoderately,'" de Selby replies with this: "One does not
readily accept the view that paradise is limited by the capacity of municipal waterworks or human happiness by water-meters manufactured by
unemancipated labour in Holland" (147).

No, human happiness cannot be limited, measured, or produced by
the municipal waterworks. De Selby is right. But it should be noted that
in fact de Selby himself is only accidentally, figuratively interested in
water as such. Social happiness, social paradise is what motivates him—
the utopian gesture. He is deluded into mistaking the material cause
(water) and the formal cause (waterworks) for the final cause, the provision of basic amenities. The efficient cause—workers, taxpayers, municipal authorities—plays no part in his experiments. De Selby's experiments

with water are stupid and funny because he is trying to distill the final cause from a premise that fails to include the final cause as a factor in causation, imagining it as instead an effect of the other causes: a logical, and here comical, impossibility. This is de Selby's mistake and, if we take this episode as a parody of Joyce, as I think we should, then according to O'Brien it is Joyce's mistake as well. A big part of the reason that de Selby is so effectively comic here is because his author is so acutely aware of the categorical mistake at the heart of de Selby's obsession. Imagine this scene as a nightmare that wakes Flann O'Brien, or Brian O'Nualláin, in the middle of the night bathed in a cold sweat: the bureaucratic unconscious. While O'Nualláin was working at his desk in the Custom House, O'Brien would have been sitting there with him, imagining "the most water-piped edifice in the world" as the caricatured sublime horror of his own job. His answer to the Joycean question "Did it flow?" is resoundingly negative, a damning report from the future, an urgent office memo lamenting the state of the Free State that Joyce, in his way, helped envision. Why didn't it flow? "A newer generation of more delicate mind has had the water turned off at the main." As exemplified in this passage and as a whole, *The Third Policeman* should be read as an angry unsent missive directed, from the Office of Public Works of the Irish Free State, to the problem space between Yeats's "fountain of nationality" and Joyce's state waterworks. For O'Brien, Joyce's expression of hope for the Free State was a literary fraud, and the proof, logically unsound as it was, was in what the state had done, and failed to do, since its foundation in 1922.

JAMMING UP THE WORKS

"The most water-piped edifice in the world"—a footnote in an unpublished book that O'Brien, whenever he was asked, always claimed to have "lost"—gave birth to all sorts of like-minded inventions and experiments in the newspaper column he took up in the same year he gave up on *The Third Policeman*. From 1940 to 1945 O'Brien wrote his weekly column for the *Irish Times*. He called it "Cruiskeen Lawn"—Irish for "little overflowing jug"—and wrote under the pseudonym Myles na gCopaleen, a name he borrowed from one of Dion Boucicault's stage-Irish characters in his melodrama *The Colleen Bawn*.[50] At first he wrote the column in Irish, but over time he began to alternate between Irish and English, and to write in English more and more. And his pseudonym became something of an open secret; many of his friends and acquaintances soon began calling him Myles. There were several recurrent and separate rubrics under which his articles could be grouped: "The Plain People of Ireland," "Keats and Chapman," and "Sir Myles na Gopaleen" appeared frequently. Another, "The Central Research Bureau," included farcical social improvement schemes that relied on inventions and advancements in technology. One was a plan to use sewer gas as fuel to illuminate streetlamps; the streetlamp poles, Myles suggests, might be made of hollow pipes connected at their base directly to the sewer underground.[51] Another proposal involved rerouting the railroads "to traverse bogland only," and to outfit all trains with "a patent scoop apparatus which would dig into the bog underneath the moving train and supply an endless stream of turf to the furnace."[52]

Two tropes that recur frequently in the "Central Research Bureau" columns were the maximization of the efficiency of machines, and infrastructural improvement. The idea of linking up city lighting with city wastage was to marry two discrete functions of the public utilities; ideally, in this understanding, some scion of progress—de Selby perhaps, or Myles himself—would invent a perpetual motion machine that would fulfill all the various functions of the public works at once, in one unified monolithic form. One of the more famous of these inventions was called "Trink." "When put on paper and dried, it emits a subtle alcoholic vapour which will hang over the document in an invisible odourless cloud for several days. A person perusing such a document is surrounded by this cloud. The vapour is drawn in with the breath, condenses on the mucous tract, gradually finds its way to the stomach and is absorbed in the blood. Intoxication ensues, mild or acute, according to how much reading is done. Later, when 'Trink' has been perfected, the whole idea is to print the *Irish Times* with it."[53] In Trink the functions of the public house and the organs of public opinion would be happily conjoined and, as a bonus, the legal limitations on the pubs' opening hours could be cheated and rendered obsolete. Such were the fantastic inventions, and such was the style of humor, that characterized O'Brien's popular column. Both the inventions and the humor descended from *The Third Policeman*.

O'Brien's Central Research Bureau had a real government counterpart and antecedent in the 1941 foundation of the Emergency Scientific Research Bureau. The purpose of that office was "to look into the feasibility of producing raw materials and commodities which were disappearing as imports dried up."[54] The Second World War—known in Ireland officially as "the Emergency"—had produced economic hardships in the form of shortages of fuel and food, and the Free State was searching for ways to alleviate them. Indeed, at this historical moment Ireland was put in mind of the Great Famine both because the food shortages threatened starvation and because the centenary of the Famine, in 1947, was fast approaching. Both government and the opposition in Ireland began to provoke "famine furore," such that "the historical memory of the famine was being cultivated" and connected menacingly to current events.[55] O'Brien's "Central Research Bureau," in its absurd humor, was a reminder of the utilitarian futility of British works in Famine Ireland and a warning not to put too much trust in the utilitarian structures of the state, even, and perhaps especially, a state with a democratic mandate.

O'Brien's shadow Research Bureau also reported on the food shortages of the Emergency and on various proposals for their relief. One of them involved the electrical production of jams—as in jellies and preserves—that could then be distributed to consumers via "the mains."

> The proposal to generate jam from second-hand electricity is being thoroughly investigated and a spokesman prominent in industrial jams—perhaps too prominent—revealed last night that experiments show that the inquiry "will not be fruitless." . . . This "raw" material will be absorbed by a factory (to be built somewhere in Ireland) where the new "jam" will be degenerated into immense watts, pardon me, vats. . . . In addition it is proposed to establish a cottage industry, probably in Donegal, where ohm-made jam will be produced for the carriage trade. A great advantage of the scheme is that it by-passes the bottling and carton problem since the new confiture will be distributed on the mains.[56]

The categorical mistake, that electricity could generate things, as opposed to generating the power to produce things from raw materials, is strikingly similar to de Selby's mistake in his experiments with water.

Human happiness as a distilled substance was never going to come out of de Selby's taps, and it seems just as unlikely that adding electricity (even "second-hand electricity" from scenic Donegal) to the mix would make it possible for jam to flow out from "the mains" of the Irish State.

This joke had another, different incarnation in *The Third Policeman.* By the end of the novel, the narrator does finally find his black box. And its contents, whose notional monetary value increases exponentially in the narrator's thoughts over the course of the novel, finally metamorphose into a fantastic and mysterious substance called "omnium." Omnium is a kind of fantasy of the universal equivalent of money. With omnium, one can produce anything at all: no labor, no capital, no social relations of production, no raw materials necessary. "If you had that box there," the titular third policeman, Fox, explains to the narrator near the end of the novel, "you could have a bucket of strawberry jam for your tea and if that was not enough you could have a bathful of it to lie in it full-length and if that much did not satisfy you, you could have ten acres of land with strawberry jam spread on it to the height of your two oxters" (186). In *The Third Policeman,* the nature of omnium is left mysterious and unexplained. But logically—and ridiculously enough—strawberry jam creates a contiguity between O'Brien's omnium and na gCopaleen's electricity, making it a safe bet that he had electricity in mind all along.

The fantasy of limitless wealth embodied in "omnium" in *The Third Policeman* could be translated, successively, from money to omnium to electricity because the Irish Free State staked, early in its existence in the mid-1920s, its legitimacy and its meager fortunes on "bringing light into darkness" through the promise of nationwide electrification. The Shannon Scheme, as it was called, was loudly proclaimed by the state as the single most important solution to Ireland's economic and cultural backwardness. It was the source and the symbol of Ireland's "great society," and it was the state's single biggest and most daring expense. So here, then, is the only logical answer to the logically unanswerable question of what is in the black box. It contains not only the electricity that the state promised the people would transform their lives for the better but also the state funds—the people's funds—spent to produce it. *Omnium*—between the funds and the electricity—is the word for that alchemy that transforms the funds into "those things that the market may leave undone."[57]

In other words, to return to Adam Smith's definition in *The Wealth of Nations,* the black box that motivates *The Third Policeman* contains, or simply *is,* the public works, and the heart of darkness around which the novel gathers its characters' motivations and its narrative motion is the connection between O'Brien's literary fictions and his civil service job financing the waterworks. The black box is thus not only an obscure representation of the public works but also a representation—as a conventional McGuffin—of the obscure zone where narrative fiction and the public works merge into one another, where, that is, the nation and the state come together. And in that latter sense, it is also, for O'Brien, a mirror in which he failed to see his own reflection.

The electrification of the whole country that was supposed to follow the construction of the Shannon Scheme was put on hold by the economic crises of the Emergency, and the scheme ended up supplying only the larger cities and towns until well after 1945. In *The Third Policeman* and in his "Central Research Bureau" columns for the *Irish Times,* Flann O'Brien voiced his dismay both at the large-scale investment in public works whose function might be more symbolic than real—one needs foodstuffs to make jam, after all, not electricity—and at their failure, in any case, to deliver on their promise of nationwide rural electrification. The Shannon Scheme and its social, cultural, and literary significance are the subject of my next chapter.

PART II

POWER

ELECTRIFICTION, OR DRAMATIZING POWER: THE SHANNON SCHEME, THE FREE STATE, AND DENIS JOHNSTON'S *THE MOON IN THE YELLOW RIVER*

FOUR

States are not "imagined" in the same way as nations, since modern *states must be materially engineered. The nation-state, as a state idea, is certainly imagined, but actual states must be something more. . . . States must be imagined, but they must also be built.*
                —Patrick Carroll-Burke, "Material Designs: Engineering
                Cultures and Engineering States—Ireland, 1650–1900"

In our country, electrification is more than merely producing light and power; it is bringing light into darkness.
                —James Larkin Jr., speaking before the Dáil in 1945

Erdnacrusha, requiestress, wake em!
                                —Joyce, *Finnegans Wake*

If *Ulysses* depicted a world on the verge of mass electrification, *Finnegans Wake* identified its hero, in Donald Theall's words, as "a citizen of our post-electric world."[1] But there were also local, Irish reasons why Joyce might have interested himself in postelectric citizenship. While writing

Finnegans Wake, he was aware of the Irish Free State's efforts to build a hydroelectric dam on the Shannon River in the southwest, just a few miles outside Limerick. The dam was constructed at a site called Ardnacrusha and eventually took the name to itself. "Erdnacrusha, requiestress, wake em!" exhorts the *Wake,* making the most of the play on words, signifying here both a celebration of "bringing light into darkness" and an act of mourning: the official end, with the bringing of the light, of premodern Ireland.[2] Joyce's exclamation also points, more simply and more profoundly, to a fundamental shift in human behavior enabled in many ways by cheap electricity like that provided by Ardnacrusha: staying up late, extending the day's activities into the night. The sound of Ardnacrusha's construction would have been enough to wake up the soundest sleeper; for most of 1926 and 1927, daily dynamite blasts punctuated the carving out of the head- and tailrace. Residents of what was formerly called Parteen Village, close to the construction site, routinely had their roofs pummeled and windows smashed by the flying rock.[3] Not only light, then, but thunder too — one of Joyce's favorite, phobic themes. Before Ardnacrusha produced domesticated electricity, its construction produced — figuratively speaking now — an electrical storm.[4]

Added to the material violence done to the geographical area around the dam during its construction was the epistemic violence done to its names. Parteen Village lost its name to the vernacular of the dam workers, who mistakenly referred to the entire area as Ardnacrusha; the name proved more durable, partly because the whole country came to know the place through the state's aggressive publicity campaign for the dam.[5] At the same time a whole new town was built exclusively to house the project's employees, of which there were, at the peak of construction, about five thousand — a small city, or in fact, given the living conditions there, a slum, with a single industrial purpose and a planned obsolescence.[6] In its time the dam was one of the largest in the world, and certainly the largest public works project ever undertaken in Ireland. When it went online in 1929, Ardnacrusha produced more than twice the energy then consumed in the Free State, including Dublin; it now produces less than 1 percent of the Republic's electricity needs. But the Shannon Scheme — as Ardnacrusha was known in its initial stages — meant and means much more than its production capacity. Certainly now its cultural significance has surpassed its utility, though this was arguably true even at the time, when few people—especially the rural agricultural workers to whom the promise of Ardnacrusha's electricity-generating potential was explicitly directed—felt that electricity would make much difference in their lives one way or the other. The dam was born a symbol; became in the 1930s, '40s, and '50s a center of electrical power production; and receded again, once electricity demand expanded well beyond its capacity, into a sleepy monumentality: not quite a ruin—Ardnacrusha is still on the grid—but probably not far from it.[7]

ELECTRIFICTION

Projects like the Shannon Scheme enjoyed an international vogue in the early part of the twentieth century. Large rich nations like the United States, the Soviet Union, and Germany were plowing money and brainpower into their hydroelectric schemes.[8] The projects and the discourses surrounding them made a promiscuous mess of what had previously been understood as clear ideological divides, and technological know-how was sought and circulated in a way that seemed practically indifferent to political rivalries. The U.S. model for the Tennessee Valley Authority was frequently associated with—read "accused of"—a kind of state socialism; and in the USSR, American consultants and project leaders were hired on for their expertise, giving the brief impression that Russia might be caving in to the free enterprise model of national development.[9] In Ireland the Shannon Scheme also engendered a fierce parliamentary and public debate about the nature of the state's role in national development, featuring communism as a predictable bogeyman. These ideological anxieties were in large part the result of the nature of the subject at hand—electricity— which carried with it a very old metaphorical load that didn't offer an easy alignment with either capital or the proletariat. But the political contests and the social anxieties raised by electricity did very little to slow the spread of electrification, as the Irish case testifies, where demand increased two hundred-fold in the years following Ardnacrusha's debut.

In 1920, five years before the Shannon Scheme was approved in Ireland, Vladimir Lenin introduced GOELRO, a Russian acronym for the State Plan for the Electrification of Russia. It was in reference to the glimmering promise GOELRO held out for the future of the proletariat that

Lenin coined his now-famous definition of communism as "Soviet power plus electrification." The idea took popular hold to such an extent that, as Susan Buck-Morss recounts, "The kilo-watt hour was proposed as 'an index of cultural progress.'"[10] Lenin's detractors, however, "are said to have ridiculed the program, suggesting that the 'a' be deleted from electrification," a little Communist party irreverence from which I derive the title of this chapter.[11] My own definition of *electrifiction,* though the term is borrowed from GOELRO's antagonists, is far less insulting than it was originally intended to be; I take it up as a serious critical term contributing to the history of the relationship between literary fiction and state power in the form of public utilities. For literary critics at least, *fiction* means much more than simply a story that is not true, and in a theoretical context *electrifiction* becomes a very compact way of describing, from a culturalist point of view, the multiple and competing discourses that circulated around the technological enterprise of electrification. Part of what I will be explaining here is why I think electricity is an exceptionally suitable emblem—what Patrick Carroll-Burke calls an epistemic engine—for modern state power, and why *electrifiction* is an exceptionally suitable critical term for some of the forms and tropes characterizing modernist literature, and modernist Irish literature in particular.[12] Electrifiction brings us closer to understanding how the relationship between modernist literature and modern power might work.

Electrifiction is also a way of understanding the nation along the lines of Benedict Anderson's imagined community, such that the term might be made to bear some of the same theoretically productive ambiguity evoked in the difference between an imaginary community and an imagined one. If the nation is a fiction in the "imagined" rather than in the "imaginary" sense, then electrifiction puts together a notion of national infrastructural engineering with a notion of the imagined character of the result: a horizontal community existing together in homogeneous, empty time, without having to have any face-to-face knowledge of each other. In chapter 3 I discussed Benedict Anderson's explanation of the way the railroads, for example, engendered a new imagination of the national landscape. The national electrical grid is an analogous—though less studied—vehicle for the imagined community of the nation. Indeed, as Joe Cleary argues, the electrification of Ireland holds the same place in the Irish national imaginary that railroads held in most other national imaginaries:

> In several of the great continental-size countries of the modern world, including the United States, Russia and India, one of the quintessential icons of modernization is the railway (symbol of the industrial conquest of time and space and of a new-found capacity to bind the hitherto far-flung locales of the national territory into a single unit). But in Ireland rural electrification has always been the favored icon of this process—as though modernity was taken to be in this instance less a matter of industrialization or state aggrandizement than a kind of quasi-religious redemption from an inchoate primeval darkness. The centrality of the motif, in other words, suggests that in the Irish context there is a particularly acute stress on modernization, not simply as a matter of technological or industrial development, but as a project that is expected to deliver cultural and psychological release from the purgatorial nightmare of Irish colonial history as well.[13]

One explanation for this phenomenon is that the railways were a sign not of Irish nationality but of British imperialism. In Ireland, the Free State—along with the popular imaginary—seized on electrification as a paradoxical sign both of the nation's equality with other modern nations and of its distinctiveness from them. The national electrical grid was an example of an Irish engineering initiative that could delineate an Irish modernity, set apart especially from its most immediate neighbor and former master, Britain. Such an "electrifiction" has not only ramifications for the concepts of nation, nationality, and nationalism but also far-reaching consequences for our notions of power in multiple senses of the term: as a question of international struggles for dominance or autonomy; as a question of the making of the modern citizen-subject, or, to put it another way, as a question of Foucauldian governmentality; and as a question of the literary forms and tropes produced contemporaneously with these new forms of power.

As Patrick Carroll-Burke puts it in my epigraph, "States must be imagined, but they must also be built."[14] Electrifiction, then, describes a problem-space between the built state and the imagined nation, a space in which much of Irish literature finds itself, obliged to say something about its strange and estranging surroundings—charged, one might say, with the task of making something of it on the one hand and making something up on the other. The work of electrifiction, then, might be defined as a way of describing and imagining the modern nation-state in fiction through its engineering cultures. Accounting for such imaginative work entails a dual, interdisciplinary focus on both engineering cultures and literary cultures.

Electrification as a model for modern nationality has an added advantage over Anderson's railway because electricity invaded the domestic space of the home in a way that the railroad did not and could not. Electrification forces a reconceptualization of the home as a domain increasingly dependent on the structures, and the engineering projects, of the state. Such dependency was understood in the public imagination as something to be very nervous about. In her book *Dark Light,* Linda Simon observes the paradoxical public reception of electricity in the nineteenth century. While many people seemed perfectly willing "to submit to the invasion of electricity into their bodies, with their own permission and administered by a physician whom they trusted, [at the same time] they were suspicious about allowing electricity to flow into their homes, where the force could stealthily invade their body in ways that they might not be able to control. It might even kill them."[15]

The ease with which people invited electricity into their bodies as a healing force is explicable partly by electricity's association in the nineteenth century with vitalism, with the belief that "electricity was the source of life itself."[16] The unease with allowing electricity into their homes has, I suspect, something to do with the anthropological division between public and private; and there is certainly a social, cultural, and legal story to be told in the strange popular belief that the home needed protection from the invading forces of electricity in a way that the body, it appears, did not. Simon's general observation about public fears over the introduction of electricity in the home was exemplified in a skeptical article about the Shannon Scheme published in London's *Morning Post* in 1929: "The present needs of Southern Ireland cannot be more than about 50 million units per annum, whereas the scheme provides for 150 million units. The Irish people . . . with such an excess of power . . . may all be electrocuted in their beds."[17] One of the most salient reasons for this common fear is suggested by Wolfgang Schivelbusch in his book *Disenchanted Night*. Speaking not of the introduction of electricity but of gas lighting, he argues that "once a house was connected to a central gas supply [or, we might add, a water supply, or electricity, etc.], its autonomy was over": "[From] now [on] these systems [of heating and lighting] were relocated outside the house, at a distance beyond the control of the paterfamilias. With a public gas supply, domestic lighting entered its industrial—and dependent—stage. No longer self-sufficiently producing its own heat and light, each house was inextricably tied to an industrial energy producer."[18]

The home, irrevocably inserted into the grid of modernity, the grid of the state, is no longer self-reliant (if it ever was); from this point on, the home relies on the public utility, on taxation, and on the urban division of labor to supply it with necessities like water, gas, and electricity. This is, to understate the matter, to put one's faith in the structures of society, to *believe* in the social imaginary or, as Schivelbusch has it, to surrender autonomy. In chapter 2 I argued that in "The Dead" Joyce turned to the gasworks as a material sign and a technological source of the imagined community of the emergent Irish nation. Belief in the nation was thus reconstructed out of the synchronic, horizontal, and infrastructural interdependence created by the public works: nationality as a function of space instead of time. Such belief—less a consciously held conviction than a kind of habitus, or what I've called, following Bollas, the unthought known—further entrenches itself with each addition of new utilities, new dependencies.[19] Electricity is exceptional in this regard because, even more than gas or water, it can be transported over tremendous distances without significant losses in transit, extending the reach of power. And in the case of rural Ireland, only after the construction of the power grid and the installation of electrical water pumps did it become possible "for the first time to install water on tap in the majority of rural dwellings."[20] In such cases electrification preceded the introduction of running water and was therefore the beginning—and not the end point—of the increasing dependence of the home on the public utilities.

Electricity may enable enlightenment, but it does so with a cost: a new, deeper dependence on the state. And the new dependence results from the relocation of the sources of power to places very distant from power's consumption. So electrification entrenches the modern state system in the sense that citizens become more dependent on it and, as a matter of habitus, they *believe* more—though perhaps not entirely consciously—in the nation-state. Belief here is something more powerful than a political opinion because whether one likes the state or not is immaterial. Once "plugged in" to the electrical grid, the citizen is dependent and reconstructs daily life around a technology that exists only as a function of national infrastructure, state owned or otherwise. As a model of Foucauldian governmentality, then, the electrification scheme in Ireland could be said to have created new kinds of citizens: not just nationalists but national subjects of the new nation-state.

One of the critically important aspects of this reconstruction of habitus is the nearly instantaneous forgetting that accompanies it. The transformation that occurs, while controversial and profoundly lived through at first, leaves everyday consciousness with astonishing rapidity. As Chandra Mukerji observes, "The glue of political regimes frequently lies precisely in modest life-worlds, with their patterned practices and the objects that sustain the moral and practical commitments pre-requisite to shared life. These collections of people and things are the infrastructures that underlie group processes—ones that may be unspoken but still sustain empire. . . . This technological activity (or tacit knowledge) may be underarticulated, but it remains deeply intelligent and provides an enduring sense of moral order that is naturalized by its physical form."[21] Carroll-Burke puts the same point more bluntly: "Key institutions of western culture silently rest upon a vast system of sanitary engineering," or again for emphasis, "*The importance of the link between drainage and civilization can hardly be overstated.*"[22] The statements appear obvious enough, leaving aside for the moment all the slippages introduced by "state," "nation," "empire," and "civilization," and also leaving aside the special importance that drainage had and has in a place with as much rainfall as Ireland. Carroll-Burke's statement is in fact a paradigmatically materialist definition of culture; and Mukerji reminds us that there is something inevitable about the forgetting involved, as if not only drainage, but also and crucially forgetting about drainage, were in some sense an enabling condition for, say, high culture. But once we factor in the forgetting, or the unspokenness, of it—the sense in which everyday life in highly organized and highly engineered states is in the main characterized by not paying any attention to drainage—public utilities reappear again and again in modernist literature as a kind of uncanny, hysterical realization. Humbert Humbert, the professor-pederast-narrator of Nabokov's *Lolita,* for example, makes the same point again, but with a sense of surprise and humor: "I felt instinctively that toilets—as also telephones—happened to be, for reasons unfathomable, the points where my destiny was liable to catch."[23] It's funny because it's true, though it is not only his destiny that is determined in this way, and the reasons are, far from unfathomable, hiding in plain sight. The real strangeness here is why this should seem strange to him, or to anybody else for that matter. The uncanny effect of remembering public utilities results from the normally instantaneous forgetting by which they incorporate themselves into the modern habitus.[24] Nabokov is able, in writing of toilet and telephone, to restate Carroll-Burke's point very economically, since the pairing makes visible the connection between communicability on one hand and communication on the other: drainage/toilet and civilization/telephone unified under the sign of the public utility.

Let us take one more example, far away again from the Irish setting, but instructive for its distance and its subject. Minke, the young native protagonist of Pramoedya Ananta Toer's *Buru Quartet*—a series of Indonesian novels that Benedict Anderson quotes often in evidence for the imagined community, and whose subject is the creation of modern subjects and nations in the former Dutch empire—proclaims his youthful dedication to the pursuit of Enlightenment through his excitement about electricity: "Oh Allah, and I couldn't really understand what electricity was."[25] The exclamation compacts the issue into a neat formula—discredited as it may be—pitting a dynastic religious worldview against an emergent understanding of the new powers of the supposedly secular nation. The mysticism associated with electricity is far from unique to the colonial subject, however; it was part and parcel of the discourse of electrification in the imperial centers as well. It's worth pointing out that electricity mystifies in some ways the European as much as the Indonesian colonial subject, though from two different directions. For Minke electricity is mysterious because he doesn't have it, and he doesn't yet understand the science behind it; for Humbert Humbert, it's mysterious because he does have it, but he has completely forgotten to think about it except in dire circumstances—the unthought known that asserts its urgency in moments of crisis. For both, it determines their fate, or, in Anderson's term, their fatality—whether as "destiny" for Humbert or "Allah" for Minke. The Irish case, as I argue below, combines the two perspectives in its anomalous postcolonial state.[26]

One of the consequences of the modern subject's habitual indifference to engineering cultures is that the commonly understood sense of "national culture," or "culture" *tout court,* can be all too easily metonymized under the sign of literature and the arts. The consequence in the Irish case, as I pointed out in chapter 1, is the underarticulation of "engineering cultures" and the overarticulation of literary cultures in the field of Irish studies. Such is the way in which the power of literature—to speak of which is of course already to speak metaphorically—appropriates "invention" as its own provenance, as if the slip between "invention" in the techno-scientific sense and "invention" in the fictional-literary sense did not happen; as if it were possible to "write" Ireland without roads and sewers and power grids; or as if building roads and sewers and power grids were not in themselves crucial modes of "writing Ireland." I would suggest, however, that what is necessary to understand these slippages better is not merely new studies of engineering cultures but studies of the relationship between inventing Ireland in literary cultures and inventing Ireland in engineering cultures. This is the project enjoined by electrifiction.

In the Irish case, there is good reason for the myopic focus on literature that both Carroll-Burke and Kincaid point out—because Ireland was invented and written, in the engineering sense now, in large part in and through British imperial institutions. The engineering cultures of Ireland were historically the product of British imperial engineering cultures and, as such, were a source of nationalist shame in many respects. "Only in the past couple of decades," Carroll-Burke goes on, "has Ireland forgotten the past sufficiently to rediscover and to embrace its engineering culture."[27] This means, too, that we are talking about another kind of forgetting as well, a forgetting of the imperial sources of Irish engineering cultures. The literary revival that took off in the late nineteenth and early twentieth centuries generated a tremendous intensity because literature was, in some ways, standing in for "culture." While "writing Ireland" is certainly something that happens in terms of engineering as it does in literature, it is also true that "writing Ireland" in the literary sense of the phrase was, during the Revival, an endeavor that integrated into itself all the magnitude and ambition of a modern national engineering culture—something that Ireland did not and could not have had at the time because it was a nation without a state. As I argued in chapter 1, the struggle to define an Irish engineering culture translated into a literary struggle to undo the racial and colonial opposition between utility and the aesthetic through generic and formal experimentation. The intensity of that struggle could in some measure explain the major achievements of Irish literature in the period—in the forty years between 1890 and 1930—which Pascale Casanova understands as the most explosive, prolific, and revolutionary literary movement ever to emerge in such a short period: "reason enough, surely," she says, "for talking of an Irish 'miracle.'"[28]

THE SHANNON SCHEME

The Shannon Scheme, commissioned by the Free State at the tail end of the Revival period, was meant to be equally miraculous and was later understood as a successful miracle. At the time it was a hope and a tremendous risk. As the *Irish Times* put it in 1976, "Never before or since has an Irish government taken such a calculated risk and never before had a single economic project assumed such importance as a fundamental act of nation-building."[29] Since 1844, the British had considered building hydroelectric dams in Ireland, and many different plans were afloat in the years leading up to 1925; the IRA had their own schemes as well. Ultimately it fell to the Free State to put a national electrification plan into motion. There were two distinct stages to the project: first the building of the dam at Ardnacrusha, and later a national program of rural electrification. The discourses surrounding the dam were from the beginning, however, suffused with the rhetoric of a democratic—and democratizing— access to the new power created on the Shannon. In 1925 the Oireachtas (Irish Parliament) passed the Shannon Electricity Bill, which authorized the funds for the Shannon Scheme, a joint venture between the German firm Siemens Schuckert and the Free State. The Electricity Supply Bill of 1927 made provision for a semistate body, the Electricity Supply Board

(ESB), to oversee the operation of Ardnacrusha as well as the sale and distribution of electricity, which according to Colin Rynne meant that Ireland became "the first country in the world to have a state-controlled national electricity grid," and which prompted one dissenting senator to speak derisively of "the cloven hoof of socialism."[30] The construction was projected to cost 5.2 million pounds, a gigantic expense for a poorly funded state that was also suffering the effects of a worldwide economic depression.

Construction began almost immediately after the act was passed. So did conflict: between the German foremen and the industrially inexperienced Irish workers; between English-speaking Irish workers and the Irish-speaking Connemara men; and finally, between the state and the Irish workers, in the form of ongoing strikes and violent labor disputes. The working conditions at Ardnacrusha were appalling. Aside from the fact that government had pegged wages with the very low average wage of agricultural labor in an effort to save money, the workers' village on the construction site was designed to house only 720 workers. This was an absurd underestimation of the initial call that went out for 3,000 workers, and of the 5,000 who actually showed up—and stuck around—hoping for a job. Most of the workers lived in "cow houses, piggeries and barns" or were simply shelterless.[31] In the senate Séamus O'Farrell decried these conditions: "Instead of creating a Gaelic Ireland these conditions will create an Irish China."[32] The specter of the Asiatic mode of production loomed up again, this time as Chinese despotism instead of Russian communism. But the most perverse nationalist rhetoric came when Paddy McGuilligan, defending in the Dáil the pay rate of Ardnacrusha workers, conjured up, whether intentionally or not, the Great Famine: "If people go to Limerick to wait on the chance of getting work . . . that's their own look out. . . . If people have to die and die through starvation . . . so be it for the good of the nation."[33] McGuilligan's gaffe inadvertently lent fire to the Labour opposition and to the strikers' cause, but at the same time it reveals that the logic of nation building that motivated the Shannon Scheme was fundamentally related not only to the Eastern despotisms against which the Free State constantly measured itself but also to the imperial despotism from which it had liberated itself less than five years earlier.

McGuilligan's notion that the nation required sacrifices ultimately prevailed, dooming the strikers to defeat. This ideological victory over labor was in part achieved through a canny and well-organized plan to shape public opinion. In July of 1928 the ESB established its Public Relations Department.

The marketing strategy assumed many forms. Bus trips to the main sites of the Shannon Scheme were organized, and in June 1928 a "Guide Bureau" was opened. The Great Southern Railways encouraged public visits with greatly reduced fares from all stations to Limerick. Altogether, this information and sightseeing campaign, complemented by advertisements in all major national newspapers and magazines, was a huge success. In the period from June 1928 to March 1932, 185,000 sightseers (or roughly 6 percent of the total population of the Irish Free State) visited Ardnacrusha. In addition, the ESB produced brochures and posters, set up showrooms and shops for electrical equipment, and conducted information presentations and slide-shows even in the smallest locations. A film was made about the scheme, and at the request of the ESB Siemens constructed a model of the power station, which was displayed from May 1929 at exhibitions throughout the Irish Free State, attracting large crowds.[34]

The film, entitled *The Eighth Wonder of the World,* is still shown on tours (now rare) of Ardnacrusha. The ESB's publicity blitz, Clair Wills argues, "produced modernist prints and photographs which would have done Russian avant-gardists or Italian futurists proud."[35] One of the original newspaper ads exhorts, "Visit the Shannon Works! See this Mighty Project in the making" (figure 2), while another entices with exoticism, "Limerick: The Mecca of Ireland" (figure 3). Figures 4 through 7 are selected from a postcard series of photographs published by the Public Relations Department. In them the sublime scale of the works is the paramount message; workers pose with the machinery to demonstrate the superhuman size of the technological apparati of turbines, penstocks, generators, and intake tunnels. Figure 4 depicts no human forms at all, only the magnitude of the destructive force mobilized to dig out the headrace.

Visit the Shannon Works!

See this Mighty Project in the making

Arrangements have been made with the Great Southern Railway to issue Return Tickets at Single Fares from all stations on its system to Limerick on week-days, available for return within three days including day of issue, from now on until the 29th of September inclusive.

Conducted Tours daily from the I. O. C. premises
Sarsfield Street, Limerick :—
1st Tour leaves at 10.30 a.m., returning 1.30 p.m.
2nd   ,,   ,,   2.30 p.m.,   ,,   6.30 p.m.
BUS FARE 4/- (Children Half-price)
Guide's services free.

Those not wishing to avail of these Conducted Tours should apply
direct for a permit, giving date of proposed visit.
Conducted Tours on SUNDAYS for large excursion parties ONLY—

Apply to The ELECTRICITY SUPPLY BOARD

GUIDE BUREAU, STRAND BARRACKS, LIMERICK

O'LOUGHLIN
PRINTER
FLEET STREET
DUBLIN

Figure 2. Generating tourism. Reproduced by kind permission of ESB Archives.

Figure 3. Exoticizing tourism. Reproduced by kind permission of ESB Archives.

In 1928 the ESB ran full-page advertisements for the scheme in George Russell's *Irish Statesman* magazine. These were the same advertisements, as I pointed out in chapter 1, that must have impressed themselves on Elizabeth Bowen as she was writing her article "Modern Lighting" for the *Saturday Review of Literature.* "Shannon electricity will lift the heavy work of industry from human shoulders to the iron shoulders of machines," says one from September 8.[36] Many of the ads stressed the same theme that Oscar Wilde stressed in his "The Soul of Man under Socialism" from 1891: the slavery of the machine as a condition of the liberation of humanity. Another ad from September 22 reiterates the formula: "In industry and in the home electricity does the heavy work easily and cheaply. It is the modern labour saver and youth saver. It converts the workman and housewife from labour slaves into directors of machinery."[37] Thus liberated from the slavery of labor, the Irish would finally be able to develop themselves and to be counted among the great modern societies of Europe: "To-day the Saorstát is the least electrified State in Europe. Next year it will have a supply as cheap and as widespread as the

Figure 4.
Blasting operations
near Clonlara.
Tourism postcard
for the Shannon
Scheme. Reproduced
by kind permission
of ESB Archives.

most modern State in Europe. This is an achievement of which the country may well be proud. This is progress!"[38]

Today a resigned modesty has replaced the hyperbole of the ESB's boosterism. "Ardnacrusha is no Disneyland," admits Seán Craig, a part-time tour guide and part-time employee at the dam.[39] But at the time of its construction it was already becoming, and was quite strategically being made into, a central symbol of and monument to the nation-state. In the inflated claims and utopian rhetoric of the ESB's publicity campaign, it

Figure 5. Penstock building. Tourism postcard for the Shannon Scheme.
Reproduced by kind permission of ESB Archives.

is not hard to discern the source for Flann O'Brien's fictional omnium, or
for Myles na gCopaleen's fantastic scheme to manufacture jam from electricity and to distribute it on the mains. For O'Brien, the problem was that
the Free State was promoting the Shannon Scheme as a kind of Disneyland, a national fantasy of laborless plenty at the end of history: an electrifiction. According to the ESB, with electricity, anything was possible.
The cheap electricity supplied by the Shannon Scheme was touted as an
all-in-one solution to the Free State's difficulties on every imaginable front.
The Shannon Scheme would put an end to the constant demographic
drain of emigration by providing industrial jobs for the working class
and by creating attractive opportunities for Ireland's professional classes.
For Irish civil and electrical engineers, the Shannon Scheme meant that
"we Irish engineers can stay in our own country instead of emigrating. In
the past we emigrated because there was nothing for us to do at home,
but now we can feel that there is a future for us here."[40]

Figure 6. Supervising the installation of a turbine. Tourism postcard for the
Shannon Scheme. Reproduced by kind permission of ESB Archives.

President William Cosgrave even suggested that the modernization
of the Free State by electrification might act as a natural magnet attracting
Northern Irish envy, thus leading finally to the peaceful achievement of
the Irish revolution's most bitter and politically divisive failure: a United
Ireland. As the *Irish Times* reported:

> That the Shannon Electricity Scheme, in addition to conferring
> widespread benefits on the people of the Free State, might play an im-
> portant part in bringing about the removal of the boundary between
> North and South, was the belief expressed by President Cosgrave at a
> dinner given by the Shannon Electricity Board in Limerick on Satur-
> day night.
>
> A difficult problem like the boundary, he said, would not be solved
> by talking about it day after day. Difficult problems of that kind might

Figure 7. Concrete work for intake building. Tourism postcard for the Shannon Scheme. Reproduced by kind permission of ESB Archives.

be more easily solved by quiet, earnest attention to their work, the work of utilising their resources and opportunities for the development of industry.[41]

The electrification of the Free State would thus not only lead peacefully to the reunification of the island but also neutralize the long-standing rift between the protreaty ruling party of Cosgrave's Cumann na nGaedhael and the opposition party of Éamon de Valera's Fianna Fáil. Cosgrave pointed to the Shannon Scheme as the economic solution to partition, implicitly arguing that modernization was the best and most realistic strategy for reunification, over and against the armed struggle. Shannon electricity, Cosgrave announced, would not only reunite Northern Ireland and the Free State but also reunite opposing forces within the Free State by vindicating the decision, in 1922, to go along with the Anglo-Irish Treaty.[42]

Official state organs like the ESB or the office of the president could not, however, be accused of producing all of the hype around the Shannon

Figure 8. Seán Keating, *Night's Candles Are Burnt Out,* 1928–29. Reproduced by kind permission of Gallery Oldham U.K.

Scheme. Indeed, it is difficult to come up with the right kind of causal grammar to describe the way in which Ardnacrusha was both producing the nation at the same time that it was being produced by it. In 1926 Seán Keating, a painter already well known in Ireland for his romantic depictions of rural Irish life and an avowed "antimodernist," went to Ardnacrusha to paint. Figure 8 reproduces the most celebrated of Keating's canvases to come out of that period, *Night's Candles Are Burnt Out* (1928–29), an allegory of electrification in which the stock characters of the Irish national imaginary—the poteen-drinking, likely Irish-speaking Connemara men at bottom left, the IRA gunman at center right, and the ambiguously placed priest at bottom right—appear as residual characters

Figure 9. Seán Keating, *Der Ubermann,* ca. 1928. Reproduced by kind permission of ESB Archives.

supplanted by the emergence of the engineer at center and the nuclear family (sensibly with only one child, as opposed to the stereotype of Irish Catholic overbreeding) at top right. At top left, the corpse of traditional Ireland hangs from a noose, and a man standing next to it holds up a now obsolete oil lamp. The concrete dam is prominently framed by all these figures as the epistemic engine powering such dramatic cultural transformation. Figure 9 reproduces *Der Ubermann* (ca. 1928), another of Keating's allegorical paintings from Ardnacrusha, featuring the engineer as hero. The rest of the series, as exemplified in figure 10, tends to omit human forms and focus, like the ESB's postcard campaign, on machinery, blasted natural landscapes, and industrial architecture.

Figure 10. Seán Keating, *Commencement of Tailrace. Excavation Work for Canal and Building of Banks,* ca. 1927. Reproduced by kind permission of ESB Archives.

The triumphalism of *Night's Candles Are Burnt Out* and *Der Ubermann,* combined with the mimetic realism of the rest of the series, leaves little room to distinguish between Keating's message and the message propounded by the ESB's Public Relations Department. "For a number of years," writes Andy Bielenberg, "it has been confidently asserted that Keating was commissioned in 1926 to execute a series of pictures illustrating the progress of the scheme."[43] But this, as Bielenberg shows, was not the case. Keating was drawn to Ardnacrusha through a "personal interest" in the "engineering and technical dimensions of the scheme."[44] Though the ESB now owns *Night's Candles Are Burnt Out,* for example, they acquired it not from Keating directly but from the Oldham Art Gallery, to whom Keating first sold the painting in 1931.[45] The fact that Keating was not, as was and still is popularly believed, commissioned to do the work speaks to the problem at the heart of electrifiction. While it is fairly easy to understand the ESB publicity department's productions as "propaganda," Keating's work, which essentially made the same nationalistic point, cannot be so easily assimilated to a story of top-down nation building, at least not without believing in the fiction of his commission with the state. In other words, Ardnacrusha was creating meaning independently of the meanings chartered by the ESB, even though those unofficial meanings may have looked very similar to the official ones.

When the power station at Ardnacrusha went online and starting supplying electricity in 1929, meaning traveled down the lines with it. On July 22, 1929, after the bishop of Killaloe gave the works his "solemn blessing," Cosgrave pressed a button that opened the intake gates of the headrace canal and allowed the waters of the River Shannon into the turbines. The *Irish Independent* accompanied its reporting of the opening ceremony with an exhortation to the Irish people: "So much public money has been sunk in the undertaking that every good citizen must hope for its success. The greater the demand for Shannon electric power the cheaper it can be sold. If the scheme is not a financial success, the consumers or the taxpayers, probably both, will bear the loss. It is, therefore, to everybody's interest to make this ambitious scheme not a leap in the dark but into the light."[46]

The economic fate not only of the Free State but of the Irish people was tied up in the success or failure of electrical modernization. If the people did not adapt to it, buy it, and use it, the Shannon Scheme would fail and the nation would remain in underdeveloped darkness. The secular destiny of the nation was articulated through the public utility, just as Humbert Humbert would later articulate it in *Lolita*—as a personal destiny dictated by toilets and telephones. The *Independent*'s secular plea for motivated national belief, however, was accompanied by the ceremonial Catholic blessing of the dam. The *Independent* quoted the blessing in full:

O Almighty and Merciful God, sole source of light and power, Who commandest the winds and the waves, and Who made streams run down as rivers from the rock in the wilderness, pour, we beseech Thee, Thy Allprotecting Blessing over this immense aqueduct, constructed in Thy Name at the cost of so much labour, so that ever guarded by Thy Provident Care it may successfully bring the waters of the Shannon to turn the Turbines, and generate the mysterious power of Electricity for Thy Glory and the benefit of the people of Ireland.[47]

Here is a queer marriage of the techno-scientific language of "turbines" and the religious language of "Almighty Merciful God" that echoes perfectly Minke's dynastic-religious exclamation: "Oh Allah, and I couldn't really understand what electricity was." As a cultural event, the Shannon Scheme embodied a postcolonial struggle to define the stakes of modernization and to navigate the ideological contradictions between a secular and a religious worldview. Modernization meant not only electrification but also the end of Irish romantic nationalism and its sudden replacement with a modern, networked sensibility of the common good. Given the spectacular failure of the public works during the Famine, and the profound and persistent distrust generated by the traumatic Irish experience of colonialism and modernization, the Free State was asking for no less than a revolution in Irish sensibilities.

RURAL ELECTRIFICATION

It took sixteen years before the Free State (since 1937 become the Republic of Ireland) dedicated the funds for the 1945 Rural Electrification Scheme Act, whose intent was to supply electricity to every home, no matter how far from already-supplied towns. The ideological focus shifted from the monumentality of nation building in the figure of the Shannon Scheme, where the people were encouraged to come and visit and gawk, to the missionary-like work of bringing national power to the people where they lived. When in 1945 James Larkin Jr. described to the Irish Dáil the state's generous attempt to "bring light into darkness," he referenced a timeworn metaphor of enlightenment.[48] So old, and so discredited, is this trope that we would not hesitate normally to dismiss it as banal, as reduced to cliché, as the most tawdry of political rhetorics. Yet in the context of electrification the frequent use of the cliché never seems to extinguish its usefulness or its power. In part this is because it is so old, so habitual. In part it is because in these contexts it is brand new: because we are speaking, when we speak of electrification, of a very modern form of the metaphor that promises its literalization through networks of power that bring light, and, what's more, that forge a new kind of dependence on the nation-state for that light. Larkin went on in his speech to elaborate the connection between electric light and enlightenment:

> The great value of this proposed scheme of rural electrification is not that we are going to have farming by electricity instead of by hand, but that we are going to put into the homes of our people in rural areas a light which will light up their minds as well as their homes. If we do that, we will have brought a new atmosphere and a new outlook to many of these people. It often appalls me to think that we have just under 2,000,000 men and women, the majority of whom are in many physical ways, debarred from mental development, the application of their mental faculties, just because they have not got the elementary physical help of a decent light with which to read. If we can get them light and nothing else, then I think we have brought about a great change.[49]

The political force of Larkin's statement lies in dismissing the economic benefits of electrification, emphasizing instead the effect on the mind of "a decent light with which to read." And the state is electricity's secular missionary, spreading enlightenment truth through the houses of Ireland's rural backwaters. A continuity between education and electricity is assumed.[50] There is, of course, hidden here a mystification as well, because the source of light—electricity—was well beyond the scientific knowledge of the imagined average Irish rural peasant on whose behalf Larkin addresses the Dáil.

To get a sense of how rural electrification was experienced as it was being implemented, in that moment before the more durable forgetting that inevitably followed, Michael Shiel quotes several newspaper and periodical reports from the "great switch-on" and synthesizes them into this general description:

> The typical scenario was a gathering of all the inhabitants in the village hall. On the stage was mounted a large switch, around which gathered leaders of the community: the local clergy, TDs, county councilors

and one or two senior representatives of the ESB. If the occasion was considered to be of sufficient importance, a government minister was present. It was usually arranged that the switch on the stage simultaneously switched on all the village houses and street lights, as well as the lights in the hall. Where this was not feasible, a signal to strategically placed operators achieved the same result. In the hall itself a number of portable high-powered lighting battens was usually installed for the occasion to reinforce the conventional installation. Speeches were made, paying tribute to the organising committee and to the ESB staff. The historic importance of the occasion was noted and hopes were expressed that the coming of the light was symbolic of the dawn of a new era of enlightenment and prosperity for the community. Almost invariably the opening verses of the Gospel of St John were quoted ". . . and the light shineth in the darkness and the darkness hath not overcome it. . . ." A blessing was given, frequently, especially in the northern counties, jointly by the clergy of different denominations, and the guest of honour was then invited to press the switch. One could anticipate a gasp of delight and a thunderous applause from the assembled crowd as the brilliant lighting took over from the existing candles and paraffin lamps. The gloomy hall was lighted as if by the noonday sun. Outside, the new public lights lit up the village street, while the brightly-lit shop windows added to the general gaiety. Far out into the countryside, bright pinpoints of light commenced to twinkle like stars against the blackness of the night as the rural "spurs" were switched on.[51]

Such high ceremony and solemn intonations accompanied every one of these occasions. The presence of the clergy, officiating side by side with government officials, conveyed the idea of an apparently easy alliance between enlightenment and religion. The banality of the discourse, however, belied the genuineness of the celebration. In Dungarvan in 1948, the great switch-on was reported by the *Leader* as a real triumph: "One old resident stated that he never saw a night of more spontaneous enjoyment. Everyone was happy and realised what a great night it was for the district when light and power, which is going to revolutionise country life, was made available."[52] A priest in Bansha asserted in his ceremonial speech that "rural electrification . . . is more than an amenity—it is a revolution which will sweep away inferiority complexes."[53] In Longford a government minister, just before flipping the switch, intoned, "May God give the light of heaven as I am about to give you light now," an uneasy moment, perhaps, for the erstwhile alliance between clergy and state.[54]

In many of these cases, the idea that Ardnacrusha—that great and greatly publicized site, pilgrimage, and event all in one—was responsible in more than just a symbolic sense for the light now flowing through rural townships appeared as a point of identification for many rural dwellers who were finally being plugged into the network.

> A continually recurring question, raised especially by the members of the older generation, was whether the electricity now lighting up their locality really came from the Shannon Scheme. When assured that this was substantially so, although of course there were now other stations also contributing, their pride and joy were obvious. For them the Shannon Scheme had been one of the first great manifestations of an independent nation and on this night they were at last partaking of its fruits in their own community.[55]

"Substantially so," assure the politicians, ESB officials, and ceremonial ringmasters. On the one hand, the older generation's desire to locate power at Ardnacrusha points to the importance of the imagined national geography. And on the other hand, the official willingness to encourage such belief points to the fiction being produced here, the way in which these people, when they inquire, are encouraged to understand the geography of power production as a fantasy of national symbolism. By all means, go ahead and *believe* that your actual electricity comes from a national symbol instead of a complex system of power stations, relays, and networks; and from a variety of sources like reservoirs, coal plants, petroleum plants, peat plants, and dams. Just believe, and leave all the rest to the experts. Here is another definition of electrifiction, one that in this case is as much about lying as it is about imagining, and to which we might add another attribute: the cult of expertise.

Of course there was opposition to electrification, though it goes mostly unrecorded. And when it was recorded, it became garbled and incomprehensible. In 1948 in Longford a heckler continually interrupted the usual spectacle of the switch-on, and the *Longford News* reported, "There

were a few idiotic interruptions by a local wit—or half wit—and an oc-
casional echo of 'the loud laugh that. . . .' It was a pity that the demon-
strator hadn't got an electric chair handy!"[56] The content of the interruption is not, for the *Longford News* anyway, worth reporting. Part of
the implication of the "idiotic interruptions" of a "local half-wit" is that
to be local—or to be militantly local, against modernization and the
interdependencies modernity implies—is to be provincial. It is also to
lack understanding, indeed to lack the ability to speak, both as a result of
repression (the words are not reprinted) and as a result of native stu-
pidity (the words don't make sense in the first place). Simply put, this
is another version of the "Irish howl" that had been sounding at least
since the years of the Famine, when the peasant population as a whole
was understood as an obstacle to progress and when their mass deaths
by starvation were understood as a necessary step toward a higher civilization.[57] Death is close by at the switch-on, too: the electric chair is
conjured—indeed, it could not have been far off in the imagination. The
state's gift to the people is also the state's monopoly on violence and its
mobilization of the new technology as a method for maintaining and
enforcing their monopoly: the Janus-face or devil's bargain of electrification. Opposition can be ignored or, if need be, destroyed. And what
more potent symbol of the state's power than the electric chair, even
though there were never any electric chairs in Ireland? The journalist's
joke speaks the repressed and unpleasant truth of power, sovereign authority over the right to life, represented in a death-machine whose origin
lies, perversely but perhaps inevitably, in the "promise" and "progress"
of technology.

THE MOON IN THE YELLOW RIVER

The state's repressive apparatus was put to work long before rural electrification, however, as a foundational gesture. The treaty with Great Britain that founded the Free State was signed on December 6, 1921. The
treaty's provision for the partition of the island into the southern counties of the Free State and the northern counties still governed by Great
Britain led to a bitter and bloody two-year civil war. The nation was di-

vided between those who accepted the treaty, and partition with it, and those who considered that independence had not been won because Ireland, all of Ireland, was not independent. The rift pitted former comrades in arms against one another. Between 1922 and 1923 Kevin O'Higgins—former IRA man, then Cumann na nGaedhael minister for justice—ordered the execution of seventy-seven IRA prisoners held by the Free State for subversive acts. The execution orders were carried out in obvious disregard for the laws of the Free State. In 1927, the antitreaty IRA assassinated O'Higgins for his part in the executions. Given this violent context, the Shannon Scheme should be understood as the Free State's effort at self-legitimation—as provider for the Irish people—which was possible only after it had finally secured its existence through extralegal murder. As Denis Johnston put it in his introduction to *The Moon in the Yellow River,* "The recrudescence of murder as a political argument had been brought to a sudden stop by means of the counter-murder of prisoners in the hands of the new native government. There was no legal or moral justification for such measures on the part of the infant Free State. But the melancholy fact remained that it had worked, and that an Irish Government had proved to be much tougher with the Irish than the English had ever dared to be."[58]

Across the Free State's threshold to modernity, there were many corpses. Denis Johnston's *The Moon in the Yellow River* asks us to contemplate the bodies while weighing the moral, ethical, and political stakes. For this reason, and for its realism, *The Moon* has been placed in the tradition of the "problem play" in the mold of Chekhov.[59] It is set just outside Dublin, next to a hypothetical hydroelectric station nearing completion on the Liffey. The political forces in conflict over this engine of modernity—for the dam is not a symbol or an emblem, as we've been seeing; it *produces* power literally and produces modernity in its cultural effects—are embodied in the characters. Tausch, the German engineer in charge of the dam project, is the rational modernizer and philanthropist; Dobelle, his disillusioned and disaffected Irish "double" (Do-belle), is a retired engineer—actually a bridge builder—with no faith left in the narrative of progress; Blake is a republican whose credo is permanent revolution; Lanigan represents the state, defending the powerhouse against republican anti-Treatyites, like Blake, who are bent on resisting modernization and undermining the Free State's legitimacy; Aunt Columba stands in for "peasant" Ireland, hostile to modernization, without pretensions to power but resistant to its incursions on an older way of life; and finally, Blanaid, Dobelle's neglected daughter, is the young, impressionable, feminine blank slate of Ireland's future (modern or not), the inheritor and ultimately the product of the conflicts that ensue. The cast is completed by George and Potts, comic-relief stage Irishmen who have spent the last four years building a giant gun as a kind of doomsday deterrent to further sectarian violence or British intervention. Blake intends to use their gun and their homemade shells to blow up the powerhouse. The central action, in fact the only action that could be called intentional in the play, occurs at the end of the second act, when Lanigan—with absolutely no warning whatsoever—shoots Blake in the back, killing him. In the end, and although Lanigan effectively thwarts the republican plot, the powerhouse is destroyed anyway—not by activists but by accident, blown up by one of George and Potts's homemade shells, thought to be defective and thrown onto the slagheap.

The Moon was Johnston's second play. His first, The Old Lady Says No!, was staged by the Gate Theatre in 1929 and was extremely well received by audiences and critics alike. It was expressionistic and surreal, its mold of drama writing entirely different from The Moon's sober realism, though it was also equally critical of Irish nationalism in general and the Free State in particular. Unlike The Old Lady Says No!, however, The Moon was not well received in Dublin: not an easy fact to explain given that both plays were equally scathing about Irish nationalism. Though it flopped in Ireland, The Moon went on to be Johnston's most internationally successful play. It was performed to rave reviews in London and New York, translated into seven languages, and broadcast as a radio play on the BBC. The Moon was unpopular in Ireland because it treated the new Irish Free State power brokers as thugs and the Irish people as stereotypes. It was popular outside Ireland because its subject, mass electrification, was timely in a world-historical sense.

On its opening night The Moon met with hisses and outbursts. The Garda were dispatched to the Abbey Theatre on the second and third nights in case of a riot, like previous ones prompted by the works of Yeats, Synge, and O'Casey. But nothing happened.[60] The most often repeated objection was to the depiction of the Free Stater, Lanigan, as a cold-blooded killer. James O'Reilly, a prominent supporter of the Free State, a barrister, and a prolific op-ed letter writer, thought it a scandal "for a man wearing a national uniform to commit a murder on the stage."[61] One night when Johnston was in attendance, the founder of the Irish Citizen Army, Jack White, accosted the playwright outside the theater. Johnston recounts that White "accused me of justifying these methods in my play. I invited him to tell me what the proper answer was, and I would put it in. 'There is no answer,' said Jack White, 'and you know it. That's why you are a traitor and a renegade.'"[62]

Such was the political atmosphere in Dublin, that even to bring up the moral ambiguity of the state was widely considered subversive. The model for Lanigan would have been clear to a Dublin audience: Kevin O'Higgins. Johnston signals this when he has Lanigan predict his own murder in turn, at the hands of a former friend and comrade in arms. In response to Tausch's threat to denounce him to the police for shooting Blake, Lanigan reasons through his ruthless commitment to protecting Tausch's engineering project:

> When I took on this job I said to myself: "Well, I'll last as long as God allows me." . . . If I don't get what's coming to me for this business, I suppose I'll be plugged sooner or later by somebody. . . . I'm a physical-force man born and bred in the movement. . . . I'm only doing my job. . . . There's no excuse for it, I daresay. . . . But I only hope that when my time comes I'll be plugged fair and clean like he [Blake] was. . . . There are times when it's best to destroy the things that are nearest to us. . . . So, shot in an attack on the works, is my report. . . . If you know better — well, I won't blame you for saying so. It'll be all the same, I suppose, for *they'll* get me in the end, if you don't. But, by God, they'll not touch this power house again! You'll see that I'm right there.[63]

This was the rhetoric of necessity (the state must be protected at all costs) and fatality (there is no other choice) that the Saorstát used to justify its execution of Irregulars. Lanigan foresees his own assassination in what had already happened, historically, to O'Higgins. And the powerhouse, then, is the melancholy monument to murder for progress: "They'll not touch this power house again!"

Dobelle presents a kind of resistance to this logic when he announces his support for Blake's scheme to blow up the dam. His words are ignored by everyone except Tausch:

> I was once like Herr Tausch here. I too built barrages and constructed power houses, until one day I found myself to be a false friend. So we parted company. . . . I will tell you, Herr Tausch, why we can never be friends. Because you are a servant of righteousness, whilst I have sworn allegiance to the other side. . . . You wish to serve something you call progress. But progress—whatever it is—is never achieved by people like you who pursue it. Progress is the fruit of evil men, with sinister motives. You and your kind can only make misery. . . . It is right that men should murder each other for the safety of progress. I admit it. That is why I am against right and believe in wrong. (150)

Dobelle cannot refute the logic of progress, so rather than try to argue against it he simply refuses to be "a servant" of it. Later in the third act, Dobelle attempts to convince Tausch that his role as state engineer for the powerhouse is deeply imbricated with Lanigan's as the state's gunman and that he bears as much guilt for Blake's murder as Lanigan does: "Lanigan is just yourself. He is your finger on the trigger. Denounce him by all means. The tribute to your works is not yet complete. . . . But before you denounce him, I say you must give me an answer to what he has said. And you won't do that. Because there is no answer and you know it" (165).

Dobelle's last line here must be the one that Johnston promised White he would write into the play after their confrontation in front of the Abbey. The stalemate of historical necessity is "solved" by Dobelle through a retreat from worldly activity into a brand of philosophical detachment, a refusal to try to tamper with the world as it is. Though Dobelle's reasoning represents the most educated and literary type in the play, and though it probably aligns itself most closely with Johnston's own opinions, it is Aunt Columba who delivers the most articulate opposition to the powerhouse in her explanation of her position:

> I [have no] objection to any ordinary factory as such. But this building is a power house, which is a quite different thing. Some people, I

know, are inclined to scoff at the significance of power houses and to dismiss them lightly as just a small matter. But it is those very people who before they realize it have become dependent on the very thing they tried to laugh off. They think that they can give them up at any time. But they never can. Never. . . . Now once you become dependent upon anything, you are a slave of the man who controls it. Expected to bow the knee to some place-hunting industrialist with a small technical education and with neither culture nor religion to guide them. And if anybody thinks I am going to do that he is very greatly mistaken. I will not be dominated or controlled by anybody, and I am very grateful to Darry Blake for what he suggests, although I don't pretend to approve of him in other ways. (146–47)

Columba has no will to power; she doesn't approve of the IRA's fight against the state any more than she approves of the state. Her main objection is to the way that the powerhouse infringes on her life-world. Machines that make things—factories—don't bother her. Machines that make power, that transmit power into the home, that create new dependencies and whole new habits and practices—epistemic engines—she will not tolerate. Her critique is the Foucauldian critique of power. The other debates between Dobelle and Tausch, between Blake and Tausch, and between Lanigan and Tausch never really deviate from the progress-versus-romance paradigm. But Columba is talking about how power operates, and though she doesn't offer a solution she does offer a different ground from which to object to the powerhouse.

The staging of the problem of modernization in *The Moon* is complex and does justice to its subject, but the resolution is simplistic and merely reestablishes the fatality of national character through a generic, racist stereotype. Blake's corpse, it turns out, is a red herring. The struggle over modernization is not, as it might appear, a struggle between statists and romantic nationalists. Modernization will fail in Ireland, so the ending predicts, because, tautologically, everything is bound to fail in Ireland—because the Irish are comic failures. It's the stage Irish who determine events in the last resort, not the serious characters like Dobelle, Tausch, Lanigan, Columba, and Blake, who can only watch—laughing, crying, or, in Blake's case, dying—as their intentions are blasted and

mocked by a racist stereotype. The ideological positions staked out by
the various representative characters, so meticulously worked up and
worked out in the play's dialogue, come to nothing. "It seems," to quote
Haines from the first chapter of *Ulysses*, "that history is to blame."[64] And
Haines, Joyce's representative imperial apologist, is a perfect stereotype to
describe the kind of figure Johnston himself cut in Dublin in the 1930s:
born of well-off Northern Irish Protestant parents, brought up in a rich
Dublin suburb, well dressed, well educated, and well traveled, Johnston
"generally had a cosmopolitan air about him that did not endear him to
some of his less privileged and more provincial colleagues and acquaintances who referred to him hostilely as a 'West Briton.'"[65]

Getting a deep sense of what Johnston was trying to do in *The Moon*
requires taking account of Johnston's identity as a member of Dublin's
Protestant middle class after their marginalization by the establishment
of the Free State. To do that it is necessary to read beyond the play's staged
philosophical and political debates, to read against the grain of the play's
didactic thrust and even its literary pretensions. The play's significance
has to be sought, that is, historically, in a geography of shifting political
power. And in this case, "political power" and "electrical power" are synonymous. Johnston set *The Moon* at a hypothetical hydroelectric station
just outside Dublin. But the Shannon Scheme is, deductively, the play's
real historical—though fictionally displaced—referent. There was no
hydroelectric station near Dublin, but there was an important coal-fired
plant there, known colloquially as the Pigeon House, that supplied electricity locally to Dublin City. The action in *The Moon* takes place "about
the year 1927" (100). In that year the Shannon Scheme was nearly complete; the powerhouse in *The Moon* is in the same stage of development,
somewhere between being finished and beginning electricity production.
On October 24, 1929, Ardnacrusha started operating commercially, feeding electricity to Dublin. For twelve days, starting on January 13, 1930,
"Ardnacrusha was synchronized with the Pigeon House power station in
Dublin and both operated in parallel." On the 25th of January, the "Pigeon House was shut down. From that date, supply for Dublin City and
most of the suburbs was from Ardnacrusha."[66] *The Moon in the Yellow
River* debuted in Dublin at the Abbey Theatre on April 27, 1931. Johnston's play, then, might have condemned the Irish to a perennial back-

wardness, but it did so just fifteen months after the national grid lit up
and took over from the local utilities—most of which, like the Pigeon
House in Dublin, were built under the British dominion in Ireland. Irish
power had become a reality even as *The Moon* was arguing that it would
never be more than a fantasy.

From this perspective, Johnston's recourse to the Irish stereotype—
and a stereotypical Irish fatality—was as much about imaginative wish
fulfillment as about any racialized opposition between Celtic incompetence and Anglo-Saxon utilitarianism. Indeed, the persistence of racialized
Irish stereotypes is perhaps even more poignantly embodied in the figures of George and Potts, who are neither Celtic nor Catholic: according to
Bernard Adams, George is an "Anglo-Irish sea-salt" and Potts a "cockney
quartermaster."[67] They may therefore appear superficially to defy the racial stereotype of the stage Irishman; but closer inspection reveals that
George and Potts inhabit the same social coordinates in Johnston's play
as the poteen-drinking Connemara men do in Keating's painting *Night's
Candles Are Burnt Out*. For Keating, these stereotypes were swept aside
by modernization as represented by Ardnacrusha; for Johnston, they persisted and determined the Irish nation's perennial backwardness. To borrow Seamus Deane's terminology once again, Johnston transposed, in his
characterization of George and Potts, the ethnic specificity of the Irish
national character into the demographic diversity of the character of the
Irish nation. *The Moon*'s stereotype of the Irish nation, in other words,
does the ideological work formerly assigned to the stereotype of the Irish
race. Structurally speaking, however, Irishness remains in *The Moon* synonymous with underdevelopment, in the face of the evidence provided
by the historical success of the Shannon Scheme.

Johnston had every reason to prefer Dublin the way it was before the
revolution, and his symbolic geography must have been seriously shaken
up by the transfer of power brought about by the foundation of the Free
State. A commonplace about the Irish Revolution is that it did little in
terms of revolutionizing living conditions or forms of domination. A
common anecdote illustrates the point: when the Dáil came to power in
1922, one of the first things it did was to order the repainting of all the
street postboxes in the Free State, from British red to Irish green. Of course,
the postbox, the mail system, all the structures remained fundamentally

the same. Beneath the Irish green of the "new" postboxes, the royal insignia of *Victoria Regina* or *Edwardus Rex* showed through as the indelible imprint of British dominion and British engineering cultures.[68] The Free State's symbolic gesture of appropriation was thus undermined by the persistence of form—the material infrastructure of the postal system. The visibility of the royal insignia mockingly suggested that the Irish Revolution was a revolution in name only, that systemic change was as elusive in Irish Ireland as under the Act of Union.

As an emblem of Irish incompetence, the Dáil's cosmetic makeover of the postboxes made the Irish Revolution seem like a bad joke—in fact the postboxes were the butt of many a bad joke at the time—especially to those who suffered the indignity of seeing their symbolic geography transformed without any apparent actual changes, except of course in their own social status. Johnston and many of his Protestant contemporaries felt contempt for, and estrangement from, these kinds of changes.[69] Or alternatively, the lack of any real changes could have served to *justify* a contempt that some Protestants undoubtedly felt regardless, before and after power changed hands: a contempt deeply rooted in the racialized opposition between utility and the aesthetic. But that contempt, whether it stemmed from a political critique or from the old racism, could not hold—or could no longer be justified—in the face of real change, which the Shannon Scheme achieved. The Shannon Scheme effectively transferred power from Dublin to Clare—literally, that is, "beyond the Pale," away from the historical seat of British rule in Ireland to the traditional and mythical realm of the Gael. Even more significant, though, was the way that the move from a local to a national network transformed the modes of production, distribution, and consumption of power: from British coal to Irish water, from the local to the national scale and, from there, spreading to embrace, with government subsidies, the poorest rural citizens. The Free State had successfully changed the form if not the content of electricity, ripping it away from British colonialism, British engineering cultures, and even private enterprise. An Irish government had finally built a better mailbox, so to speak, as opposed to just painting it a different color. In writing *The Moon*, Johnston expressed not so much the theory that the Irish were incapable of a real transformation of power as his wish that the attempt would fail, along with a disavowal of its already achieved success.

Where, then, do we find the corpse on the threshold? Where are electrification's victims? One answer I suggest here is that in the dramatic action of *The Moon,* it was in the end Johnston himself whose identity was
shattered, not by electrification per se but by the drama of power enacted
in the electrification schemes of the Free State. If the revolution swept
away the privileges of the Protestant middle class, the Shannon Scheme
swept away whatever remained of the *reasons* behind those privileges.
And this, of course, is the real blow to identity: beyond the loss of entitlement, the unwanted knowledge that the entitlement was never more than
arbitrary in the first place. The Irish, it turned out, were perfectly capable
of piloting a modern nation just as well as—if not, in the case of electrification, better than—their former patrician masters. This is not to say
that the dam was an unmitigated success—we've seen some of its casual-
ties, as well as the state's other victims, throughout—but from the Protestant middle-class point of view, Ardnacrusha proved something that
they might not have been eager to believe.

Johnston was always far too eager to pretend that *The Moon*—his
most well-known play outside of Ireland, and the one that made his international reputation—had nothing whatsoever to do with electricity
or even, for that matter, history in general. Even though *The Moon* was
his only play that could be described as realist, he insisted that, of all his
plays, it was the only one that should not be considered "historical."[70] And
even though it is a play set in and around a powerhouse, he insisted that
the powerhouse had nothing at all to do with the dramatic action or the
ultimate meaning of the play. When he met with New York producers to
discuss a staging of the play on Broadway, they asked him to explain "what
this scene between the father [Dobelle] and the daughter [Blanaid] has to
do with the play about the power house." "This isn't a play about a power
house," he snapped, "it's a play about people."[71] Though true in a way,
of course, Johnston's answer is about as evasive as they come, wielding a
kind of literary humanism as a club to quash questions about the stakes of
writing a play set around the construction of an electrical plant. It's not an
answer, really: it's a defensive denial. One of the first things the New York
producers of *The Moon* asked Johnston to do when he arrived was to
"please begin by drawing a plan of the fort in which the play was set, and
add to this a sketch-map of the countryside for some miles around." Johnston's reaction is telling too: "This was a pleasure. I drafted out a plan of

the Pigeon House, together with all the topographical aspects of the sur-rounding slob-lands of Sandymount."[72] The pleasure he took in draw-ing a picture of the Pigeon House had nothing to do with realism; he was dismissive of the questions that followed on the request and that sought to deepen a realist sensibility: "But there were other things they wanted to know. How many people were hurt in the explosion? How far away did the life-saving exercises take place? How old was Blanaid's mother when she died? . . . I failed [read: refused] to answer some of Broadway's more searching probes."[73]

Johnston had no interest in answering these last questions; he did, however, have an interest, a "pleasure," in the Pigeon House. In New York, however, and for an American audience he might have reasonably as-sumed had little knowledge of Irish power politics, Johnston could pre-sent his Pigeon House as if it were a reality, as if it were still a source of power, as if it still *mattered*. His drawing of the Pigeon House has an im-mediate analogue in the scaled model of Ardnacrusha that Siemens made for the ESB and that toured the country; they are both miniaturizations of regimes of power, techno-fetishes intensely tied to the identities of their bearers. And power—in this case, its transfer to another, and the nostalgic recreation of its heyday—is at the heart of the curious exception John-ston made to his otherwise principled decision not to explain himself to Broadway. If he was right to say that *The Moon* is not a historical play, that is because it is a denial of history in the form of a historical play. More accurately, *The Moon* might be considered a counterhistorical or allo-historical play, a counterfactual fiction, what we could call—because it deals, or refuses to deal, with the politics of electrification—an "electrific-tion," in the limited and negative sense given the term by Lenin's critics.[74]

Dobelle's bookshelves, however, tell a different story than *The Moon* ul-timately does, "filled," as Johnston describes them, "with books on tech-nical engineering mixed with a hotchpotch of modern and classical lit-erature" (101).[75] That "hotchpotch" represents the domain of what I've been calling electrifiction in the theoretical sense, the place where—to re-turn once more to Nabokov—Dobelle's destiny and, as I've been trying to suggest here, ours as well, is "liable to catch," or be caught out.

OTHER ROUGH BEASTS:
COMPARATIVE POSTCOLONIALISM
AND THE DREAM OF INFRASTRUCTURE

FIVE

It is said that the dialectical method consists in doing justice each time to the concrete historical situation of its object. But that is not enough. For it is just as much a matter of doing justice to the concrete historical situation of the interest *taken in the object.*
—Walter Benjamin, *The Arcades Project*

In the preceding chapters, Irish modernism revealed its attentiveness to municipal and national infrastructure, an attentiveness shaped by the experience of the colonial imposition of utilitarian institutions and structures in Ireland. That imposition in turn produced, reproduced, and reinforced a racialized opposition between the poetic Celt and the pragmatic Anglo-Saxon that had a double effect. Some Irish writers seized on their purported superiority in the realm of the aesthetic as a mandate, embracing the opposition and producing works that cleaved closely to its tenets. Others confronted the opposition head on, attempting to dismantle it with the invention of new generic strategies. In my readings, Joyce undid the opposition; O'Brien challenged it but struggled within its confines; the Free State challenged it on the extraliterary grounds of its massive electrification project; and Johnston used it in his drama as an excuse for political despair.

In this final chapter I follow Benjamin's injunction to "do justice to the concrete historical situation of the *interest* taken in the object," the representation of public utilities in postcolonial Irish modernism. That is, I account for my present interest in the object and for what I want to show should be our ongoing interest in the object. I move therefore from the early twentieth century to the turn of the twenty-first century, and I focus my attention on a postcolonial novel, Patrick Chamoiseau's *Texaco*, that takes up the form of the postcolonial comedy of development as a genre suited to representing the twenty-first-century cities of the Global South. I draw on a connection here between the underdeveloped city of Dublin at the turn of the twentieth century—a colonial metropole— and the key characteristics it shares with new forms of urbanization at the turn of the twenty-first century. In *Texaco*, the networked supply of electricity—from the official city of Fort-de-France to the shantytown of Texaco—figures a celebratory moment of political recognition. The story of Texaco's struggle for political recognition is the story of what in chapter 1 I followed Gayatri Spivak in calling the emergence of agency through the demand for infrastructure. Of course, infrastructure can mean many things, and one of the aims of this chapter is to show why electricity signifies so powerfully in *Texaco* and elsewhere as a metonym for infrastructure, its promises and its dangers. To do so will require a preliminary investigation of the historical meanings attaching to electricity in relation to the rise of republicanism in the eighteenth century; in relation to Romantic tropes of aesthetic experience; and in relation to the Victorian spread of the discourses and projects of town planning and public health.

I conclude by arguing that *Texaco* makes a case for a reformulation of human rights discourse through an insistence on infrastructure not only as a human right but as the minimal material prostheses of democratic participation and the formation of citizen-subjects. For this reason, infrastructure is thematically—and in *Texaco*'s case, formally—central to postcolonial literatures and to the literatures of the cities of the Global

South. I end by considering a popular cultural form—the choreographed martial art of *parkour* and its recent visibility in American and French action cinema—that expresses, I argue, the demand for infrastructure from the ghettos, suburbs, shantytowns, and bidonvilles of both the post-imperial metropole and the postcolonial cities of the Global South.

The story of *Public Works* culminates in the Irish case with the national electrification of the Free State. But as I pointed out in chapter 4, Ireland's experiment with electrification was contemporaneous with electrification projects in Europe, the United States, the Soviet Union, and elsewhere. It is important to realize that electrification transformed early twentieth-century understandings of modern political power. The democratization of electricity—that is, not the discovery of electricity so much as the technological mediation of electricity in massive distributional grids—was one of the most imaginatively profound events in the history of technological modernization. Electricity was a perfect metonymic stand-in for enlightenment in nearly every context into which it was introduced; the very concept of "power" as we now understand it has a nearly reflexive reference to electricity built into it, so that to speak in the twentieth century of "the power of the state" is in some sense to speak of electrical power and of the national electrical grid. In the popular imagination electricity held simultaneously the secret of life and the threat of violent death. The force with which electricity-became-enlightenment-became-power was so overwhelming that ideologues from every camp between communism and capitalism professed their belief in its transformative powers. In chapter 4, I pointed to V. I. Lenin's 1924 slogan "Communism = Soviet Power + Electrification of the Whole Country." Lenin's idea, that electrification would make Russians into modern citizen-subjects of the communist state, was equally applicable in the Western capitalist nations; and the Irish case was in that respect an anomalous example of how applicable such rhetorics of electrification were in postcolonial states as well. The power of the nation-state in the twentieth century is bound up with electricity and specifically with national electrical grids in ways that we still do not really understand very well. But we could say that electricity bears a relationship to power something like the relationship that Coke bears to soda or Kleenex to tissue: electricity was the brand name, so to speak, of power in the first half of the twentieth century.

ELECTRICITY, POLITICS, AESTHETICS

From breast to breast th'electric ardour ran
And in full glare display'd the rights of man.

—St. John Honeywood,
"Poetical Address to the Citizen Adet" (1801)

The conceptual linkage between the abstract ideals of Enlightenment republicanism and the utopian promise of electricity dates back to the American Revolution, long before the arrival of large-scale electrical grids at the turn of the twentieth century. James Delbourgo, in his book *A Most Amazing Scene of Wonders,* explores "the rhetorical career of electricity in the American Revolution," when, he argues, "electricity lent itself readily to political use because it provided a language of power through which to articulate the meaning of revolution."[1] So strong was the connection between electricity and revolution in the American popular imagination that in 1790 John Adams could complain about it as a vulgar and widespread fictionalization of history: "The history of our Revolution will be one continued lie from one end to the other. . . . The essence of the whole will be *that Dr. Franklin's electrical rod smote the earth and out sprung General Washington. That Franklin electrized him with his rod—and henceforward these two conducted all the policy, negotiation, legislation, and war.*"[2] This should forcefully recall the Soviet joke about "electrifiction." But Adams was writing against the popular current, so to speak; according to Delbourgo, "From the pens of Patriots, electricity became for the first time anywhere a language of radicalism, republicanism, and revolution."[3] By 1799 the French would speak of the "electric example of the American Revolution," using a metaphor of electrical conductivity to express the politics of influence that led from America to France.[4]

Just as the discourse of electricity infiltrated the discourse of republican politics in Revolutionary America, it became a major trope in the discourse of Romantic poetry and aesthetics in the years that followed. In his essay "Romantic Electricity, or the Materiality of Aesthetics," Paul Gilmore offers many examples from the Romantic period in which "the elec-

tric . . . seems to refer to some intensified level of consciousness connected
to the insights of poetic genius." And that intensified level of consciousness, figured through the mysteries of electricity, led to "the individual's
momentary suspension in a sense of a larger whole": a collective experience of the imagined community of the nation.[5] This is why, according
to Gilmore, Shelley believed that technological advances in electricity
"would virtually emancipate every slave, and would annihilate slavery
for ever." But it was not the idea of electricity as a network, as a constructed environment, that motivated these ideas; it was something more
like electricity as a vital life force that was both cause and effect of the
revolutionary forces of American and French republicanism. The material network—in particular for Gilmore the network of the telegraph—
inspired the idea of "a boundaryless, yet embodied, social collective."[6]
But to do so, the telegraphic network's limits in a bounded and defined
built infrastructure had to be ignored or downplayed. Delbourgo points
to the same discursive desire to make the machinic mediation of electricity invisible in the American Revolutionary era: "Electrical politics
was a discourse of science and politics that omitted mention of the machines by which electrification was actually experienced. That omission
was not absentminded but studied, and ideologically significant. The
discourse of electrical politics could not incorporate the mediating technologies involved in making electrical knowledge because it sought to
naturalize and sacralize revolution as the artless work of higher cosmic
forces."[7] Gilmore makes a similar point for the Romantic discourse of aesthetics: electricity was a mystical force, the province of "genius" as opposed to "talent and industry."[8]

The popular Romantic concept of an electrical aesthetic experience
was subsequently challenged when the boundaries of constructed networks became much harder to ignore. By the end of the nineteenth century, as Chris Otter shows, municipalities and private enterprise—and
the discourses of town and city planning—had succeeded in creating an
urban, built environment dedicated to "making liberalism durable." Sewer
systems, street lighting, waterworks, and the rest were, in Otter's account,
forms of Foucauldian governmentality that produced "environmental
and sensory conditions through which liberalism as a modality of government could be made possible."[9] In his account, "Infrastructure functions

as environmental technology, regulating the habitats within which subjectivity is produced. In short, it normalizes."[10] While such infrastructural
systems "cannot in and of themselves determine positively any form of
human conduct . . . they do . . . produce certain spectra of possibility" that
for Otter amount to the construction of the liberal bourgeois subject.[11]

Thus, if the electrical trope began with an idea of electricity as a mystical, total experience of mind, body, and collective—whether in political or aesthetic discourses—by the Victorian era the built environment
began to attenuate that ecstatic experience by revealing its limits in the
engineering cultures of states, municipalities, and private enterprise. The
connection between electricity and "poetic genius" loosened as electricity
began to be associated with urban planners, engineers, and politicians,
as opposed to Shelley's poetic "unacknowledged legislators." Joseph Pax-
ton's Crystal Palace, constructed for the 1851 Great Exhibition in London, indexes for Marshall Berman a shift in the popular imagination from
Romantic poetic genius to "the primacy of engineering" as a "symbol of
human creativity."[12] This meant a certain amount of trouble for the literary sphere, whose claim to electrical experience was henceforth challenged by the engineers who were delivering electrical experience in the
realm of the utility networks. Thus on the one hand there was Oscar
Wilde, who could assert in perfect continuity with Shelley in 1891 that
"great storages of force for every city" meant the end of "human slavery"
but who at the same time saw no connection—unlike Shelley—between
those stores of energy and the new art that the liberated individual would
produce; the energy stores themselves were for Wilde entirely banal. And
on the other hand there was James Joyce, who in 1916 used the metaphor of electricity, as I pointed out in chapter 2, as a figure for boredom,
counterintuitively opposing everyday electricity to Stephen's poetic genius: "The droning voice of the professor continued to wind itself slowly
round and round the coils it spoke of, doubling, trebling, quadrupling
its somnolent energy as the coil multiplied its ohms of resistance."[13] As
electricity became more and more a part of the normalizing processes of
"making liberalism durable," it became less and less a part of literature's
claim to producing an aesthetic experience that transcended the everyday. Electricity became, that is to say, boring.

Joyce would, however, reclaim the public utility as an ecstatic experience for literature in *Ulysses,* where he embraced the role of engineer

as a metaphor for authorship. Even as *Ulysses* depicts Stephen Dedalus locked in an opposition between engineering and poetry, the author of *Ulysses* conceived himself as an artist who had surpassed the opposition and thereby reclaimed the Romantic electrical experience for both engineering and the literary. Whereas the mundanity of the public utility threatened for a time to nullify electricity's claim to transcendent aesthetic experience, some writers in the modernist period championed the old connection between electricity and the aesthetic, but in a new conjunction with the emergent electrical grid. In 1935 Walter Benjamin could invoke, through Paul Valéry's 1928 essay "The Conquest of Ubiquity," that new conjunction of electricity as both an aesthetic experience and as a social technology, precisely in the image of the public utility. Benjamin quotes Valéry in his 1935 essay "The Work of Art in the Age of Its Technological Reproducibility": "Just as water, gas, and electricity are brought into our houses from far off to satisfy our needs with minimal effort, so we shall be supplied with visual or auditory images, which will appear and disappear at a simple movement of the hand, hardly more than a sign."[14]

Valéry's essay is really about a technological fantasy of transmitting a worldwide musical experience, but Benjamin uses it here as a segue to his argument that "around 1900, technical reproduction not only had reached a standard that permitted it to reproduce all known works of art, profoundly modifying their effect, but it also had captured a place of its own among the artistic processes."[15] The last part of Benjamin's argument is key; technology had for him "a place of its own" as part of the artistic process. Valéry is proposing nothing, in his statement, about a relationship between public utilities and the technological stream of visual and auditory images; the comparison rests as an homology with structural similarities but without points of contact—a parallelism. But we might hear something, based on the argument of this book, with more significance: the "song" of the gas jet for Stephen Dedalus in *A Portrait of the Artist as a Young Man*, for example, which matches up with Benjamin's assertion—that the technological means had a "place of their own" in artistic processes—via Valéry's suggestion that technological means and artistic processes were somehow alike, if essentially unrelated.

It is as if, in thinking about the technological dissemination of new media, Valéry cannot help but think also about the structures that underlie the delivery of such media, though in a way that remains confined to homology, never becoming the object of analysis. In the foreword to his 1931 book *The Outlook for Intelligence,* however, the issue of electricity as a networked public utility becomes finally an object of analysis while at the same time remaining fairly obscure:

> Nothing is easier than to point out in history books the omission of remarkable phenomena that have occurred so slowly as to be imperceptible. They escape the historian, since no document mentions them expressly. They could be perceived and noted only by means of a preestablished system of prior questions and definitions, which so far have never been conceived. An event that takes place over a century does not figure in any document or any collection of memoirs. For example, the immense and singular role of the city of Paris in the life of France after the Revolution. Or the discovery of electricity and the conquest of the earth by its different uses. The latter events, unequaled in human history, appear in it, when they do, less prominent than some other affair more *scenic,* more in conformity (this especially) with what traditional history customarily reports. In Napoleon's time electricity had about the same importance as Christianity at the time of Tiberius. It is gradually becoming obvious that this general *energizing* of the world is more pregnant with consequences, more capable of transforming life in the immediate future than all the "political" events from the time of Ampère to the present day.[16]

Notice that in this passage the "conquest of the earth" by the different uses of electricity shifts its status from a single example of "remarkable phenomena" to a singular example, one of the most significant motor forces of history, more powerful than "all the 'political' events" combined. By invoking André-Marie Ampère's work on electromagnetism, Valéry asserts that the discovery of electricity marked a historic shift in how and where history was made, from the domain of politics to the domain of technology. And because Ampère's life straddles both sides of the French Revolution, Valéry suggests—if not that the one was more important than the other—that the French Revolution and the discovery of electricity were imbricated with one another: something very similar to Delbourgo's argument about America, but with a more technological awareness. He locates us, that is to say, in a conceptually difficult zone between liberty, equality, and brotherhood on the one hand and water, gas, and electricity on the other. If we combine this with Valéry's hopes, in "The Conquest of Ubiquity," for the aesthetic possibilities of electricity, then we are situated at a nexus where aesthetics, politics, and engineering come together to form a new kind of historical, and historiographical, problem.

Thomas Hughes, in the first pages of his introduction to one of the few detailed histories of electrification in the West, *Networks of Power*, notes the dearth of scholarship on the subject. "Historians interested in technology," he writes, "have written only a few monographs that concentrate on the evolution of the massive, extensive, vertically integrated production systems of the modern industrial world."

> Although the public senses the strong organizing forces that originated in these systems and that today influence their lives, they only dimly perceive the nature of these forces. The technological, or man-made, world awaits a Darwin to explicate the origins and dynamics of the forces that pervade it. Quoting Paul Valéry, historian Marc Bloch chides traditional historians for not taking up the task of explicating "the conquest of the earth" by electricity, one of those notable phenomena that have "greater possibilities of shaping our immediate future than all the political events combined."[17]

Echoing Valéry's sense of historical magnitude in asserting that the electrical grid would require a "Darwin" to explicate its impact on the lives of the public, Hughes reveals his own sense that the significance of the networked electrical utility "eludes the historian" still. But following Valéry, it is necessary not only to take the measure of the historical impact of electricity's evolution into a massive production system but also— the point I wish to stress here—to take the measure of its *possibilities* for shaping our immediate future. That is why I am focused on a fiction of electrification: a novel.

Hughes was writing in 1983. Today, as historian Chris Otter argues, "Infrastructure, as a material technology of rule, is beginning to receive the attention of historians."[18] But to the extent that Otter focuses on the ways that the infrastructure of the Victorian city was calculated to produce "liberalism as a modality of government," he highlights the project of Foucauldian governmentality, neglecting the utopian element inhering in the infrastructural developments he describes. Writing about the infrastructure of transport and transit in the context of disability studies, Celeste Langan has emphasized, not the coercion of liberalism's built environment, but its democratic possibilities. Her project is to recognize "in the artificial form of the citizen a *prosthetic* subject, whose capacities for liberty depend on the built environment of the public sphere."[19] Borrowing from Langan's thesis about public transportation as an infrastructural prosthetic guarantee for the democratic equality of the citizen-subject, I think it possible to make the same claim for the institution of the public utility: water, gas, and electricity. And in the reading of Patrick Chamoiseau's *Texaco* that follows, I wish to show how the provision of electricity functions in that novel precisely as such a democratic prosthesis, enabling the postcolonial subject's emergence into agency, as Spivak puts it, and enabling recognition between Fort-de-France's municipal authorities and the residents of Texaco.

TEXACO AND THE PLANET OF SLUMS

Texaco is about the founding and flourishing of a fictional shantytown, called Texaco, just outside Fort-de-France in Martinique. The setting of *Texaco* is also its subject; Texaco is a paradigmatic instance of what Mike Davis has called, in his seminal 2004 essay (and subsequent book), the "Planet of Slums."[20] There Davis proclaimed 2005 the watershed year during which the planet would become urban as opposed to rural, since by that time demographers predicted that more than 50 percent of the world's population would be living in cities. He described the emergence of the mega- and hypercity, cities like Lagos and Mumbai, where population density and poverty levels were exponentially greater than anything first-world cities had ever experienced, and where, in the absence of infrastructural development to match the demographic explosion, a series of outlying shantytowns, bidonvilles, and favelas would sprout like fungi or cancer on the older, more structured city they surrounded and infiltrated. Critics in the humanities have been quick to take up Davis's sociohistorical work. Brent Edwards and Ashley Dawson's coedited special issue of *Social Text* entitled "Cities of the Global South" is one example;[21] Patricia Yeager's *PMLA* special issue "Cities," and especially her accompanying introduction, "Dreaming of Infrastructure," is another.[22] Looming over this trend is yet another text: the novel *Texaco* itself, published in French in 1992 and translated into English in 1998.[23] Davis cites it, as do Dawson, Edwards, and Yeager, making it a kind of de facto representative literary text for the "Planet of Slums" in Anglophone literary criticism. While not representative of the new hypercities like São Paulo or Mexico City, the evolution of Fort-de-France is, in fact, exemplary of the demographic trend Davis is talking about, which involves not so much the hypercities, which "have actually declined in relative share of urban population," as the "secondary cities" with a population of between one hundred thousand and five hundred thousand inhabitants. In these places "urbanization must be conceptualized as structural transformation along, and intensified interaction between, every point of an urban-rural continuum."[24]

In such places the new urban subject of the Planet of Slums comes into being. Despite "the diminutive size of Martinique's capital," Ashley Dawson observes, "*Texaco*'s picaresque narrative records a paradigmatic experience for the many millions experiencing urbanization in the global South: displacement."[25] For Dawson the emergent subject of *Texaco* is, furthermore, the "squatter citizen," and it is this subject whose "struggles . . . for resources and legitimacy will define the form and character of the global cities of the South and, by extension, the shape of modernity in the twenty-first century."[26] There are thus several reasons for considering *Texaco*'s slum-urban vision as exemplary, to which I would add another: the novel's treatment of the public utility, particularly electricity. I wish to argue that electricity is central to *Texaco*'s telos as a postcolonial comedy of development whose ultimate protagonist is the shantytown of Texaco itself, and further, that *Texaco* gets taken up as a representative text of the literature of the Planet of Slums *because* the public utility—in the form of electricity—is the end point of the plot's development. Marie-Sophie, the founder of Texaco, names her city for the American oil company that owns the gasoline reservoirs, and the land, on which she has decided to settle. "Texaco" announces itself therefore as on the one hand a representative of Valéry's "general *energizing* of the world" and on the other as "a kind of enterprise." In Marie-Sophie's Texaco, "that enterprise was about living" (386).

TEXACO AS POSTCOLONIAL COMEDY OF DEVELOPMENT

Light! More light!
— Goethe's last words (apocryphal)

Chamoiseau's novel is what I call a postcolonial comedy of development in part because it has a happy ending. The shantytown of Texaco, slated for destruction by the municipal authorities of Fort-de-France, is saved through the efforts of the protagonist, Marie-Sophie, to get the settlement officially recognized by the city. She does this through a series of interviews with "the Urban Planner," who has come to survey the settlement and make his recommendation to the city, presumably to raze Texaco and relocate its inhabitants somewhere chosen, zoned, and chartered by city officials. But the story that Marie-Sophie recounts to the Urban Planner, the epic history and mythology of Texaco, converts him to her side; and through a combination of his efforts and Marie-Sophie's, Texaco is finally recognized by the city as a legitimate settlement. Along the way, the Urban Planner is converted to a new understanding of the relationship between the shantytown and the official city of Fort-de-France. The novel is interspersed with excerpts like this one from the Urban Planner's notebooks: "The Western urban planner sees Texaco as a tumor on the urban order. Incoherent. Insalubrious. A dynamic contestation. A threat. It is denied any architectural or social value. Political discourse negates it. In other words, it is a *problem*. But to raze it is to send the problem elsewhere or worse: not to consider it. No, we must dismiss the West and re-learn to read: learn to reinvent the city" (269). The urban slum is denied, negated, and unrecognized by the traditional urban order.

For the Urban Planner, however, relearning how to read the city means recognizing that the urban slum is an integral, vital part of the official city, that "City draws strength from Texaco's urban mangroves" (263). And Texaco, in turn, needs recognition from the official city of Fort-de-France. As the Urban Planner puts it, "To reach its potential and its function of renaissance, Texaco needs City to caress it, meaning: it needs consideration" (263).

The Urban Planner casts the problem of what might constitute "consideration" for Texaco in terms of reading and of learning to read: a point that will return in the context of the struggle to obtain electricity for Texaco. In the final pages of the novel, the crowning act of that process the Urban Planner calls "consideration" turns on the flow of municipal electricity into Texaco's homes. Marie-Sophie records the event: "The E.D.F. appeared one day along the Pénétrante West [the new road from Fort-de-France into Texaco], stuck its poles, and plugged us some electricity. It was an unblemished joy. . . . City was from now on taking us under its wing and admitting our existence. . . . City would integrate Texaco's soul. . . . Everything would be improved but . . . everything would remain in accordance with its fundamental law, with its alleys, places, with its so old memory which the country needed" (381). "An unblemished joy." This is not the usual language of mourning, longing, loss, and struggle that characterizes the novel's tone and narrative arc, from slavery to abolition to urban migration to the founding of Texaco. It is impossible to characterize, for example, abolition as an unblemished joy, since its enactment almost automatically entails a remembering of the slave trade, of families broken, lives taken, years lost. This is the way *Texaco* in general remembers the past, so that an "unblemished joy" like the one Marie-Sophie describes here demands attention. Unblemished joys are not common in Texaco, and this is the only one to be found in *Texaco*. Nor, perhaps, ought this one to be taken without a suspicion of irony. But my gamble here is that "une joie sans faille," "an unblemished joy," says exactly what it means, and that explaining why this should be so is the key to understanding the novel as a whole.[27] Coming as it does a few pages from the end of the novel, this moment is the culmination of the novel's telos. This is not independence *tout court* but recognition: "City was taking us under its wing and admitting our existence." Not "freedom from," say, the impositions of City and the city's authorities, but freedom *in* them: "Everything would be improved but . . . everything would remain in accordance with its fundamental law." The last part is important; in the end it is Texaco's own governing body that decides issues of planning and development. The municipal authorities supply electricity, they recognize Texaco as a part of the municipality, but they don't—from this point forward—otherwise interfere. And as I argue in what follows, the "unblemished joy" recorded by Marie-Sophie as the collective sentiment expressed when the lights go on in Texaco is in large part a reference to—and a continuation of—both the electric politics of Revolutionary America and the electric aesthetics of the Romantic poets.

Taking the "unblemished joy" as an authentic feeling, however, does not mean that it is the right feeling, or that Marie-Sophie ought to take electricity as the unequivocal sign of recognition, as if the power supply could make up for centuries of oppression and exploitation. Could we not consider electricity as the sign merely of a giddy historical amnesia brought on by the thrill of admittance to consumer luxuries long denied Dawson's "squatter citizens," or, in Robert Kurz's formulation, "monetary subjects with no cash"?[28] We could, but again we would have to read Marie-Sophie, tough and dedicated as she is, as finally defeated, bought out by the comforts of commodity culture.[29] And that won't do either, because this moment of joy is altogether more complicated, and it is, moreover, intricately woven into the plot structure of *Texaco*. It emerges proleptically at the moment when Marie-Sophie teaches herself to read with the cast-off books of her first employer in the city: "Caméléon Sainte-Claire offered me my first book (a technical manual which must have bored him). I used it to find this or that word, to spell it, to copy it, but never read it: it offered nothing but discussions of electricity, something about screws, wire, switches, and volts and watts. It was from Monsieur Gros-Joseph [Marie-Sophie's second employer] himself that I would develop a taste for the books-to-read, devoid of pictures, in which writing becomes the sorcerer of the world" (216).

Here is an echo, in Marie-Sophie's literary education, of Gayatri Spivak's evocation of "infrastructure in the colloquial sense" on the one hand and "Humanities education" on the other: the key elements, for her, of the emergence of subaltern agency. The electricity book is Marie-Sophie's

primer, in her description of it, for literature: high literature, world literature. Her disavowal of the importance of the intellectual value of electrical know-how, for which she swears she "never read," is meant to signal her intellectual ambition in the context of her shameful sense of her
own ignorance. She goes so far as to equate "picture books" with child's
play and to equate books "devoid of pictures" and dense with text with
intellectual maturity, a touchingly naive distinction that is instantly recognizable as the young upstart's aggressive insecurity. Not for her the trades-
man's knowledge of "screws, wire, switches, and volts and watts." This is
plebeian knowledge compared to the transcendence of great literature.
Yet of course the culminating passage of *Texaco* gives the lie to such a position by depicting the "unblemished joy" that comes with the turning on
of the current, the connection to and the recognition by City. And we can
see, even in the way that she characterizes high literature as "the sorcerer
of the world," that electricity is already the metaphor through which she
comes to understand literature's effects on her.

This metaphor only becomes more pronounced as she puts more and
more "good" books in front of her memory of her first book: the process
by which the metaphor of electricity, though time, distance, and forget-
fulness, becomes a commonplace or cliché. Her literary education con-
tinues and deepens with her second employer, Monsieur Gros-Joseph:
"With him I embarked upon the unknown world of books. . . . When circumstances lent themselves, I skimmed many books, read lots of poems,
bits of paragraphs, spellbinding moments. To Gros-Joseph's great despair, I could never tell what was by whom, nor if someone was worth
more than another. For me, each book released an aroma, a voice, a time,
a moment, a pain, a presence; each book cast a light or burdened me with
its shadow; I was terrified feeling these souls, tied up in one hum, crackling under my fingers" (218).

In the "one hum" and in the "crackling under [her] fingers," we cannot help but hear the echo of that first book about electricity, the buzz of
watts and volts and wires and switches. Each book, as she says, "casts a
light" and a shadow. The electricity of her first book is a current that runs
through all her subsequent reading of literature—again, despite her claim
never really to have read it for its contents. This formative reading experience is also a genealogy of a metaphor. For Marie-Sophie, reading is an

electrifying experience, first as a matter of fact, later as a matter of feeling. There are, as we've seen, origins for this trope that go back to revolutionary republicanism and Romantic poetry. But the metaphor of literature as somehow electrifying is in *Texaco* traced back instead to a more local origin, which for Marie-Sophie is also very literal: the electrician's handbook.

And at an intermediate distance from the electrician and the writer as "sorcerer[s] of the world"—between the engineer and the artist—is the politician, the very role that Marie-Sophie fulfills for her constituents in Texaco. "I proposed a plan which everyone adopted," she recounts, "to pay a visit to [Aimé] Césaire, not to the town council where his dogs kept watch, but at his home. . . . There I would speak to him about getting us water, electricity, a path over the mud, solid steps, cement scuppers. The thing was voted through by the women (the men thinking us basically crazy but avoiding opposing me)" (366–67). Encouraged by the inhabitants of Texaco—especially the women, as she notes—Marie-Sophie's path from engineering (the electricity primer) to humanities education (writing as "the sorcerer of the world") leads her finally to politics, where, remarkably, she encounters in the fiction of *Texaco* a "real" historical, recognizable person: Aimé Césaire, who himself combined the roles of poet and politician.

The approach on Césaire's private life is also, in the end, a literary approach. Marie-Sophie gets him to listen to her only after she has recited— as she says, "with all the energy in the world"—a few lines from his "Notebook of a Return to a Native Land," lines whose central trope has to do with reconceptualizing the cosmos as centered on humankind and its intentions: "and room there is for all at the rendezvous with conquest and we now know that the sun revolves around our earth, lighting the parcel that only our will has fixed and that any star shall plummet from sky to earth at our limitless command" (368). Again, electricity seems to be the point of these lines, at least in isolation. More than just proving her literacy and her familiarity with Césaire's poetry, Marie-Sophie chooses— with poetic attention to her own political intent—a passage that expresses exactly what she is asking for: a star to light a parcel that her will has fixed. She appeals to Césaire as mayor through an appeal to Césaire as poet; she wants her constituents, too, to have "limitless command" of the light of the stars.

Césaire is obviously a key figure here.[30] As mayor of Fort-de-France and a representative of Martinique in the French National Assembly from 1945 to 1983, and as the founding poet of négritude with the publication of *Cahier d'un retour au pays natal* in 1947, he represented both the political and the poetic hopes of the people of Martinique to such an extent that he was known to most Martinicians as "Papa Aimé." His career sketched the contours of Marshall Berman's Faustian developer. In Césaire's original poem, the "convocation of conquest" that Marie-Sophie quotes is preceded by this passage, where the speaker makes a demand for development and recognition much like Marie-Sophie's:

Oh friendly light
Oh fresh source of light
Those who have invented neither powder nor compass
Those who could harness neither steam nor electricity
Those who explored neither the seas nor the sky but those
Without whom the earth would not be the earth

. . . .

Pity for our omniscient and naïve conquerors!

Eia for grief and its udders of reincarnated tears
For those who have never explored anything
For those who have never conquered anything

And here at the end of these wee hours is my virile prayer that I hear neither the laughter nor the screams, my eyes fixed on this town which I prophesy, beautiful . . .[31]

The speaker of the *Cahier* pretends to accept the idea that technological inventions (powder, compass, steam, electricity) are the province of the European colonial powers, that his own people "never explored" and "never conquered anything." But the curious construction of the idea of a "rendez-vous," or—as Eshelman and Smith translate—a "convocation of conquest," in the later lines quoted by Marie-Sophie describes a transformation by which such conquests become the communal property of all.[32] If the colonizer "invented" electricity, it would fall to the colonized to make electricity a part of the commons at the convocation of conquest, thus concretizing the ideals inscribed in the discourse of revolutionary republicanism. If for Shelley and Wilde electricity promised the end of human slavery, then Césaire—and through him Marie-Sophie—makes it clear that to signify as the end of slavery, electricity will finally have to be made to serve the ends of the formerly enslaved. Then and only then will the republican and Romantic rhetoric of liberation—the end of slavery—finally make sense. If the colonizer was responsible for conquest, the colonized are responsible for insisting on its convocation, the culminating action of Hegelian universal history. What in 1801 Toussaint Louverture did for the Rights of Man, Marie-Sophie's struggle for electricity does for its material counterpart, the public utility. As Césaire put it in his 1960 *Toussaint Louverture,*

> When Toussaint Louverture came on the scene, it was to take the Declaration of the Rights of Man at its word; it was to show . . . that there can be no excepted peoples. It was to incarnate and particularize a principle; that is to say, to vivify it. In history and in the domain of the rights of man . . . Toussaint Louverture fought for the transformation of formal rights into real rights, his was a combat for the recognition of man, and that is why he inscribed himself and the revolt of the black slaves of Saint-Domingue within the history of universal civilization.[33]

Taking the French Declaration of the Rights of Man at its word, Louverture made it conform for the first time to its own ideals. His reading would "incarnate and particularize a principle," it would "vivify"; in other words, it would "take the Rights of Man literally."[34] The constitution he wrote for Haiti in 1801 would, as Susan Buck-Morss writes, "take universal history to the farthest point of progress by extending it to all residents" and to "any person who entered its territory."[35] Such literalization is also the meaning behind the supply of electricity into Texaco, the reason for its "unblemished joy." It is not about consumer comforts but about the fulfillment—by way of Louverture and Césaire—of the Hegelian concrete universal. The supply of electricity is an unblemished joy for Texaco because it literalizes—two centuries later—the eighteenth century's trope of electric politics just as Louverture literalized its political ideals.

Getting electrical supply into Texaco is the end point of a long struggle. Marie-Sophie's intervention with Césaire yields quick results; Césaire convinces the city authorities to run water into Texaco. But still, no electricity. He is impressed by Marie-Sophie's recitation but not convinced. "Tell me, Madame Laborieux, have you read the *Notebook*? Or is it just a quotation that . . ." he begins to ask her as she is about to leave him. "I read it, Monsieur Césaire," she interrupts, but then concludes on reflection that "he must not have believed me" (368). We are just short of recognition here, just short of the "unblemished joy" of electricity; water doesn't satisfy. And it almost seems that Césaire is uncertain about supplying electricity as a consequence of his suspicious admiration for Marie-Sophie's erudition, as if her literacy were a kind of precondition for Texaco's "consideration." In many ways, Marie-Sophie is Césaire's unofficial counterpart. She too is a writer, and she too is a mayor of a city, though in both capacities she is unofficial: unpublished and unelected.

Once the water utility arrives, Texaco's residents are more than ever driven by the dream of electricity. And so is Marie-Sophie, though she dissimulates by pretending to act merely as their representative:

> As he climbs the tree, the macaque is never happy with his fate: more committee sessions were demanded of me to study the question of electricity. Ti-Cirique, the secretary, had dispatched thirty-and-three missives to the director of SPEDEM [now E.D.F., Électricité de France], but that personage had not even bothered to reply: Texaco did not exist for him. I went down to see him once and tried to force my way into his office. Another time, we went there at night and smeared his walls with our demands. But it was like pissing on a violin to make it play. (369)

Marie-Sophie is now obliged to "study the question of electricity," something that, though she would pretend otherwise, she has already been doing for quite some time, both literally and literarily. To admit it openly she feigns dis- and uninterest. We can almost hear the sigh of resignation from the put-upon politician bowing to the demands of her clamorous constituents, combining with the sharp edge of the insult likening them to greedy monkeys. And again, Marie-Sophie's language couples recognition to electricity: "Texaco did not exist for him [the director of SPEDEM]." When Césaire fails to recognize Marie-Sophie, it is because he doesn't believe she can read; when SPEDEM's director fails to recognize her, it is because he doesn't know how to read the demands she and her constituents have "smeared" or written on his walls. In both cases, the novel is making electricity the sign—or even the language—of recognition, intimately tied into the questions of translation, literacy, and literature, and setting us up for the "unblemished joy" at the end: something that Marie-Sophie, along with her political opponents, also fails to recognize.

The moment of unblemished joy is not, therefore, a moment of characterological realization. To account for the distance between Marie-Sophie's perspective and the reader's, we might call the moment of Texaco's electrification an epiphany in the Joycean sense of the word: something that the reader and writer are in on, while the protagonist remains either entirely unaware of the significance of the moment or unaware of the real meaning of the significant moment. *Texaco* keeps its full story—its formal coherence shaped by recognition through electricity—confined to the level of narrative plot. The version of the story we have as readers of plot is not the same as the characters' experience. The "unblemished joy" of electrification is, in the original French, rendered as "une joie sans faille." *Faille* in French means variously a break, a fault, a rift, default, or even bankruptcy. "Une joie sans faille" is less common in continental French than the more standard colloquial "une joie sans tare," a joy without stain, and the English translation, "blemish," is probably following this more current usage. "Une joie sans faille" is an older usage in standard French that remains current in Creole French.[36]

But *faille* instead of *tare* is a significant choice of words for another reason. Peter Brooks uses the term in his *Reading for the Plot* to describe "the central gap or split—the *faille* or fault—of the text: the time and place that the protagonist, and the text, never can account for, a black hole [in *Texaco*'s case we must think, perhaps, more in terms of a blinding illumination] that is also animating of plotting and meaning since it provokes the reader's search."[37] In that sense, we might think of the narrative plot of *Texaco* as something like a photographic negative of Brooks's explanation of narrative *faille*. Like the narrator's black box in Flann O'Brien's *The Third Policeman*—which as we saw in chapter 3 contained and obscured the public works in the figure of omnium, a fantasy of limitless national wealth—Marie-Sophie's "une joie sans faille" marks a moment of rupture between plot and story, or *récit* and *histoire,* that is felt by Texaco's inhabitants as its opposite: a joy without rupture. Her electricity primer is a textual mark of "meanings that depend on energy [narrative plot, Valéry's "general *energizing* of the world"] as well as form [the postcolonial comedy of development, the unity of Hegelian universal history]."[38] To put it another way, we might say that for the inhabitants of Texaco, history itself—their particular and traumatic experience of history as displacement, enslavement, self-emancipation, urbanization, endemic poverty, social death and the continuing failure of political recognition—is the constant (as opposed to Brooks's periodic or singular) narrative *faille* that is then momentarily *felt* as repaired, made whole, and made coherent through the provision of electricity. The lighting up of Texaco is the symbolic and narrative fulfillment of the process of liberation and recognition begun two centuries before with Toussaint Louverture's Haitian Revolution: the telos (narrative) and the unity (form) of the Hegelian dialectic of history.

In this sense it is important that the E. D. F., Électricité de France, is the local arm of the national electrical utility that "plugs" Texaco with electricity. Marie-Sophie's appeals to SPEDEM, a regional energy agency, fail because for SPEDEM's director "Texaco didn't exist." In Metropolitan France, electricity was nationalized through the E. D. F. in 1946, but it wasn't until 1975 that nationalization came to Martinique, absorbing SPEDEM and offering subsidies and lower rates for the poor that matched the national policies within France's European borders.[39] French electricity, then, for recognized French citizens: Toussaint's Haitian Revolution, his "literalization" of the Declaration of the Rights of Man and of the Citizen, was remarkable not only for its success but for its insistence, as an integral part of that literalization, that he was claiming his constituents' rights as French citizens. Where Toussaint succeeded in winning liberation he failed in winning recognition; Marie-Sophie, through Aimé Césaire and through the E. D. F., achieves recognition for Texaco and for Texaco's urban poor from the French nation-state. Yoann Pélis demonstrates that the E. D. F. takeover of electrical distribution in Martinique effected the democratization of electricity in the French *département.*[40] In Martinique the E. D. F. depended wholly on petroleum-fueled electrical generation, which meant that cost and price were significantly bound to international oil markets.[41] This fact, however, gives a special resonance to Texaco's name and its location on land owned by the oil company Texaco. Embedded in name and location is a reappropriation or expropriation of energy resources, a demand for consideration beyond the meager buying power of Texaco's residents. The word *Texaco* becomes a name for an enterprise—Valéry's utopian "general energizing of the world"—that is henceforth "about living," no longer about profit. Marie-Sophie's naming of Texaco enacts the demand for recognition not only against the French welfare state (the E.D.F.) but also against the transnational corporation (Texaco). In so doing, she dwells in the ambiguity of public works as a supplemental agency, tarrying between, and struggling to differentiate itself from, both the state and the market.

CITING JOYCE'S CITY

Elle a tellement pénétré le quotidien, qu'on sait l'électricité sans le savoir. [So much has it penetrated daily life, that one knows electricity without knowing one knows it.]
> —Marie-Odile Briot, "Electra-mémoires:
> Électricité en large de la modernité"

Texaco's developmental telos owes something also to the generic conventions of the Bildungsroman. Joseph Slaughter has described this convention as a "temporal contortion" common to the form in which "the novel concludes where it began after bringing the past into conjunction with the present and the earlier protagonist self into correspondence with the later narrative self, producing the *Bildungsheld* as the narrator-protagonist (citizen-subject) of its story."[42] Such is the micronarrative arc of Marie-Sophie's experience from her first book about electricity to Texaco's recognition through electricity. Of course, Marie-Sophie differs fundamentally from the traditional *Bildungsheld*; first of all she's a she, and she is a part of the first generation of Africans in the Caribbean born after the abolition of slavery. That is, she is one of the first of her people for whom some relationship to the state—beyond the absolute command of obedience and the absolute threat of death—is even possible. Nevertheless, *Texaco* seems to follow the same developmental narrative as the European Bildungsroman, with the crucial qualification that, rather than remaining fixated on the personal development of an individual protagonist, *Texaco*'s narrative opens up explicitly to a collective, corporate, and economic development narrative; Marie-Sophie's story turns out to be the story of a literary figure turned developer, and the protagonist turns out to be Texaco as a whole. Removed from the characterological schema of *Faust*—to go back to Berman's example, in which the character of Faust becomes, in the last acts, a self-conscious developer— in *Texaco* the story of artistic and economic development is about a city, not a character. To whatever extent Marie-Sophie is unaware of her prophetic role in bringing electricity and recognition to her city, Texaco's unblemished joy at being plugged in reveals a collective awareness of the significance of the event.

We might think also of the dissonance—as I argued in chapter 2— between Joyce's embrace of the fusion of artist and engineer and Stephen's ironically distanced refusal of it. Slaughter focuses in his essay on the German tradition of the Bildungsroman. But the fictions of James Joyce are in fact frequent points of reference for Marie-Sophie in *Texaco*. She speaks of reading Joyce as a way of accompanying him "in Dublin's City where the infinite was being envisioned" (366). Joyce's literary vision for Dublin thus inspires a literary vision for Texaco. As Ti-Cirique—a Haitian living in Texaco and one of Marie-Sophie's many literary mentors—suggests, what "the Caribbean calls for [is] a Cervantes who has read Joyce" (327). In the call for a generic form capable of rendering Texaco's experience, he gestures toward what is, according to Mike Davis, a real similarity between Dublin as a colonial slum at the turn of the twentieth century and Fort-de-France as a postcolonial slum at the turn of the twenty-first: "Most cities of the [Global] South . . . more closely resemble Victorian Dublin, which, as historian Emmet Larkin has stressed, was unique amongst 'all the slumdoms produced in the western world in the nineteenth century . . . [because] its slums were not a product of the industrial revolution.'"[43] Thus what Marie-Sophie perceives as a literary affinity is also a function of Texaco's position, and Dublin's former position, in the world economic system, though at opposite ends of the century. And there are further similarities between Stephen's reactions to and experiences with the public utility, and Marie-Sophie's reaction to her electricity primer. As a boy coming into language, as we saw in chapter 2, Stephen Dedalus has a childish fascination with the public utility. Marie-Sophie's story of literacy betrays the same connection between the public utility and the writing life: in Stephen's "song" of the gas jet we ought to hear Marie-Sophie's electrical description of reading, "one hum, crackling under [her] fingers." And just as Marie-Sophie misses the fateful significance of her earlier confrontation with electrical engineering in her first book, so Stephen misses his later confrontation with it in his university lecture about electricity. Through the young Stephen Dedalus we can see that Marie-Sophie's predicament, her ignorance of the narrative dynamo that drives her to plug Texaco into the grid, has a kind of precedent in *A Portrait of the Artist as a Young Man.*

In the ambivalence of both Stephen and Marie-Sophie toward electricity is a genealogy of a trope of the Bildungsroman or, in both these cases, the Kunstlerroman. For the artist conceived within the confines of this generic tradition, there is no room for public utilities, engineering, or infrastructure. This may even be true not only for our protagonists but for literary critics as well. Bruce Robbins offers a provisional story for why this should be the case.

> The modern study of literature, much like Romantic literature itself, was arguably born from nineteenth-century resistance to the criterion of utility. . . . The concept of culture emerges in reaction against the proindustrial ideology of utilitarianism. . . . If the humanities in the era of cultural studies took up Foucault instead of Arnold as our inspiration, and did so without missing a beat, this is in large part because of a constitutive disgust for Bentham and utilitarianism, lodged deep in the interdisciplinary unconscious, a disgust that prepared us to recognize ourselves in Foucault's gesture of singling out Bentham's Panopticon to stand for what is most wrong with the modern world, or at least for what we are here on earth to make right.[44]

This could be the literary and literary-critical legacy that makes Marie-Sophie discount her electricity primer as boring and that makes Stephen mock his electricity lecture as terminally dull.[45] Though electricity might be generally a figuration for excitement, when used as a figure *for itself,* it appears to short out into its opposite: boredom, dullness. That boredom is symptomatic of the truth of Robbins's claim. Many artists and critics are disgusted by utility, steeped in a tradition stretching back to the nineteenth-century antagonism between utilitarianism and aesthetics. In its unthought power, that tradition works practically to force Stephen to be uninterested in the lecture and Marie-Sophie to be uninterested in her primer. As we've seen, however, looking further back into the history of electricity as a rhetorical trope yields a slightly more complicated explanation, in which the rise of utilitarianism—as the coercive construction of the liberal subject through the built environment—interrupted a much older and much more sympathetic connection between electrical, aesthetic, and political discourses, one that gets taken up variously by writers like Joyce, Valéry, Benjamin, and Chamoiseau. Stephen and Marie-Sophie both misunderstand themselves as protagonists of a Kunstlerroman as opposed to a postcolonial comedy of development; the narrative thrust of both novels is less toward the personal development of the artist than toward the Faustian fusion of artist and developer. By contrast to Stephen in Dublin, however, Marie-Sophie eventually takes up responsibility for bringing electricity into Texaco. She literally becomes a developer, bringing a victory for the town that, nevertheless, does not enlighten her to the special nature of the relationship between her political and her aesthetic experience. But that victory does enlighten her and the rest of Texaco's inhabitants in other ways, and, by revealing the plot's structure, it enlightens the reader of *Texaco* as well.

THE RIGHTS OF MAN, HUMAN RIGHTS,
AND THE PUBLIC UTILITY

To the deepest needs there corresponds a superficial approach.
—Bertolt Brecht, in conversation with
Walter Benjamin, Paris, 1938

There are some interesting counterexamples to the reflexive dismissal of the public utility by the protagonist of the Bildungsroman, but they tend, symptomatically, to the other extreme: fetishism. Ralph Ellison's 1952 novel *Invisible Man* is a stunning example.[46] There the narrator begins writing his story at the same time that he begins his "battle" with the electric company, Monopolated Light and Power, from his basement squat in a Harlem tenement. This battle he wages by stealing as much electricity as possible; collecting several gramophones and upwards of a thousand lightbulbs; and running them all simultaneously in order to siphon off electricity from the corporate giant while providing himself with a synesthetic buzz. "I love light," he reports, "that is why I fight my battle with Monopolated Light and Power. The deeper reason, I mean: It allows me to feel my vital aliveness."[47] Vital aliveness, somnolent energy, the crackle of souls; we seem to arrive at the same conclusion via very different orientations toward both writing and the public utility. In another example, at the start of Henry Roth's 1934 *Call It Sleep,* the child-protagonist stares in wonder at the water taps of the kitchen sink.[48] Near the end, David jams a metal dipper into the third rail of a Lower East Side elevated train track, causing a power outage, electrocuting himself, and only narrowly avoiding death, all in order to touch the power embodied in the public utility. Bruce Robbins, in an article published in 1983, calls David's obsession a "cult of the public utilities."[49] I would stick to "fetishism" because it describes much better the counterpathology that Robbins identifies later, that institutionalized hatred for the public utility from the vantage point of culture, especially literary culture.

Outside of literary culture, electricity has a tendency—especially in situations where it is not in constant supply—to figure recognition, just as it does in *Texaco.* In his 2003 film *Power Trip,* a documentary telling the story of the denationalization and consequent privatization of electricity in post-Soviet Tbilisi, the capital city of Georgia, Paul Devlin interviews a local resident on the question of what electricity means.[50] The answer echoes Marie-Sophie's: "If you don't have power, it means that you are hungry. And you are cold. And you are in the dark. No information. This is like . . . being dead, you know?" His "being dead" to Marie-Sophie's "we still didn't exist"; can we not hear in both of these statements a way of equating being supplied with electricity with being recognized as citizens, as the difference between social life and social death? In 2004 in another Georgian city, Kutaisi, protestors motivated by rolling blackouts took to the streets shouting, "Give us light!" In response, the deputy governor, Gia Tevdoradze, uncomprehendingly blurted before the crowd, in a near-perfect echo of *Texaco's* residents: "You haven't had electricity for thirteen years, [so] why do you remember it?"[51] Marie-Sophie: "We began to feel the need for certainties and for conveniences which, strangely enough, we would sorely miss all the sudden." A paradox: How is it possible to miss what one never had in the first place?

Marie-Sophie groups electricity with "certainties" and "conveniences." Unlike access to clean water, electricity is not a human necessity. It nevertheless emerges from these fictions as a non-negotiable demand made by citizens on the state. Kutaisi's protesters announce the demand for positive rights, not "the right not to be killed" or "the right not to be tortured" but "the right to light": the right to be seen, to be recognized, to be supplied.[52] A right of consumption, modeled perhaps on the excesses of the West, but enacted in an entirely different context, an entirely different relationship to power. The demand is staged as an ambiguous but emphatic "before": "remembering" electricity *from before*, missing "certainties and conveniences" *from before* that cannot logically have come from before. This is, among other things, the very grammatical structure of human rights, rights that can be enacted only by declaring their anteriority to the moment of their declaration.[53] Slaughter refers to such apparent tautologies as "legal conventions of the obvious":

> For example, the 1986 Declaration on the Right to Development formulates its developmental common sense as a perfect tautology. Its final preambular paragraph *confirms* "that the right to development is an inalienable human right," anticipating article 1, which now *proclaims,* "The right to development is an inalienable human right." . . . Each of the preambular statements of recognition and confirmation has a corresponding statement in the body of the text that articulates the same content (often verbatim) in the declarative mode. These two speech acts—the constative that confirms and the declarative that enacts—interact to imbue the hermetic legal tautologies with kinetic energy and a temporal dimension that initiates a sort of teleology in tautology.[54]

We've seen this temporal dimension in the way Marie-Sophie's personal development and economic development remain split in her own mind while also appearing as a gradual—that is to say temporal—drawing into coherence through the plot structure of *Texaco*'s postcolonial comedy of development.

Electricity is assumed by Kutaisi's protestors, and by Marie-Sophie and the residents of Texaco, to be a right: a right to recognition beyond necessity, which is, arguably, the very moment where human recognition really begins. This is pointedly not a claim on metaphysical recognition; it is a claim to recognition made through public utilities and utilitarianism, through Jeremy Bentham's "project," as Frances Ferguson puts it, "of replacing metaphysical notions with physical environments."[55] Or, to repeat Langan's formulation, it is to recognize "in the artificial form of the citizen a *prosthetic* subject, whose capacities for liberty depend on the built environment of the public sphere." The electrical grid in *Texaco* defines a physical environment of recognition. There is a clear if somewhat canned connection between light and enlightenment, a trope so old that neither Stephen nor Marie-Sophie can really credit it, as if its lack of originality (something that the upstart artist of the Bildungsroman tends by convention to overvalue) were by extension the proof of its bankruptcy. Their narrators do credit it, however, and so, I think, should we, in the face of what Robbins points out as our old institutional prejudices.

There's an important difference, then, between taking up water as an exemplary public utility and taking up electricity in the same way. Unlike water and sanitation, the demand for electricity is a call not for necessity or survival but for something else altogether. As Orlando Patterson has pointed out, public works in the European context were, from their earliest history there until "well into the nineteenth" century, characterized by "penal slavery, beginning with galley slavery and continuing with its replacement by the Bagnes, or penal slavery in public works."[56] But by the time Adam Smith defined the public works in *The Wealth of Nations*, political economy had renounced slavery theoretically and excluded it as a category of "social utility."[57] That renunciation functioned as a repression so successful that Patterson expresses genuine dismay that most historians of Europe, well into the twentieth century, had failed to make the connections between European slavery and public works. "It is truly extraordinary that European scholars have either neglected this whole aspect of the subject or defined it as something other than slavery when they have recognized it. When we look for reasons, it is too easy to claim that there has been a conspiracy of silence, or worse, a deliberate attempt to distort the historical facts. My own feeling is that there has been a genuine failure to recognize the institution for what it is owing to the pervasiveness of the intrusive conception of slavery in the Western intellectual consciousness."[58]

The connection, then, between slavery and public works must be acknowledged historically. As I have been arguing in the case of *Texaco*, however, the electrical public utility and its promise of social recognition transformed the idea of the public works from an institution of labor regulation connected to the penal system into the promise of universal rights of access to common property. This was a transformation led not from above but from below, in a historical process of imminent critique exemplified by Marie-Sophie and Texaco's residents. The pioneers of the electrical grid systems of the late nineteenth and early twentieth centuries were hardly revolutionaries or even social reformers. "Generally," Thomas Hughes concludes, "before 1930, [electrical] supply was limited to those who could afford to pay." "But," Hughes notes briefly, "in the decade after 1930, interest in introducing a more complex set of values into the design of electric power systems increased."[59] That "interest" came not from technocrats but from the architects of the welfare state and their constituents. It came also from writers and artists of the early twentieth century—as we've seen—like Joyce, Valéry, and Benjamin, such that by the end of the twentieth century electrical supply could be nearly reflexively understood as a demand for consideration, for rights of access, for a "convocation of conquest" that recreated the public utility as a question of the rights of the citizen-subject and, ultimately, the rights of the squatter citizen.

Electricity thus stands at a very difficult and precarious conceptual position: on the one hand a kind of luxury good provided by state, municipal, or private authorities, and on the other a powerful metaphor for state power—and, crucially, as a real weapon of state power. Torture by means of electrocution, for example: Ellison's Invisible Man develops his fetish out of traumatic experience, from torture on an electrified carpet to electroshock therapy. Yet his hopes for becoming politically visible are nevertheless expressed through electrical supply. The death penalty in the United States has its history tied into the history of the national electrical grid. At the turn of the twentieth century, Thomas Edison lobbied for capital punishment by electrocution using Westinghouse's alternating current. Edison hoped that associating alternating current with the threat of death would guarantee that the as-yet-unbuilt national electrical grid would adopt his own direct current supply method. In effect Edison wanted to create a difference in the popular imagination between state power as repressive apparatus (alternating current) and state power as public utility (direct current). His motivations were entrepreneurial, not philosophical, and he was ultimately unsuccessful because alternating current proved to be far more efficient than direct current. But what is interesting is that he was able for a time to exploit an imaginative distinction—that is to say, a distinction more wished for than real—between the state as executioner and the state as supplier of the common good.[60]

Electricity, it seems, figures what we might want from the state at the same time that it figures what we know we don't. It is an ambiguity, following Ferguson, Langan, Robbins, and Spivak, worth contesting and differentiating, as opposed to renouncing. The postcolonial literatures I have presented here, Irish and otherwise, contest the legitimacy of state systems at the same time that they demand something—public works—from them. The demand is for the concrete fulfillment of the ideals upheld in the Declaration of the Rights of Man and of the Citizen and the Declaration of Human Rights: an immanent critique that does as much to reveal the contradictions of state systems as any Foucauldian critique of power and governmentality. The argument is not that government is good but only that it could be, if forced to resolve its contradictions in concrete universal manifestations of its abstract universal ideals. In this struggle, the public utility serves as a representative figure for what it means to force interstate organizations, states, and municipal authorities to confront their failures and resolve their contradictions.

FREE RUNNING

The body, enlightened by electricity, was not docile, but ecstatic.
    —James Delbourgo, *A Most Amazing Scene of Wonders*

In the 2005 French action film *District B13*, screenwriter Luc Besson offers up a merely vehicular script through which to showcase the spectacular acrobatics of Paris's—more accurately, the *banlieues* of Paris's—newest offering to choreographed martial artistry, *parkour*. A cop, Damien (Cyril Raffaelli), and a badass *banlieusard* called Leïto (David Belle) square off in an abandoned factory in a Paris ghetto for a climactic confrontation.[61] Before they engage each other, the cop shouts his abstract allegiance to the state—"Liberté, égalité, fraternité!"—and the ghetto youth responds with his material allegiance to the city's decaying slums: "Eau, gaz, électricité!" The battle begins, rages awesomely, and then ends in an alliance between the two characters when they realize, in the middle of the action, that they are on the same side after all, that the ideals of liberty, equality, and brotherhood need to be unified with the material infrastructure of water, gas, and electricity for the ideals to have any real weight or meaning. The scene is a perfect reduction of the problem this chapter addresses, the essential tension between democratization and modernization, and, in particular, the status within global modernity of what I have been calling public utilities: water, gas, and electricity.

It's not just the neat trinitarian fit between freedom-equality-brotherhood and water-gas-electricity that motivates Leïto's response to Damien. As we have seen, the relationship goes deeper historically. The French national slogan was derived later from the original 1789 Declaration of the Rights of Man and of the Citizen. Article 1 of the declaration reads: "Les hommes naissent et demeurent libres et égaux en droits. Les distinctions sociales ne peuvent être fondées que sur l'utilité commune." *L'utilité commune* usually gets translated into English as "the common good," but the idea of the "public utility" in the restricted sense—water, gas, electricity—is there: anachronistically, to be sure, but there in the sense that the term must have attached itself to modern American "public utilities" from this origin. The story becomes rather complicated in this regard because the French do not usually refer to their "public utilities" as such (they call them "services publics"),[62] nor do the British (they say "utility," not "public utility"); but Americans do. So we might imagine a complex and international recirculation of the idea of the public utility, from the American Revolution to the French declaration to British utilitarianism, then to the American idiom and back, finally, to *District B13* and Leïto's utilitarian retort to Damien's lofty republicanism. In 1789 the *utilité commune* in Article 1 was a kind of escape clause for social distinction; the social "utility" of slavery, for example, justified its continuation—whether legal or extralegal—for nearly seventy years after the declaration.[63] In the present, however, the *utilité commune* vacillates between the abstraction of the public good and the concretion of the public utility. It may be the origin of "infrastructure" in the colloquial sense, the source for its commonplace trinitarian formulation in "water, gas, electricity." It points, furthermore, to what is arguably the most important "social distinction" of the twenty-first century: the divide between the squatter citizen and the citizen-subject, or, to put it another way, between those who have public utilities and those who do not.

Consider, as a fantastic embodiment of this thesis by way of its satirical negation, a contemporary architectural project, proposed by Peter Sloterdijk and Gesa Mueller von der Hagen, called the "pneumatic parliament." The project, part of Sloterdijk's and von der Hagen's collaborative architectural initiative "Global Instant Objects," was showcased at an exhibition curated by Bruno Latour and Peter Weibel in 2005 called "Making Things Public: Atmospheres of Democracy."[64] The idea behind the pneumatic parliament was to solve the problem of exporting democratic forms to failed states, postcolonies, and other "sponsors of international terrorism." The structure could be airdropped into these global hot spots nearly fully constructed; it consisted of an inflatable transparent bubble with riser seating arranged in a circle, complete with solar- and battery-powered lighting and air-conditioning. "On entering the building," the inventors write, "parliamentarians first encounter a pneumatic air lock: an intermediate chamber as mediator between the public subject outside and objective affairs of state inside." In what they describe as a unique and useful feature of the structure, the parliamentary "chamber can be filled with colored air, which allows adaptation to the mood or atmosphere prevailing in the country where it is dropped." In attempting to embody the pure form of transparent parliamentary democracy, the designers of the pneumatic parliament created their mock-ups of its insertion into failed-state situations as computer-generated images that depicted the building without any people inside or outside of it, and without connecting it in any way to the built environment into which it was inserted. Usually, it was imaged in the middle of a desert, empty and autonomous. Entirely self-generating and self-sustaining, the pneumatic parliament bore none but the most alienated and alienating of relationships to the social and political life-worlds into which it pretended to intervene.

And that, of course, was the pneumatic parliament's whole point. The atmosphere on the street and the atmosphere in the chamber were rigorously separated by air locks, even as the "mood" outside was mockingly simulated with colored air inside. What the pneumatic parliament lacked entirely, and what its designers wished to highlight in their roaring absence, were the social infrastructures that served as prosthetic bodies for the democratic citizen-subjects: subjects—in Spivak's term from chapter 1, agents—that the pneumatic parliament assumed would magically be created by the top-down imposition of the pure form of democracy. The critique that motivated the suggestion of the pneumatic parliament is the same terse debate that launches Leïto and Damien in *District B13* in mortal combat: the political ideals of liberty, equality, and brotherhood pitched against a demand for water, gas, and electricity.

The pneumatic parliament was proposed as a critique of the U.S. invasion of Iraq in 2003 and the broader U.S. policy and ideology of "spreading democracy." In Baghdad, one of the consequences of the destruction wrought by the U.S. occupation was the undermining of the public utilities networks. Competing claims for political legitimacy started to play out on the terrain of "basic amenities": "a standard—and, according to many here, crucial—counterinsurgency tactic [in Iraq] is to appeal to a skeptical population after fighting through an area, by restoring and improving basic services."[65] Political legitimacy rested, as Michael Gordon argues, on the provision of infrastructural development to a much greater extent than the U.S. military had anticipated.

> "He who is able to fix the public utilities holds the keys to the kingdom in terms of winning the support of the Iraqi people and ultimately ending this conflict," said Sgt. Alex J. Plitsas of the 312th Psychological Operations Company, who met with Sadr City representatives. . . . "People tell me time and time again that they see their basic needs as being more than food, clothing and shelter," said the sergeant, whose team is attached to Company B, First Battalion, 14th Infantry Regiment. "They include electricity, water and sewage. And until the Iraqi government provides them with such basic services, they won't trust them."[66]

Again, the imposition of political forms from above seems to provoke a demand from below for the social services and public utilities that
would connect the political structure with the social situation. This adds
something to Otter's critique of infrastructural governmentality in Victorian England; instead of seeing the creation of the liberal subject through
the built environment, we might see as well the creation of consent and
dissent—in other words, participation—in liberal government through
the provisioning of basic amenities. And instead of a Foucauldian understanding of "normalizing," we might see instead a call for normalization.
In the absence of infrastructure, the idea of the imagined community
becomes almost inconceivable. The technological prostheses necessary
for democratic participation, for the construction of the citizen-subject,
are glaring in their absence: "When there was no electricity in Baghdad,
the reason was that as soon as copper cable was laid, the Iraqis came out in
the night and stole it. Copper brought a good price. When the troops ex-
postulated with those caught and tried to make them see that their theft
was against the 'Iraqi People,' the indignant thieves demanded to know
who these 'Iraqi People' were who stood between them and the feeding
of their starving families."[67] The implication is obvious: that in the break-
down of the built environment of public utilities, the national imagined
community becomes very hard to imagine, and political legitimacy and
political participation are thrown into radical crisis.

The film *District B13* is a popular representation—and, it should be
said, a popular exploitation—of that crisis of political legitimacy and
participation occasioned by the absence and/or the breakdown of infrastructure. In her introductory article for the January 2007 *PMLA* special
issue entitled "Cities," Patricia Yeager asks, "What is it like to be stuck,
night and day, dreaming of infrastructure?"[68] The question emerges from
the "premise" that "our intellectual apparatus, like the wage puzzle, is inadequate for describing the pleasures and pounding of most urban lives,
or the fact that many city dwellers survive despite all odds."[69] Leïto in
District B13 is one of Yeager's dreamers, not just because he makes the
demand for infrastructure in speech, but also because his practice, *parkour,* makes that demand palpable in movement, exemplifying the "pleasures and pounding" of urban life. *Parkour* was born in the decay and
neglect of the Parisian suburb. Its name is a derivation of the French mili-

tary *parcours,* or obstacle course, an obsession David Belle—*parkour's* founder—picked up from his career-military father. Belle adapted *parcours* into a slum-urban art form something like break dancing, in which the *traceur* leaps from rooftops, moves from building to building, jumps through windows, scales terraces and balconies. The *traceur* looks for anything and everything that can help him make his way—pipes, cables, windows, fire escapes, electric and telephone poles—and, as part of the challenge, makes a virtue of turning any obstacle to his path into a part of the path itself. Rock climbing for the dispossessed: the *traceur,* unlike the rock climber, must move both vertically and horizontally through a thoroughly lived-in though broken-down environment, crowded with others. A new and artistic "use" is made of structures and infrastructures that no longer work; they are turned into part of the spectacle. And to the extent that *parkour* has made a name for itself in action cinema, the *traceur* is generally running for his life, from authorities of some kind, often enough the police. The physical grammar of *parkour* turns evading the police into a martial art and, by aestheticizing its choreography, into a fine art. The *traceur* is a twenty-first-century urban flâneur who has turned the economists' "wage puzzle"—and the breakdown of infrastructure in the urban slum—into a spectacularly choreographed performance of survival. *Parkour,* like Marie-Sophie's Texaco, is "about living" in the Planet of Slums.

Belle had a partner in *parkour* boosterism early on, Sébastien Foucan, who also makes some spectacular appearances on film, notably in the 2006 James Bond outing *Casino Royale.*[70] There he plays Mollaka, an African terrorist-bomber whom Bond shoots and kills at the end of the very first, very long, and very expensive chase scene in the film. Most of the scene takes place on a construction site that, the film tells us only in textual overlay, is somewhere in Madagascar. "Madagascar" and "construction site" both function without specificity; we are located, as far as we need to know, in a development site in darkest underdeveloped Africa, and in a situation of what economist Amartya Sen has dubbed "infrapoverty."[71] Aside from the incredibly choreographed action in the sequence, far better than most action sequences in most films and by far the best thing about *Casino Royale,* what is interesting is the juxtaposition of *style* between Mollaka as the third-world *traceur*-terrorist and

Bond as the agent of Western power. Mollaka moves through this land-scape of development *without breaking anything,* a fact that might go un-noticed were it not for Bond's destruction of everything that stands in his way. Mollaka jumps a high fence in what looks like one fluid and grace-ful gesture; Bond jumps into a bulldozer and plows through the fence, causing tremendous collateral damage in the process. Mollaka jumps feet first through a high transom window; Bond crashes through the *wall* the window is set in, pauses for effect covered in drywall dust, and con-tinues the chase. There are many more examples. The point is that with-out giving us any actual context, the film codes the African Mollaka's movements to acknowledge Africa's desire and need for development. Mollaka doesn't break anything because this is, in a metaphorical sense, his home, his nation, or his continent. Bond breaks everything because he represents Western power and the systematic development of under-development in the former colonial territories of the Western powers. He is just doing his job, which is not so much to stop terrorists as it is to destroy the "African" "construction site." This is the "cycle of creative de-struction that permits the most exploitative forms of capitalism to thrive," which is how Yeager describes Naomi Klein's notion of "disaster capital-ism."[72] Transnational capital is engaged by poor African country through IMF loans to develop Africa; Bond destroys construction site on pretext of terrorist threat; transnational capital is engaged by (now even poorer) poor African country through IMF loans to develop Africa; and so on. The secret agent doesn't have a target or a goal; his mission is nothing more than ongoing destruction. Mollaka, on the other hand, traces Leïto's vocal demand for infrastructure—water, gas, electricity—in movement.

Parkour in *Casino Royale* renders Naomi Klein's "disaster capitalism" in spectacle. *Parkour* in *District B13* renders Mike Davis's "Planet of Slums" in spectacle. In both films *parkour* renders Yeager's "dream of infrastruc-ture" in spectacle. All of which is to say that to follow Yeager's call for an "intellectual apparatus" adequate "for describing the pleasures and pound-ing of most urban lives," we need some method for accounting for the structures of feeling that the public utility generates, and of which *par-kour* is a popular kinetic expression. The *traceur* spatializes, in the land-scape of the urban slum, the temporal lag in the Declaration of Human Rights between the preambular constative statement of human rights

and their postambular declarative enactment. The motion of *parkour* is
the expression of the "kinetic energy"—that is, the political struggle—
necessary to overcome the gulf between them: an aesthetic representation of the emergence into agency of the squatter citizen.

In *Public Works* as a whole I have proposed some tentative reading
strategies for teasing out that struggle as a function of literary representation, first in the context of Irish postcolonial modernism—in the four preceding chapters—and finally in the context of comparative postcolonial
modernism. In the Irish case I grounded my claims for the importance
of the literary role of the public utility in a historical background of the
proliferation of experimental, traumatic and deadly utilitarian structures in nineteenth-century Ireland. The project of recuperating "utility"
in the Irish case meant the literary invention of an Irish utility that served
Irish postcolonial political aspirations. In the case of the literary and
other artistic representations of the public utility in the context of the
Planet of Slums, I have grounded my claims in the enlightenment invention and/or discovery of the Rights of Man and of the Citizen; I have traced
the idea of the public utility to the conception of universal rights in the
American and French Revolutions, revealing their dialectical realization in
the Haitian Revolution and—in my reading of *Texaco*—in the contemporary demand from systematically underdeveloped zones of the globe
for "basic amenities" in the context of the discourse of human rights. In
both the Irish and the Martinician cases, I have identified a generic form,
the postcolonial comedy of development, that emerges as a literary ar-
ticulation of postcolonial liberation through the development of the common good. The figure that defines the common good in the postcolonial
comedy of development is the public utility. The literary figure of the
public utility has a tendency toward literalization that is activated by the
discourse of the Rights of Man and of the Citizen and by the discourse of
human rights. We've seen many versions of that literalization: in the narrative arc from Marie-Sophie's electrical textbook to the electrification
of Texaco; in the Invisible Man's quest for enlightenment in lightbulbs;
in David's attempt to access the concrete universal through electrocution; and in the *traceur*'s kinetic expression of the infrastructural deprivation of the urban slum. The fact that the formula can be repeated so often,
so insistently, and from so many different spheres of discourse—high

modernism, postcolonial theory, the postcolonial novel, state propaganda, installation art, urban youth culture, and a popular action movie—suggests some of the confusion out of which the formula emerges, the intensity of feeling it generates, and the importance of deciphering it. "Water, gas, and electricity," in all these instances, appears as a linguistic commonplace and as a symbolic invocation that, in gesturing to the materially basic, points to something often elusive of theory.

NOTES

ONE. The Postcolonial Comedy of Development

1. Colin Rynne, *Industrial Ireland, 1750–1930: An Archaeology* (Cork: Collins Press, 2006), 431.

2. I document this claim and explore its implications in chapter 4. Thomas P. Hughes makes it briefly here: "Historians interested in technology have written only a few monographs that concentrate on the evolution of the massive, extensive, vertically integrated production systems of the modern industrial world." Thomas P. Hughes, *Networks of Power: Electrification in Western Society, 1880–1930* (Baltimore: Johns Hopkins University Press, 1983), 5.

3. Adam Smith, *An Inquiry into the Nature and Causes of the Wealth of Nations,* ed. R. H. Campbell and A. S. Skinner, 2 vols. (1776; repr., Indianapolis: Liberty Fund, 1981), 2:723.

4. It's important to note that the term *capitalism* does not, according to Amartya Sen, appear even once in *The Wealth of Nations.* Amartya Sen, "Capitalism beyond the Crisis," *New York Review of Books,* March 26, 2009, 28.

5. See Jacques Derrida, *Of Grammatology,* trans. Gayatri Spivak (Baltimore: Johns Hopkins University Press, 1998).

6. Sen, "Capitalism," 28.

7. Rynne, *Industrial Ireland,* 411.

8. Daniel T. Rodgers, *Atlantic Crossings: Social Politics in a Progressive Age* (Cambridge, MA: Harvard University Press, 1998), 130.

9. Amanda Claybaugh, "Government Is Good," *Minnesota Review* 70 (Spring 2008): 162.

10. See Michael Szalay, *New Deal Modernism: American Literature and the Invention of the Welfare State* (Durham: Duke University Press, 2000).

11. Bruce Robbins, *Upward Mobility and the Common Good: Toward a Literary History of the Welfare State* (Princeton: Princeton University Press, 2007), 235.

12. Christopher Bollas, *The Evocative Object World* (London: Routledge, 2008), 19. In context, as an argument for free-associative psychoanalysis, Bollas wants the "unthought known" to stand for unique individuality and intimate

psychic truths about the self. But I find his term striking for its value in thinking, in terms of the self's experience with public utilities, about communion with the state as well.

13. Benedict Anderson, *Imagined Communities: Reflections on the Origin and Spread of Nationalism* (London: Verso, 1991).

14. David Lloyd, *Anomalous States: Irish Writing and the Postcolonial Moment* (Durham: Duke University Press, 1993).

15. Achille Mbembe, *On the Postcolony* (Berkeley: University of California Press, 2001).

16. Marshall Berman, *All That Is Solid Melts into Air: The Experience of Modernity* (New York: Penguin, 1982), 43.

17. Ibid., 43.

18. Ibid., 40.

19. Ibid., 49.

20. Ibid., 48.

21. Ibid., 60–61.

22. Ibid., 45.

23. Ibid., 60.

24. Ibid., 40.

25. Gayatri Spivak, "The Subaltern and the Popular: The Trajectory of the Subaltern in My Work," paper presented at the University of California, Santa Barbara, February 7, 2008, video posted at www.youtube.com/watch?v=2ZHH4ALRFHw&feature=channel_page; Gayatri Spivak, "Can the Subaltern Speak?" in *Marxism and the Interpretation of Culture,* ed. Cary Nelson and Lawrence Grossberg (Champaign: University of Illinois Press, 1988), 271–313.

26. Spivak, "Subaltern and the Popular."

27. Aravind Adiga, *The White Tiger* (New York: Free Press, 2008), 80.

28. Dilip Parameshwar Gaonkar, "On Alternative Modernities," in *Alternative Modernities,* ed. Dilip Parameshwar Gaonkar (Durham: Duke University Press, 2001), 17.

29. James Ferguson, "Decomposing Modernity: History and Hierarchy after Development," in *Postcolonial Studies and Beyond,* ed. Ania Loomba et al. (Durham: Duke University Press, 2005), 180.

30. Nirvana Tanoukhi, "The Scale of World Literature," *New Literary History* 39 (2008): 609–10.

31. David Lloyd, *Irish Times: Temporalities of Modernity* (Dublin: Field Day Publications, 2008), 5.

32. Ibid., 5.

33. Joe Cleary, "Introduction: Ireland and Modernity," in *The Cambridge Companion to Modern Irish Culture,* ed. Joe Cleary and Claire Connolly (Cam-

bridge: Cambridge University Press, 2005), 9; Mike Davis, *Late Victorian Holocausts: El Niño Famines and the Making of the Third World* (London: Verso, 2000).

34. Lloyd, *Irish Times,* 5.

35. Cleary, "Introduction," 9.

36. For more on the distinction, see Seamus Deane, "National Character and the Character of Nations," in *Strange Country: Modernity and Nationhood in Irish Writing since 1790* (Oxford: Oxford University Press, 1997), 49–99. Deane defines "the character of nations" as "the story of a progression from the narrow ambit of the national place into the territory or space of the state." The national character, on the other hand, is a discourse of particularity whose "largest ambition is to formulate a coherent idea of a nation and to keep that distinct from the idea of the state" (49–50).

37. James Joyce, *Ulysses,* ed. Hans Walter Gabler et al. (New York: Vintage Books, 1986), 7:489–95.

38. Matthew Arnold, "On the Study of Celtic Literature," in *Lectures and Essays in Criticism,* ed. R. H. Super (Ann Arbor: University of Michigan Press, 1962), 344.

39. Ibid., 346.

40. Laura O'Connor, *Haunted English: The Celtic Fringe, the British Empire, and De-Anglicization* (Baltimore: Johns Hopkins University Press, 2006), xv.

41. Patrick Carroll-Burke, "Material Designs: Engineering Cultures and Engineering States—Ireland, 1650–1900," *Theory and Society* 31 (2002): 97. Carroll-Burke quotes Grey from his aptly titled *Observations on House and General Sewage, and on an Improved Plan for Cleansing and Ventilating House Drains by a Self-acting Mechanism: with a Description of the Apparatus, as applied in the North Dublin Union Workhouse, under the Superintendence of the Poor-law Commissioners: Being the Substance of a paper read at the Royal Dublin Society* (Dublin: Hodges and Smith, 1855), 30.

42. Slavoj Žižek, "Knee Deep," *London Review of Books,* September 2, 2004.

43. Carroll-Burke, "Material Designs," 97.

44. Flann O'Brien's 1941 novel *The Poor Mouth* offers a darkly comic vision of the national school. The protagonist, Bonaparte, is on his first day of school rechristened as Jams O'Donnell by the vicious schoolmaster. Every student, in fact, is renamed Jams O'Donnell with an accompanying crack on the head. The schoolmaster "continued in this manner until every creature in the school had been struck down by him and all had been named *Jams O'Donnell.* No young skull in the countryside that day remained unsplit. Of course, there were many unable to walk by the afternoon and were transported home by relatives. It was a pitiable thing for those who had to swim back to Aran that evening and were without a bite of food or a sup of milk since morning" (31).

Flann O'Brien, *The Poor Mouth*, trans. Patrick Power (Normal, IL: Dalkey Archive Press, 1996). One of the most well-known dramatic accounts of the competition between the hedge school and the national school is Brian Friel's 1981 play *Translations* (London: Faber and Faber, 1995).

45. See Michel Foucault, *Discipline and Punish: The Birth of the Prison,* trans. Alan Sheridan (New York: Vintage Books, 1995).

46. A. R. G. Griffiths, "The Irish Board of Works in the Famine Years," *Historical Journal* 13 (December 1970): 638; R. F. Foster, *Modern Ireland, 1600–1972* (New York: Penguin, 1989), 326.

47. Foster, *Modern Ireland,* 326.

48. Ibid.

49. Cormac Ó Gráda, *Black '47 and Beyond: The Great Irish Famine in History, Economy, and Memory* (Princeton: Princeton University Press, 1999), 41.

50. Ibid.

51. David Lloyd, *Nationalism and Minor Literature: James Clarence Mangan and the Emergence of Irish Cultural Nationalism* (Berkeley: University of California Press, 1987), 53.

52. As quoted in Seamus Deane, gen. ed., *The Field Day Anthology of Irish Writing,* vol. 2 (Derry: Field Day Publications, 1991), 177.

53. John Mitchel, *Jail Journal* (Dublin: M. H. McGill and Son, 1914).

54. Lloyd, *Nationalism,* 49.

55. Mitchel, *Jail Journal,* 60.

56. Ibid., 74.

57. Ibid., 79.

58. Ibid., 86.

59. See Richard Ellmann, *James Joyce* (New York: Oxford University Press, 1959), 528. "To [Woolf] it was 'underbred,' 'the book of a self-taught working man,' of 'a queasy undergraduate scratching his pimples.'"

60. Victoria Rosner, *Modernism and the Architecture of Private Life* (New York: Columbia University Press, 2008), 7.

61. Ezra Pound, "Suffragettes," *Egoist* 1 (July 1, 1914): 255, quoted in Bruce Robbins, "The Smell of Infrastructure," *boundary 2* 34 (2007): 31.

62. Carroll-Burke, "Material Designs," 103. He refers here to David Cairns, *Writing Ireland: Colonialism, Nationalism, and Culture* (New York: Manchester University Press, 1988); Susan Shaw Sailer, ed., *Representing Ireland: Gender, Class, Nationality* (Gainesville: University Press of Florida, 1997); Declan Kiberd, *Inventing Ireland: The Literature of the Modern Nation* (London: Jonathan Cape, 1995); and Brendan Bradshaw, ed., *Representing Ireland: Literature and the Origins of Conflict, 1534–1660* (New York: Cambridge University Press, 1993).

63. Andrew Kincaid, *Postcolonial Dublin: Imperial Legacies and the Built Environment* (Minneapolis: University of Minnesota Press, 2006), xiv.

64. Joe Cleary, *Outrageous Fortune: Capital and Culture in Modern Ireland* (Dublin: Field Day Publications, 2006), 93–94.

65. Emer Nolan, "Modernism and the Irish Revival," in Cleary and Connolly, *Cambridge Companion*, 167.

66. Cleary, *Outrageous Fortune*, 94. According to Cleary the one exception to the confinement of Irish modernism to the literary was "a very modest modernism in painting" (93).

67. Ibid., 213.

68. Joseph Lee, *The Modernisation of Irish Society, 1848–1918* (Dublin: Gill and Macmillan, 1973), 139.

69. Ibid., 138.

70. Ibid.

71. Ibid., 139.

72. Quoted in ibid., 147.

73. Ibid., 148.

74. Ibid., 148.

75. Oscar Wilde, "The Soul of Man under Socialism," in *The Soul of Man under Socialism and Selected Critical Prose*, ed. Linda Dowling (New York: Penguin, 2001), 141.

76. Samuel Beckett, "First Love," in *The Penguin Book of Irish Fiction*, ed. Colm Tóibín (New York: Penguin, 2001), 566. In the original French: "Vous n'avez pas l'électricité? dis-je. Non, dit-elle, mais j'ai l'eau courante et le gaz. Tiens, dis-je, vous avez le gaz." *Premier amour* (Paris: Éditions de Minuit, 1970), 40.

77. Beckett, "First Love," 567. "Savez-vous où sont les cabinets? dit-elle. Elle avait raison, je n'y pensais plus. Se soulager dans son lit, cela fait plaisir sur le moment, mais après on est incommodé. Donnez un vase de nuit, dis-je." Beckett, *Premier amour*, 44.

78. James Joyce, *A Portrait of the Artist as a Young Man* (New York: Penguin, 1992), 3.

79. See Seán Kennedy, "The Beckett Country Revisited: Beckett, Belonging and Longing," in *Ireland: Space, Text, Time*, ed. Liam Harte, Yvonne Whelan, and Patrick Crotty (Dublin: Liffey Press, 2005), 135–45.

80. Elizabeth Bowen, "Modern Lighting," *Saturday Review of Literature*, October 27, 1928, 294. Thanks to Allan Hepburn for sharing this article with me. It is reprinted in Allan Hepburn, ed., *People, Places, Things: Essays by Elizabeth Bowen* (Edinburgh: Edinburgh University Press, 2008), 26–28.

81. Hepburn, *People, Places, Things*, 418.

TWO. Aquacity

Portions of this chapter were previously published, and I thank the publisher for permission to reproduce them here: " 'The Waters of Civic Finance': Moneyed States in Joyce's *Ulysses*," *Novel: A Forum on Fiction* 36 (Summer 2003): 289–306. The epigraph for the section "Collective Structures of Invention," from Giedion's *Building in France* (*Bauen in Frankreich* [Leipzig: Klinkhardt and Bierman, 1928]), is quoted from Walter Benjamin, *The Arcades Project,* trans. Howard Ei-land and Kevin McLaughlin (Cambridge, MA: Harvard University Press, 1999), 390–91.

1. *The Third Man,* dir. Carol Reed (British Lion Film Corporation, 1949).

2. Franco Moretti, *Modern Epic: The World-System from Goethe to García Márquez* (New York: Verso, 1996), 123.

3. The name is actually Martins in the film, and the quote above is slightly inaccurate (it's actually as I reproduced it later in this chapter, "Do you believe, Mr. Martins, in the stream of consciousness?").

4. Joyce, *Portrait of the Artist,* 276. Subsequent page citations to this work are given parenthetically in the text.

5. Marjorie Howes and Derek Attridge, introduction to *Semicolonial Joyce,* ed. Derek Attridge and Marjorie Howes (Cambridge: Cambridge University Press, 2000), 7.

6. Ibid., 10.

7. Pierre Bourdieu, "Pour un savoir engagé," *Le Monde Diplomatique,* February 2002, 3. "What might be the role of activists here and now [in the age of globalization]? That of working for the collective invention of collective structures of invention" (my translation).

8. For more on this argument, see Rebecca L. Walkowitz, *Cosmopolitan Style: Modernism beyond the Nation* (New York: Columbia University Press, 2006), especially ch. 2, "Joyce's Triviality."

9. Joyce, *Ulysses,* 17.160–82. Subsequent chapter and page citations are given parenthetically in the text.

10. Fredric Jameson, "*Ulysses* in History," in *James Joyce and Modern Literature,* ed. W. J. McCormack and Alistair Stead (London: Routledge and Keegan Paul, 1982), 126–41.

11. Joep Leerssen, *Remembrance and Imagination: Patterns in the Historical and Literary Representation of Ireland in the Nineteenth Century* (Notre Dame: University of Notre Dame Press, 1997), 230.

12. Jameson, "*Ulysses* in History," 140–41.

13. Ibid., 140.

14. Ibid.

15. Ibid., 126.

16. Leerssen, *Remembrance and Imagination*, 230.

17. Ibid., 231, emphasis in original.

18. Leo Bersani, "Against *Ulysses*," in *James Joyce's "Ulysses": A Casebook*, ed. Derek Attridge (Oxford: Oxford University Press, 2004), 227.

19. Walkowitz, *Cosmopolitan Style*, 64.

20. Ariela Freedman, "Did It Flow? Bridging Aesthetics and History in Joyce's *Ulysses*," *Modernism/Modernity* 13, no. 1 (2006): 858.

21. James E. McClellan and Harold Dorn, *Science and Technology in World History* (Baltimore: Johns Hopkins University Press, 1999), 31.

22. See ibid., ch. 3, "Pharaohs and Engineers." Several descriptive passages from their chapter reveal deep resonances with Joyce's waterworks, making it seem probable that Joyce had this long history of the Urban Revolution in mind when he wrote it: "Simple gardening was superceded by field agriculture based on large-scale water-management networks constructed and maintained as public works by conscripted labor gangs (the corvée) under the supervision of state employed engineers. . . . Subsistence-level farming gave way to the production of large surpluses of cereals . . . that could be taxed, stored, and redistributed" (31). They further emphasize that "large-scale hydraulic engineering projects" were the main motivation behind "the formation of large, highly centralized, bureaucratic states" (32). There is therefore every reason to see the waterworks as a kind of master-metaphor for the modern state.

23. Freedman, "Did It Flow?" 857.

24. Joseph Brady, "Dublin at the Turn of the Century," in *Dublin through Space and Time (c. 900–1900)*, ed. Joseph Brady and Anngret Simms (Dublin: Four Courts Press, 2001), 221–81, especially 238–41.

25. Jacinta Prunty, *Dublin Slums, 1800–1925* (Dublin: Irish Academic Press, 1999), 71.

26. John Norwood, "On the Working of the Sanitary Laws in Dublin, with Suggestions for Their Amendment," *Journal of the Social and Statistical Inquiry Society of Ireland* 6, no. 43 (1873): 232, quoted in Prunty, *Dublin Slums*, 71.

27. See Kincaid, *Postcolonial Dublin*, especially ch. 1, "*Dublin of the Future* and the Emergence of Town Planning in Ireland," 1–57.

28. Prunty, *Dublin Slums*, 14.

29. Ibid., 71.

30. Charles Cameron and Edward Mapother, "Report on the Means for the Prevention of Disease in Dublin," *Reports and Printed Documents of the Corporation of Dublin* 1 (1879): 346, quoted in Prunty, *Dublin Slums*, 71.

31. I am indebted to Kevin Whelan for first demonstrating to me the political geography of the Dublin waterworks, and Joyce's presentation of it in this passage, when I presented a version of this chapter to the Notre Dame Irish Studies Summer School in Dublin in June of 2005.

32. Bruce Robbins, "The Sweatshop Sublime," *PMLA* 117 (January 2002): 84–97.

33. We will have good reason to return to the "sweatshop sublime" in its global significance later, but for now the term needs slight modification since we are talking exclusively about municipal finance, municipal tax structures, and a municipal division of labor.

34. See entries for *solvent* and *sound* in the *Oxford English Dictionary Online,* www.oed.com, June 1, 2008.

35. Martin Heidegger, "The Question Concerning Technology," in *The Question Concerning Technology and Other Essays,* trans. William Lovitt (New York: Harper Perennial, 1977), 6–7.

36. Ibid., 7. In a footnote on the same page, the translator, William Lovitt, remarks on the German verb *vershulden,* which "has a wide range of meanings— to be indebted, to owe, to be guilty, to be responsible for or to, to cause. Heidegger intends to awaken all these meanings and to have connotations of mutual interdependence sound throughout this passage."

37. The difference between the "public" as a classical category and "society" or the social whole as a purely modern category—entirely foreign to Greek and Roman thought—is outlined in Hannah Arendt, *The Human Condition* (Chicago: University of Chicago Press, 1998), 22–78.

38. Enda Duffy, "Disappearing Dublin," in Attridge and Howes, *Semicolonial Joyce,* 37–38.

39. Leerssen, *Remembrance and Imagination,* 231.

40. I borrow the term *messianic power* loosely from Walter Benjamin, "Theses on the Philosophy of History," in *Illuminations,* ed. Hannah Arendt, trans. Harry Zohn (New York: Schocken Books, 1969), 254.

41. See also Vincent Cheng's discussion of the Milkwoman scene in his *Joyce, Race, and Empire* (Cambridge: Cambridge University Press, 1995), 156–57. Cheng describes the scene as "a wonderful parody of ethnographic encounter with a tribal culture," a spot-on description that nevertheless fails to account for the alternatives that Joyce, as I'm arguing, offers.

42. Freedman, "Did It Flow?" 857.

43. Erich Auerbach, *Mimesis: The Representation of Reality in Western Literature,* trans. Willard R. Trask (Princeton: Princeton University Press, 2003), 6.

44. Ibid., 7.

45. Ibid., 5.

46. Ibid., 552–53. Thank you to Michael Sayeau, who invited me to partici-pate in his seminar "Modernist Simplicity" at the November 2007 Modernist Studies Association Conference in Long Beach, California, where he drew my attention to Auerbach's work and particularly to the final passage of *Mimesis*.

47. Declan Kiberd, *Irish Classics* (Cambridge, MA: Harvard University Press, 2001), 468.

48. Ibid.

49. Clive Hart, "Wandering Rocks," in *James Joyce's "Ulysses": Critical Essays*, ed. Clive Hart and David Hayman (Berkeley: University of California Press, 1974), 193.

50. Ibid., 196.

51. Ibid., 199.

52. Michael Seidel, *Epic Geography: James Joyce's "Ulysses"* (Princeton: Princeton University Press, 1976), 183.

53. See Chris Stillman, Robert Barklie, and Cathy Johnson, "Viking Iron-Smelting in Dublin's Temple Bar West," *Geology Today* 19 (November–December 2003): 216.

54. For more about the play between time and space in "Wandering Rocks," see also Luke Gibbons, "Spaces of Time through Times of Space: Joyce, Ireland, and Colonial Modernity," *Field Day Review* 1 (2005): 71–86.

55. The term is Homi Bhabha's, from his "Sly Civility," *October* 34 (Autumn 1985): 71–80. See especially 77–78, where Bhabha quotes the missionary frustration at recalcitrant natives who persist in their own religious beliefs by reinterpreting Christianity as capacious enough to accommodate them. I would simply suggest that in inventing a talking sewer, Joyce is working from within such sly civility.

56. The closest analogue that comes to mind is Bruno Latour's thought experiment in his *Aramis, or, The Love of Technology,* trans. Catherine Porter (Cambridge, MA: Harvard University Press, 1996), where he intersperses— throughout his account of an automated public transportation system intended (but never implemented) in Paris—first-person narrative vignettes that suppose the transit system itself as a narrating voice. That voice insists on *being:* "I am lying in the middle of the large circle they are making around me, these ministers, cabinet heads, municipal officials, public employees, and engineers large and small. At the center of this big circle, I am the deep well into which they are tossing their wishes, their hopes, and their curses. Blessed, cursed. Loved, hated. Indifferent, passionate. Plural, singular, masculine, feminine, neutral. I am waiting for them all to grant me being. What is a self? The intersection

of all the acts carried out in its name. But is that intersection full or empty? I exist if they agree, I die if they quarrel. . . . How can I become a being, an object, a thing—finally a self, yes, a full set, saturated with being—without them, without their agreement, without their coming to terms (since I myself am made from them, flesh of their flesh, a rib extracted from theirs). . . . How can I interest them all in me when they all love me differently? I can give them only what they have given me. I can hold them assembled together only if they keep me assembled. The 'I' that humans receive at birth—that is precisely what has to be created for me. I am in a prebirth state. I do not yet have a body. The dismemberment humans encounter in the tomb is my condition even before the cradle [. . .] The breath of life to which I aspire in order to make of my scattered members and my whitened bones a being that is not of reason—my soul—awaits your agreement, O you hors-d'oeuvres-eaters, who all agree today to defer my genesis until later. Indifferent to what you love. Rubicon-crossers who set up camp in the middle of the ford. Human beings contemptuous of things and thus contemptuous of yourselves" (200–202).

57. For more on the myths and meanings of the sewer, not in Dublin but in a comparative study of Paris and London, see David Pike, *Subterranean Cities: The World Beneath Paris and London, 1800–1945* (Ithaca: Cornell University Press, 2005), especially ch. 3, "Charon's Bark." See also, by the same author, *Metropolis on the Styx: The Underworlds of Modern Urban Culture, 1800–2001* (Ithaca: Cornell University Press, 2007).

58. D. A. Miller, *The Novel and the Police* (Berkeley: University of California Press, 1988), 24. Miller argues that the Victorian novel fulfills a policing function and that what he calls "panoptical narration" is "a kind of police." "Panoptical narration" fully situates what is otherwise known as omniscient narration within the ambitions of Victorian engineering culture and Benthamite utilitarianism. In Joyce's case, however, I would further gloss *police* as *polis* in order to drop the Foucauldian association with discipline, and I would assert, somewhat in contradistinction to Miller, that in *Ulysses* water and sanitation function as panoptical narrators whose mission is not discipline per se but governmentality more broadly. In *Ulysses,* a strong utopian element persists in the institution of the public works such that critics like Jameson, Leerssen, and Kiberd all pick up on it. The panoptical narrator in *Ulysses* is therefore not the same panoptical narrator of the Victorian novel, though Miller's term is tremendously instructive, in slightly modified form, for talking about modernism and Joyce in particular.

59. Ann Banfield, *Unspeakable Sentences: Narration and Representation in the Language of Fiction* (London: Routledge and Kegan Paul, 1982), 69–70.

60. Ann Banfield, "L'Imparfait de l'Objectif: The Imperfect of the Object Glass," *Camera Obscura* 24 (Fall 1990): 77, quoted in Martin Jay, "Experience without a Subject: Walter Benjamin and the Novel," in *The Actuality of Walter Benjamin,* ed. Laura Marcus and Lynda Nead (London: Lawrence and Wishart, 1993), 153.

61. In Jürgen Habermas, "Consciousness-Raising or Redemptive Criticism—The Contemporaneity of Walter Benjamin," *New German Critique* 17 (Spring 1979): 46, also quoted in Jay, "Experience without a Subject," 155.

62. Jay, "Experience without a Subject," 155.

63. Victor Hugo, *Les Misérables,* trans. Lee Fahnestock and Norman Mac-Afee (New York: Penguin, 1987), 1261. Hugo's French reads: "L'égout, c'est la conscience de la ville." See Victor Hugo, *Les Misérables,* 4 vols. (Paris: Éditeurs Nelson, 1930), 4:191. My thanks go to Ann Banfield for directing me to this passage in Hugo's novel.

64. Bernard Stiegler, *Technics and Time,* vol. 1, *The Fault of Epimetheus,* trans. Richard Beardsworth and George Collins (Stanford: Stanford University Press, 1998), 1.

65. Ibid., 13.

66. It is of interest to me that Alex Woloch uses this passage from *Ulysses* as an epigram to his chapter on Dickens's *Great Expectations,* "Partings Welded Together: The Character-System in *Great Expectations,*" in *The One vs. the Many: Minor Characters and the Space of the Protagonist in the Novel* (Princeton: Princeton University Press, 2003), 178–243. He seems to imply, without performing a reading of the passage, that the "beingless beings" Stephen evokes in reference to the power plant might be part of his proposed novelistic "character-system" in some way. I would say: as a character, or as a part of the character-space, in the sense that, like Bloom but with more ambivalence, Stephen thinks of machines as beings that talk "in their own way" (*Ulysses,* 7.175).

67. Ellmann, *James Joyce,* 25.

68. Critics have interpreted this passage variously. Andrew Gibson sees in Stephen's "two roaring worlds" another allusion to his struggle against two masters, the Catholic Church and the British Empire. Andrew Gibson, *Joyce's Revenge* (Oxford: Oxford University Press, 2002), 99. Daniel R. Schwarz is the only other critic I've come across who really emphasizes the importance of the rapidly expanding technology of electricity in this passage: "Influenced by the Futurists and perhaps, too, by Constructivists and Suprematists, Joyce was fascinated by the possibilities of machines; as Stephen responds to the energy and power of machinery, we realize that the technique of 'mechanics' has a celebratory function [albeit one that goes seemingly unrecognized by Stephen here]. We

recall, too, that Bloom had responded to the printing machines in 'Aeolus' in terms which anthropomorphized them. . . . Isn't the pumping heart a metaphor for the throbbing dynamos of the Dublin Corporation Electric Light Station which circulate—in the form of electricity and light—the necessary nourishment to the industrial city? That his heart responds rhythmically to the pulsations of the machine . . . not only validates his aesthetic credo for the man of genius—'He found in the world without as actual what was in his world within as possible'—but stretches it to include experiences beyond encounters with other people (U.213; IX.1041–2). . . . By using the heart as signifier of machinery and vice versa, Stephen is growing into the writer who might write the Irish epic." Daniel R. Schwarz, *Reading Joyce's "Ulysses"* (London: Macmillan, 1987), 156–57.

69. See Don Gifford, *"Ulysses" Annotated: Notes for James Joyce's "Ulysses"* (Berkeley: University of California Press, 1988), 276.

70. Luke Gibbons, "Ghostly Light: Spectres of Modernity in James Joyce's and John Huston's *The Dead*," in *The Blackwell Companion to James Joyce,* ed. Richard Brown (London: Blackwell, 2008), 359. Thanks to Luke Gibbons for allowing me to cite from the proofs.

71. The word *paraheliotropic* is richly suggestive for thinking about the consequences of public lighting. Turning night into day, which was the way many commentators at the time described such public street lighting, would have a profound effect on the diurnal rhythms of everyday life, so profound that the conversations about that effect are neutralized in repetition and banality— exactly the effect that the alienating reportage of "Ithaca" has on the particular conversation between Bloom and Stephen. The term *paraheliotropic* is not one of Joyce's pseudoscientific neologisms, scattered throughout "Ithaca." It was first used by Darwin in his *Origin of the Species* to describe plants that control their exposure to sunlight by turning their leafage at an angle to the sun's rays. As an evolutionary adaptation, this is a brilliant metaphor to describe human adaptations to the new, modern metropolis. See entry for *paraheliotropic* in the *Oxford English Dictionary Online,* www.oed.com, June 1, 2008. For more on Joycean pseudoscience in "Ithaca," see Gibson, *Joyce's Revenge,* 243–46.

72. See Nolan, "Modernism," 167. Nolan reads the passage as a parody in which "even dreams of Nirvana have been overtaken by images of a domestic paradise," and as Joyce's attempt to trace "the relationship between all sorts of material and spiritual deprivation, and concomitant fantasies of plenitude and pleasure" (167). Though I agree with Nolan about the import of the passage itself, I am arguing here that the humor of the passage is the symptom of the post-Socratic relationship to modern technology that *Ulysses* as a whole thor-

oughly critiques; the passage is not, in other words, Joyce's last word on "all modern conveniences," but rather like MacHugh's watercloset joke, as we saw in chapter 1, the beginning of an investigation into and a dismantling of the joke's assumptions.

73. At least one other Joycean has identified the punning play in "aquacity." See Robert Adams Day, "Joyce's AquaCities," in *Joyce in the Hibernian Metropolis: Essays,* ed. Morris Beja and David Norris (Columbus: State University of Ohio Press, 1996), 3–20.

74. Quoted in Donald F. Theall, *James Joyce's Techno-Poetics* (Toronto: University of Toronto Press, 1997), 34.

75. Stanislaus Joyce, *Recollections of James Joyce* (New York: James Joyce Society, 1950), 20, quoted in Kevin Whelan, "The Memories of 'The Dead,'" *Yale Journal of Criticism* 15, no. 1 (2002): 69.

76. James Joyce, *Dubliners* (New York: Penguin, 1996), 219. Subsequent page citations to this work are given parenthetically in the text.

77. Gibbons, "Ghostly Light," 359.

78. Ibid., 360–61.

79. Ibid., 361.

80. Rynne, *Industrial Ireland,* 430.

81. For more on the question of Gretta's social mobility and her status as an internal migrant worker before her marriage to Gabriel, see Marjorie Howes, "How Many People Has Gretta Conroy Killed?" in her *Colonial Crossings: Figures in Irish Literary History* (Dublin: Field Day Publications, 2006), 79–93. Her essay focuses on Gretta as a figure for the Irish migrant woman whose difficult choices leave in their wake a number of broken hearts, violated class boundaries, and dead bodies.

82. All this would seem like a classic case of "gaslighting"—"to manipulate a person by psychological means into questioning his or her own sanity"—if it weren't for the fact that the term doesn't come into usage until after the release of George Cukor's 1944 film *Gaslight,* which starred Ingrid Bergman, Charles Boyer, and Joseph Cotten. (In *The Third Man* Cotten coincidentally played Holly Martins, whose character is significant to this chapter only for having nothing to say about the theory of the novel, or the stream of consciousness, or James Joyce). The film was based on Patrick Hamilton's 1938 play *Angel Street.* Patrick Hamilton, *Angel Street: A Victorian Thriller in Three Acts* (Los Angeles: Samuel French, 1966). *Gaslighting* is an anachronism as far as "The Dead" is concerned, though clearly apt as a description of the role of gaslight in Gabriel's psychological agonies. See "gaslighting," *Oxford English Dictionary Online,* January 20, 2009, www.oed.com.

83. Kevis Goodman, *Georgic Modernity and British Romanticism: Poetry and the Mediation of History* (Cambridge: Cambridge University Press, 2004), 17–18. Goodman cites Aristotle's definition of medium in his *De Anima*, given as a visual example and wholly applicable to Joyce's use of gaslight in "The Dead": "Democritus is mistaken in thinking that if the intervening space *[to metaxu]* were empty, even an ant in the sky would be clearly visible; for this is impossible. For vision occurs when the faculty of sense is affected; as it cannot be acted upon by the seen color [i.e., of the object] itself, there only remains the medium *[to metaxu]* to act on it. So that some medium *[metaxu]* must exist; in fact, if it *[metaxu* implied from previous clause] were empty, sight would not only be not accurate but we would see nothing altogether" (*De Anima* 419a, 16–21, quoted in Goodman, *Georgic Modernity*, 18).

84. K. Whelan, "Memories of 'The Dead,'" 65.

85. Ellmann, *James Joyce*, 500–501. "Ithaca" evolved until the very last minute before publication, though the waterworks passage remained remarkably similar throughout the proofsheets. See Michael Groden, ed., *James Joyce's "Ulysses," "Ithaca" and "Penelope," a Facsimile of Placards for Episodes 17–18* (New York: Garland, 1978).

86. Duffy, "Disappearing Dublin," 49.

87. This passage remained entirely unchanged in the proofsheets for "Ithaca," like the waterworks passage, which underwent only minimal changes. See Groden, *James Joyce's "Ulysses."*

88. Jameson, "*Ulysses* in History," 131.

89. Emer Nolan, "State of the Art: Joyce and Postcolonialism," in Attridge and Howes, *Semicolonial Joyce*, 93.

90. Ibid.

91. Jameson, "*Ulysses* in History," 140.

92. Ibid., 139.

93. For the origins of the term *fetish* in John Atkins's *A Voyage to Guinea, Brasil, and the West Indies*, written in 1735, see Patrick Brantlinger, *Fictions of State: Culture and Credit in Britain, 1694–1994* (Ithaca: Cornell University Press, 1996), 42. Atkins originally used the term to infantilize and "barbarianize" the natives he encountered on his journeys; Freud used it in an ostensibly depoliticized way; and Marx used it as a condemnation of capitalism. But the point is perhaps that "fetishism" of one sort or another may be the founding gesture of any given imagined community and ought not be considered an aberration or perversion of sexuality, or capitalism, or barbarism, or social organization, and so on.

THREE. A Fountain of Nationality

1. By proposing the "allegory of the nation-state," I seek to define a third way of thinking about allegory in postcolonial literature that borrows and differentiates itself from Fredric Jameson's understanding of national allegory on one side and Abdul JanMohamed's understanding of the colonial and anticolonial Manichean allegory on the other. See Fredric Jameson, "Third-World Literature in the Era of Multinational Capitalism," *Social Text* 15 (1986): 65–88; and Abdul JanMohamed, "The Economy of Manichean Allegory: The Function of Racial Difference in Colonialist Literature," in *"Race," Writing and Difference,* ed. Henry Louis Gates (Chicago: University of Chicago Press, 1986), 78–106.

2. Douglas Hyde, "The Necessity for De-Anglicising Ireland," in *Language, Lore and Lyrics: Essays and Lectures,* ed. Breandán Ó Conaire (Dublin: Irish Academic Press, 1986), 153–70.

3. O'Connor, *Haunted English,* xvii. I borrow, somewhat polemically, the title of my chapter, "Haunted Infrastructure," from the title of her book.

4. W. B. Yeats, "The De-Anglicising of Ireland," *United Ireland,* December 12, 1892, repr. in *Yeats's Poetry Drama and Prose,* ed. James Pethica (New York: W.W. Norton, 2000), 261.

5. Ibid., 262.

6. Ibid.

7. Chinua Achebe, "English and the African Writer" (*Transition* 4, no. 18 [1965]), repr. in "The Anniversary Issue: Selections from *Transition,* 1961–1976," special issue, *Transition* 75–76 (1997): 345.

8. "Fountain," *OED* Online, www.oed.com, April 15, 2009.

9. Ellmann, *James Joyce,* 102–3.

10. Ibid., 104.

11. Anthony Cronin, *No Laughing Matter: The Life and Times of Flann O'Brien* (New York: International Publishing, 1998), 75.

12. Clair Wills, *That Neutral Island: A Cultural History of Ireland during the Second World War* (Cambridge, MA: Harvard University Press, 2007), 33. The decline of the language was concurrent and consonant with other demographic trends. "Between 1911 and 1936 the number of agricultural labourers dropped from 300,000 to 150,000. Emigration accelerated from an average level of around 23,000 during the first two decades of the century to over 33,000 during the 1921–31 period, and there was an absolute fall of 89,000 in the size of the population." See also Andrew MacLaran, *Dublin: The Shaping of a Capital* (London: Belhaven Press, 1993), 52–53.

13. Cronin, *No Laughing Matter*, 74–75. I said "Kafkaesque," but this is to point to the fact that even the idea of the "Kafkaesque" highlights the relative neglect of O'Brien's work on the theme of bureaucratic alienation, the self lost, or, it might be better to say, the self defined in the "seemingly endless, identical corridors" of the state.

14. Ibid., 74.

15. Quoted in ibid., 75.

16. Garvin's Joyce scholarship was originally published under the pseudonym Andrew Cass and was later republished under his real name. John Garvin, *James Joyce's Disunited Kingdom* (Dublin: Gill and Macmillan, 1976).

17. Quoted in Cronin, *No Laughing Matter*, 78–79.

18. O'Brien was often merciless on the subject of the language revival and its consequences. He was later to insult his former professor at University College Dublin, Douglas Hyde, who had founded the Gaelic League and was generally venerated for his principal role in the attempt to revive the Irish language, claiming that Hyde spoke Irish "inaccurately and badly," and again that he "spoke atrocious Irish" (Cronin, *No Laughing Matter*, 53–54). For some other examples of O'Brien's mockery of academic Gaelic in his *Times* column, see Flann O'Brien [Myles na gCopaleen, pseud.], *The Best of Myles* (Normal, IL: Dalkey Archive Press, 1999), esp. 276–79. The paradox here is that without the revival O'Brien's dexterity in Irish would never have earned him a job with the state, and his Irish works might never have been published or even written. Clearly this is the result of some constitutive ambivalence about the language question, an ambivalence that hinges on the state and the state's role in imposing or reimposing Irish on the Irish people.

19. Kiberd, *Irish Classics*, 501.

20. The argument that the Gaelicization of Ireland amounted to nothing more than an empty nominalism had an emblem in the Irish postbox. In 1922 the Irish Free State ordered all the red British postboxes to be painted over in Irish green, "covering although not obliterating the Royal insignia of *Victoria Regina* or *Edwardus Rex*." By extension, many of the name changes seemed only to highlight rather than to diminish the persistence of old forms. See Yvonne Whelan, *Reinventing Modern Dublin* (Dublin: University College Dublin Press, 2003), 117–18.

21. Kiberd summarizes these events more or less as I have. For more details about the recession and the economic war with Britain, see Joseph J. Lee, *Ireland, 1912–1985: Politics and Society* (Cambridge: Cambridge University Press, 1989), 175–270; and MacLaran, *Dublin*, 52–56. For the social and cultural formations connected to these economic factors, see also Terence Brown,

Ireland: A Social and Cultural History, 1922–1985 (London: Fontana Press, 1985), 13–171.

22. Kiberd, *Irish Classics*, 500.

23. Brown, *Ireland*, 81.

24. Kiberd, *Irish Classics*, 500.

25. Cronin, *No Laughing Matter*, 49.

26. Ibid., 53–54.

27. See John Wyse Jackson, introduction to *Flann O'Brien at War: Myles na gCopaleen, 1940–1945*, ed. John Wyse Jackson (London: Gerald Duckworth, 1999), 16.

28. Wills, *That Neutral Island*, 290.

29. The first result of Beckett's turn to French was the 1945 short story "Premier Amour," or "First Love," whose vulgar attention to the public utilities I read in chapter 1.

30. Cronin, *No Laughing Matter*, 105.

31. Ibid.

32. Anne Clissmann, *Flann O'Brien: A Critical Introduction to His Writings* (Dublin: Gill and Macmillan, 1975), 156. For a reading of the novel through the strict lens of its use and abuse of modern scientific discovery, see Andrew Spencer, "Many Worlds: The New Physics in Flann O'Brien's *The Third Policeman*," *Eire-Ireland* 30 (Spring 1995): 145–58.

33. Quoted in Clissmann, *Flann O'Brien*, 151.

34. Quoted in Benedict Anderson, *The Spectre of Comparisons: Nationalism, Southeast Asia, and the World* (London: Verso, 1998), 59.

35. Ibid., 64.

36. Ibid., 64–65, emphases mine.

37. There is precedent for the comparison in Kiberd's *Inventing Ireland*. There he compares O'Brien's *An Béal Bocht* (*The Poor Mouth*), his only novel written in Irish, to Kafka's *The Trial*. Kiberd calls Bonaparte, the protagonist of *An Béal Bocht*, "the peasant equivalent of Kafka's nameless citizen, a Joseph K. of the western world" (511). Also notable is his claim that O'Brien's novel is "the Irish version of *One Hundred Years of Solitude*, a book in which identities are fluid and interchangeable, as characters are trapped in repetitive cycles of time and rains that pelt down without mercy" (503). Whether these specific claims are sustainable is perhaps less important than that they establish O'Brien as a writer of minor literature, in the sense elaborated by Deleuze and Guattari and also, specifically in the Irish case, by David Lloyd. The kinship to the genre of magical realism, however, is in many ways just as true, if not more so, for *The Third Policeman* as it is for *An Béal Bocht*.

38. In their book *Kafka: Toward a Minor Literature,* Deleuze and Guattari refer to Joyce and Beckett as exemplary figures for the practice of minor literature. "As Irishmen, both of them lived within the genial conditions of a minor literature. . . . But the former never stops operating by exhilaration and over-determination and brings about all sorts of worldwide reterritorializations. The other proceeds by dryness and sobriety, a willed poverty pushing deterritorialization to such an extreme that nothing remains but intensities." Gilles Deleuze and Félix Guattari, *Kafka: Toward a Minor Literature* (Minneapolis: University of Minnesota Press, 1986), 19. While O'Brien is not mentioned, it may be worth pointing out that his marginal status in the English canon is itself a paradoxical indicator of his supreme representativeness for minor literature. Assuming that it is somehow, somewhere, generally agreed that he is less talented or less accomplished than Joyce or Beckett, then the case only becomes stronger by their logic: "Indeed scarcity of talent [in a minor literature] is in fact beneficial and allows the conception of something other than a literature of masters" (17).

39. Cronin, *No Laughing Matter,* 106.

40. Flann O'Brien, *The Third Policeman* (Normal, IL: Dalkey Archive Press, 1999), 15. Subsequent page citations to this work are given parenthetically in the text.

41. Joyce, *Ulysses,* 12.1561. Subsequent chapter and page citations to this work are given parenthetically in the text.

42. Marjorie Howes, "'Goodbye Ireland I'm Going to Gort': Geography, Scale, and Narrating the Nation," in Attridge and Howes, *Semicolonial Joyce,* 60.

43. Quoted in K. Whelan, "Memories of 'The Dead,'" 67. Whelan quotes from W. Dillon's *Life of John Mitchel,* 2 vols. (London: K. Paul, Trench, 1888), 211. Dillon quotes from Mitchel's newspaper the *United Irishman.*

44. As Joseph J. Lee points out, such a conflation was in part due to some constitutional wavering over how exactly to define the nation. "The very structure of the constitution betrays the difficulties of the de Valera dialectic on the crucial question of identity. Articles 1–2 deal with 'The Nation.' Articles 4–11 deal with 'The State.' But de Valera makes no attempt to define 'The Nation.' The definition contained in Article 2 is not of the nation, only of the national territory" (Lee, *Ireland,* 205). For more detail on constitutional issues, see also Joseph J. Lee, "The Irish Constitution of 1937," in *Ireland's Histories: Aspects of State Society and Ideology,* ed. Seán Hutton and Paul Stewart (London: Routledge, 1991), 80–93. There Lee points to Article 8 of the constitution, where Irish is proclaimed the national language, and where as a result the constitution "found itself embroiled in the potential conflict between nation and people, as

opposed to 'nation' and 'state'" (87). "Theoretically, Irish would presumably remain the 'national language' even if nobody at all spoke it. Does the idea that *the nation exists wholly independently of reality* at any given time inform the assumptions underlying this article? ... It seems clear from the text that the nation exists independently of the 'national territory.' It is unclear whether it exists independently of the people" (88, emphasis mine).

45. Anderson, *Spectre*, 64.

46. Ibid., 37.

47. Michael Warner, "The Mass Public and the Mass Subject," in *Habermas and the Public Sphere*, ed. Craig Calhoun (Cambridge, MA: MIT Press, 1992), 382.

48. For Brantlinger's original analysis of the link between the public sphere and the public debt, from which I borrow heavily, see ch. 3 of his *Fictions of State*, 88–135.

49. O'Brien would make de Selby, along with James Joyce, central characters of his 1966 novel *The Dalkey Archive* (Normal, IL: Dalkey Archive Press, 2006).

50. Jackson, introduction, 13.

51. O'Brien, *Best of Myles*, 116–17.

52. Ibid., 114.

53. Ibid., 118.

54. Wills, *That Neutral Island*, 250.

55. Ibid., 257.

56. O'Brien, *Best of Myles*, 125.

57. Sen, "Capitalism beyond the Crisis," 28.

FOUR. Electrifiction, or Dramatizing Power

1. Theall, *James Joyce's Techno-Poetics*, 10.

2. James Joyce, *Finnegans Wake* (New York: Penguin, 1939), 262. Thanks to John Bishop for showing me this passage and offering the triple interpretation of the line I reproduce here.

3. Michael McCarthy, *High Tension: Life on the Shannon Scheme* (Dublin: Lilliput Press, 2004). See especially ch. 6, "Trouble by the Mile."

4. See figure 4, part of the ESB's postcard series promoting the Shannon Scheme, which depicts blasting operations near Clonlara and is discussed later in this chapter.

5. McCarthy, *High Tension*, 27–28.

6. Ibid., 77.

7. On the dam's original symbolic value, see Mark Maguire, "Socialists, Savages and Hydroelectric Schemes: A Historical Anthropological Account of the Construction of Ardnacrusha," *Irish Journal of Anthropology* 3 (1998): 60–77. As Maguire puts it, "Ardnacrusha possessed a symbolic value far in excess of any economic benefit" (61). Maguire took a tour of Ardnacrusha in 1995. His tour guide, Seán Craig, revealed that the operation of the dam was becoming automated, reducing its number of workers by half. When asked if "there was any chance of closure," however, Craig insisted, "in a mystical tone," that "Ardnacrusha will keep going" (60).

8. On hydroelectric schemes in the United States, see David Nye, *Electrifying America: Social Meanings of a New Technology, 1880–1940* (Cambridge, MA: MIT Press, 1990). On such schemes in Germany, see David Blackbourn, *The Conquest of Nature: Water, Landscape and the Making of Modern Germany* (London: Jonathan Cape, 2006).

9. See Harold Dorn, "Hugh Lincoln Cooper and the First Détente," *Technology and Culture* 20 (April 1979): 322–47; Susan Buck-Morss, *Dreamworld and Catastrophe: The Passing of Mass Utopia in East and West* (Cambridge, MA: MIT Press, 2000), 316 n. 10. Buck-Morss quotes the Russian electrical engineer Gleb Krzhizhanovskii on the necessity of adapting Western technologies of electrical production: "[Abroad] stand opponents, equipped with all the attributes of the strongly developed capitalist economy. It is perfectly clear that in the economic struggle we must be armed in the same areas they are. . . . If we do not work from a base of electrification, our position will be extremely disadvantageous."

10. Buck-Morss, *Dreamworld and Catastrophe*, 140.

11. Dorn, "Hugh Lincoln Cooper," 332. The insult works the same in the original Russian, *elektrifikatzia* becoming *elektrifiktzia*. Thanks to Joshua Rubenstein and Boris Katz for confirming this for me.

12. Patrick Carroll-Burke, "Tools, Instruments, and Engines: Getting a Handle on the Specificity of Engine Science," *Social Studies of Science* 31 (August 2001): 593–625.

13. Cleary, *Outrageous Fortune*, ch. 6, "Modernization and Aesthetic Ideology," 205.

14. Carroll-Burke, "Material Designs," 79.

15. Linda Simon, *Dark Light: Electricity and Anxiety from the Telegraph to the X-Ray* (New York: Harcourt, 2004), 7.

16. Ibid.

17. Quoted in Michael Shiel, *The Quiet Revolution: The Electrification of Rural Ireland, 1946–1976* (Dublin: O'Brien Press, 2003), 18.

18. Wolfgang Schivelbusch, *Disenchanted Night: The Industrialization of Light in the Nineteenth Century* (Berkeley: University of California Press, 1995), 28.

19. I take my understanding of "habitus" from Loïc Wacquant, "Habitus," in *The International Encyclopedia of Economic Sociology,* ed. Jens Beckert and Milan Zafirovski (London: Routledge, 2005), 315—19.

20. Shiel, *Quiet Revolution,* 194. According to him, "In over 90% of [rural] homes every drop of water used in the house had to be carried over the threshold, most of it from a considerable distance, usually by the farmer's wife or children," and "Every drop of hot water had to be heated over the fire" (195).

21. Chandra Mukerji, "Intelligent Uses of Engineering and the Legitimacy of State Power," *Technology and Culture* 44 (October 2003): 659.

22. Carroll-Burke, "Material Designs," 78, 85.

23. Vladimir Nabokov, *The Annotated Lolita* (New York: G.P. Putnam's Sons, 1970), 213.

24. Another way to understand this uncanny effect in literary-theoretical terms would be through Victor Shklovsky's concept of "defamiliarization." I am, however, trying to defamiliarize the literary-critical notion of defamiliarization in order to argue for a special resonance between engineering cultures and literary cultures, because they are both products of *tekhne*—a restricted class of objects crafted by humans. Shklovsky, by contrast, makes no distinction among the objects that art defamiliarizes: "Art is a way of experiencing the artfulness of an object; the object is not important" (12). Victor Shklovsky, "Art as Technique," in *Russian Formalist Criticism: Four Essays,* ed. Lee T. Lemon and Marion J. Reis (Lincoln: University of Nebraska Press, 1965), 3—24.

25. Pramoedya Ananta Toer, *This Earth of Mankind,* trans. Max Lane (New York: Penguin, 1990), 17.

26. The term is David Lloyd's, from his *Anomalous States.*

27. Carroll-Burke, "Material Designs," 106.

28. Pascale Casanova, *The World Republic of Letters,* trans. M.B. DeBevoise (Cambridge, MA: Harvard University Press, 2004), 304.

29. Quoted in Lothar Schoen, "The Irish Free State and the Electricity Industry, 1922—1927," in *The Shannon Scheme and the Electrification of the Irish Free State,* ed. Andy Bielenberg (Dublin: Lilliput Press, 2002), 47.

30. Rynne, *Industrial Ireland,* 431; Senator Séamus O'Farrell as quoted in Maguire, "Socialists, Savages," 61.

31. Senator John T. O'Farrell, quoted in Maguire, "Socialists, Savages," 64.

32. Quoted in McCarthy, *High Tension,* 41.

33. Quoted in Maguire, "Socialists, Savages," 66.

34. Schoen, "Irish Free State," 46.

35. Wills, *That Neutral Island,* 18.

36. Electricity Supply Board, "Energy! 90,000 Horsepower," *Irish Statesman,* September 8, 1928, 2.

37. Electricity Supply Board, "Electricity Does the Heavy Work," *Irish Statesman,* September 22, 1928, 53.

38. Electricity Supply Board, "Progress," *Irish Statesman,* October 20, 1928, 133.

39. Quoted in Maguire, "Socialists, Savages," 60.

40. "Scope for Irish Engineers: No Longer Necessary to Emigrate," *Irish Times,* September 10, 1928, 5.

41. "Success of the Shannon Scheme: Mr. Cosgrave Hopes for the Unity of Ireland," *Irish Times,* September 10, 1928, 5.

42. The response from hardline antitreaty republicans to Cosgrave's arguments for modernization—and electrification in particular—as a means of Irish reunification was not, for the most part, enthusiastic. A telling fictionalized account is Cathal Black's 1996 film *Korea,* which depicts a rural electrification switch-on ceremony. When the officials turn on the public lights, a crusty veteran of the Civil War quips, "It wasn't for streetlamps we fought." Cathal Black, dir., *Korea* (Black Star Films, 1996). Cleary analyses this scene at some length in his chapter "Modernization and Aesthetic Ideology" in *Outrageous Fortune,* 203–6.

43. Andy Bielenberg, "Seán Keating, the Shannon Scheme and the Art of State-Building," in Bielenberg, *Shannon Scheme,* 115.

44. Ibid., 127.

45. Ibid.

46. "The Shannon Scheme," *Irish Independent,* July 23, 1929, 1.

47. "The Religious Note," *Irish Independent,* July 23, 1929.

48. Quoted in Shiel, *Quiet Revolution,* 29.

49. Ibid., 29–30.

50. There may be a particularly Irish historical precedent for the connection: the Irish National School System, established in 1831 under British rule, "was the first national school system of government funded popular education in the world." Carroll-Burke, "Material Designs," 98.

51. Shiel, *Quiet Revolution,* 142–43.

52. Ibid., 143.

53. Ibid., 143–44.

54. Ibid., 144.

55. Ibid., 149.

56. Ibid., 144.

57. See Christopher Morash's chapter on John Mitchel in his *Writing the Irish Famine* (Oxford: Clarendon Press, 1995), 70. There he quotes from Mitchel's *Jail Journal* the following "definition" of the "Irish howl": "Success confers every right in this Enlightened Age; wherein, for the first time it has come to be admitted and proclaimed in set terms, that Success is Right and Defeat is Wrong. If I profess myself a disbeliever in that gospel, the Enlightened Age will only smile, and say, 'The defeated always are.' Britain being in possession of the floor, any hostile comment upon her way of telling the story is an unmannerly interruption; nay, is nothing short of an *Irish howl*."

58. Denis Johnston, "Let There Be Light," in *The Selected Plays of Denis Johnston,* ed. Joseph Ronsley (Washington, DC: Catholic University of America Press, 1983), 94.

59. Gene A. Barnett, *Denis Johnston* (Boston: G.K. Hall, 1978), 42.

60. Bernard Adams, *Denis Johnston: A Life* (Dublin: Lilliput Press, 2002), 114–15.

61. Ibid., 115.

62. Johnston, "Let There Be Light," 94.

63. Denis Johnston, *The Moon in the Yellow River,* in *Selected Plays,* 162–63. Subsequent page citations to this work are given parenthetically in the text.

64. Joyce, *Ulysses,* 1.649.

65. Joseph Ronsley, introduction to Johnston, *Selected Plays,* 7.

66. Bob Cullen, "Some Notable Features of the Design and Operational History of Ardnacrusha," in Bielenberg, *Shannon Scheme,* 141. This was all part of the plan for national electrification: "From small beginnings," Cullen goes on, "load demand increased significantly as more towns were gradually connected to the network and small utilities were closed down." Though the Pigeon House did briefly come back into operation, to make up for drought shortages when the Shannon was running too low for Ardnacrusha to meet demand, the national plan was always, nevertheless, to replace local power with national power.

67. Adams, *Denis Johnston,* 112.

68. Y. Whelan, *Reinventing Modern Dublin,* 117–18.

69. This was true, too, for Samuel Beckett, who records his discomfort with the new street names that went up all over Dublin after the war of independence, memorializing the heroes of the revolution. See Seán Kennedy, " 'In the street I was lost': Cultural Dislocation in 'The End,' " in Seán Kennedy, ed., *Beckett and Ireland* (Cambridge: Cambridge University Press, 2009), 135–61.

70. Denis Johnston, "Period Piece," in *Selected Plays,* 259.

71. Johnston, "Let There Be Light," 95.

72. Ibid.

73. Ibid.

74. See Catherine Gallagher, "War, Counterfactual History, and Alternate-History Novels," *Field Day Review* 3 (2007): 53–66.

75. The observation originally comes from Veronica O'Reilly, "The Realism of Denis Johnston," in *Myth and Reality in Irish Literature,* ed. Joseph Ronsley (Waterloo, Ontario: Wilfrid Laurier Press, 1977), 286. O'Reilly suggests that the books are "suggestive of the complexity as well as the clash of values in the play." Of the toy train, O'Reilly remarks that it "indicates [Dobelle's] remove from what others consider the 'real' world."

FIVE. Other Rough Beasts

Portions of this chapter were previously published, and I thank the publishers for their permission to reproduce them here: "Light Reading: Public Utility, Urban Fiction and Human Rights," *Social Text* 97 (Winter 2008): 31–50.

1. James Delbourgo, *A Most Amazing Scene of Wonders: Electricity and Enlightenment in Early America* (Cambridge, MA: Harvard University Press, 2006), 131–32.

2. Quoted in ibid., 139.

3. Ibid., 141.

4. Ibid., 139.

5. Paul Gilmore, "Romantic Electricity, or the Materiality of Aesthetics," *American Literature* 76 (September 2004): 473.

6. Ibid., 478 and 479. On Shelley, Gilmore is quoting Thomas Jefferson Hogg, *The Life of Percy Bysshe Shelley* (New York: Dutton, 1933), 51–52.

7. Delbourgo, *Most Amazing Scene,* 140–41.

8. Gilmore, "Romantic Electricity," 472–73.

9. Chris Otter, "Making Liberalism Durable: Vision and Civility in the Late Victorian City," *Social History* 27 (January 2002): 14.

10. Ibid., 6.

11. Ibid., 4.

12. Berman, *All That Is Solid,* 242. Berman speculates that Dostoyevsky's 1864 *Notes from Underground* may be the first literary admission that engineering had become that primary symbol of human creativity.

13. Joyce, *Portrait of the Artist,* 210.

14. Quoted in Walter Benjamin, "The Work of Art in the Age of Its Technological Reproducibility," in *Selected Writings,* vol. 4, *1938–1940,* ed. Michael W. Jennings, trans. Howard Eiland et al. (Cambridge, MA: Harvard University Press, 2003), 253. The quote from Valéry's essay appears only in the third and

latest version of Benjamin's essay, a strange inclusion given that the public utilities do not seem immediately to pertain to Benjamin's subject, the work of art.

15. Ibid., 253.

16. Paul Valéry, *The Outlook for Intelligence,* trans. Denise Folliot and Jackson Mathews (New York: Harper and Row, 1962), 10.

17. Hughes, *Networks of Power,* 5.

18. Otter, "Making Liberalism Durable," 5.

19. Celeste Langan, "Mobility Disability," *Public Culture* 13, no. 3 (2001): 464–65.

20. Mike Davis, "Planet of Slums," *New Left Review* 26 (March–April 2004): 5–34, and *Planet of Slums* (New York: Verso, 2006).

21. Brent Edwards and Ashley Dawson, eds., "Cities of the Global South," special issue, *Social Text* 22 (Winter 2004).

22. Patricia Yeager, "Introduction: Dreaming of Infrastructure," *PMLA* 122 (Winter 2007): 9–26.

23. Patrick Chamoiseau, *Texaco,* trans. Rose-Myriam Réjouis and Val Vinokurov (New York: Vintage Books, 1998), originally published as *Texaco* (Paris: Gallimard, 1992). All subsequent page citations are to the Vintage English translation of this work and are given parenthetically in the text.

24. Davis, "Planet of Slums," 7.

25. Ashley Dawson, "Squatters, Space, and Belonging in the Underdeveloped City," *Social Text* 22 (Winter 2004): 18.

26. Ibid., 18–19.

27. I quote the French text from Patrick Chamoiseau, *Texaco* (Paris: Gallimard, 1992), 486.

28. The phrase is Robert Kurz's, quoted in Roberto Schwartz's review of *City of God,* dir. Fernando Meirelles, *New Left Review* 12 (November–December 2001): 112.

29. Indeed, Aimé Césaire thought that the *département* status granted to Martinique after the Second World War—a status that he argued for over independence from France—brought with it new forms of "economic oppression" combined with "cultural dependency." See Colin Dayan, "Out of Defeat: Aimé Césaire's Miraculous Words," *Boston Review,* September-October 2008, March 3, 2009, www.bostonreview.net/BR33.5/dayan.php.

30. Chamoiseau's literary relationship to Césaire was and is a complicated one. To Césaire's *négritude* Chamoiseau and other French Caribbean writers of his generation counterposed their notion of *créolité.* The Créolistes denounced *négritude* for replacing "the illusion of Europe for the illusion of Africa." Lucien Taylor, "*Créolité* Bites: A Conversation with Patrick Chamoiseau, Raphaël Confiant, and Jean Bernabé," *Transition* 74 (1997): 128.

31. Aimé Césaire, "Cahier d'un retour au pays natal," in *Aimé Césaire: The Collected Poetry,* trans. Clayton Eshelman and Annette Smith (Berkeley: University of California Press, 1983), 67, 69.

32. Ibid., 77.

33. Quoted in Nick Nesbitt, "Troping Toussaint, Reading Revolution," *Research in African Literatures* 35 (Summer 2004): 29.

34. Quoted in Dayan, "Out of Defeat."

35. Susan Buck-Morss, *Hegel, Haiti, and Universal History* (Pittsburgh: University of Pittsburgh Press, 2009), 94.

36. Thanks to Katherine Anderson for bringing this translation issue to my attention.

37. Peter Brooks, *Reading for the Plot: Design and Intention in Narrative* (Cambridge, MA: Harvard University Press, 1984), 315.

38. Ibid., xiv.

39. See Yoann Pélis, *Les nouveaux défis de l'énergie à la Martinique* (Paris: Éditions Publibook, 2007), 33–38.

40. Ibid., 35. Pélis states that in 1975, when the E. D. F. took over the electrical utilities in Martinique, one person out of seven lived in a household with electricity; by 1990 the ratio was one to three, and by 2004 a little higher than one to two.

41. Ibid., 34.

42. Joseph Slaughter, "Enabling Fictions: The *Bildungsroman* and International Human Rights Law," *PMLA* 121 (October 2006): 1415.

43. Davis, *Planet of Slums,* 16.

44. Robbins, "Smell of Infrastructure," 27.

45. I'm following through on Robbins's notion of literary distaste for utility here, but it is important to note that Slaughter makes a kind of counterargument in his "Enabling Fictions." There he makes the case that the Bildungsroman was and is an underappreciated model not only for the 1948 Declaration of Human Rights but also for the 1986 Declaration of the Right to Development, a claim that would superficially seem to contradict Robbins. Rather than see it as a contradiction, however, I would mark the moment as a crucial intersection for further conversation and debate.

46. Ralph Ellison, *Invisible Man* (New York: Vintage Books, 1995).

47. Ibid., 6–7.

48. Henry Roth, *Call It Sleep* (New York: Farrar, Straus and Giroux, 1991).

49. Bruce Robbins, "Modernism in History, Modernism in Power," in *Modernism Reconsidered,* ed. Robert Kiely (Cambridge, MA: Harvard University Press, 1983), 245.

50. *Power Trip,* dir. Paul Devlin, 2003.

51. See Molly Corso, "Promises Still Power Georgia's Electricity System," *EurasiaNet,* January 24, 2005, www. Eurasianet.org.

52. See Jacques Rancière, "Who Is the Subject of the Rights of Man?" *South Atlantic Quarterly* 103 (Spring–Summer 2004): 297–310. Rancière speaks of Arendt's suspicion that "the Rights of Man [were] a mere abstraction because the only real rights were the rights of citizens, the rights attached to a national community as such." Or again that human rights are "the rights of those who have no more property left than the property of being human. . . . They are the rights of those who have no rights, the mere derision of right" (298).

53. See Slaughter, "Enabling Fictions," 1414. See 1412–15 for his full explanation.

54. Ibid., 1414.

55. Frances Ferguson, *Pornography, the Theory: What Utilitarianism Did to Action* (Chicago: University of Chicago Press, 2004), 6.

56. Orlando Patterson, *Slavery and Social Death: A Comparative Study* (Cambridge, MA: Harvard University Press, 1985), 44. Also quoted in Buck-Morss, *Hegel, Haiti,* 88.

57. Buck-Morss, *Hegel, Haiti,* 89.

58. Patterson, *Slavery and Social Death,* 45.

59. Hughes, *Networks of Power,* 464.

60. See Mark Essig, *Edison and the Electric Chair* (New York: Sutton, 2003).

61. *District B13,* screenplay by Luc Besson and Bibi Naceri, dir. Pierre Morel (TF1 and Canal+, 2004).

62. The nature of the French *services publics* differs significantly from the British civil service and the American public utility. For more on the deep cultural sense of the institution in France, see Jacques Fournier's "Public Services," Embassy of France in the United States, June 1, 2008, www.ambafrance-us.org/atoz/public_services.asp.

63. Buck-Morss points out that the notion of slavery as a "social utility" predated but did not discursively survive the republican Revolutionary era. Thus the *utilité commune* of the French declaration had links to slavery, though they had been decisively conceptually severed. See Buck-Morss, *Hegel, Haiti,* 89.

64. Peter Sloterdijk and Gesa Mueller von der Haegen, "Instant Democracy: The Pneumatic Parliament," in *Making Things Public: Atmospheres of Democracy,* ed. Bruno Latour and Peter Weibel (Cambridge, MA: MIT Press, 2005), 952–57.

65. Michael R. Gordon, "In Sadr City, Basic Services Are Faltering," *New York Times,* April 22, 2008. For an account of how electricity is provisionally

supplied in Iraq since the invasion, as a dual function of the national grid and independently operated generating stations, see Kirk Semple, "As Iraqi Lights Flicker, 'Generator Man' Feels Heat," *New York Times,* September 25, 2006.

66. Gordon, "In Sadr City."

67. Robin Fox, "The Kindness of Strangers," *Harper's Magazine,* November 2007, 15–21.

68. Yeager is talking about something like wishing for infrastructure. Though I do not have time to address the issue directly here, I think it important to note that, from the perspective of those who do have infrastructure, the "dream" of destroying it is often as powerful or more so than the dream of building it or having it. Hollywood action cinema is the most obvious example. But this is to get into a psychoanalytic argument that would take us too far away from the generic and historical points that I will be making here.

69. Yeager, introduction, 15.

70. *Casino Royale,* dir. Martin Campbell (Columbia Pictures, 2007). Belle and Foucan parted ways in 1998, with Belle claiming to practice a kind of spiritual form of *parkour* and Foucan calling his version "free running." Belle has accused "free running" of being too sensational and commercial. Foucan has sold his image to K-Swiss to market a "free running" shoe. So it goes. If nothing else, this all signals the way in which *parkour* looks like the "next big thing" in the commercial appropriation of urban street culture, and the way in which such appropriation, through French-to-English translation, strips the form of its historical origins. In this sense "free running" is a wishful translation of *parkour,* whose name has roots in French imperialist adventures in Vietnam and Africa, where the French military developed their physical fitness programs.

71. Amartya Sen, "Infrapoverty," April 20, 2009, Regional Academy for Research and Renaissance, www.rarre.org/documents/sen/Sen-%20Infra%20 Poverty.pdf, a summary of a lecture delivered at the United Nations in New York at the launch of the Japan–United Nations Development Programme report, "Making Infrastructure Work for the Poor," March 8, 2006.

72. Yeager, introduction, 10. See Naomi Klein, *The Shock Doctrine: The Rise of Disaster Capitalism* (New York: Metropolitan Books, 2007), and the excerpt from the book, "Disaster Capitalism: The New Economy of Catastrophe," *Harper's Magazine,* October 2007.

BIBLIOGRAPHY

Achebe, Chinua. "English and the African Writer." *Transition* 4, no. 18 (1965). Reprinted in "The Anniversary Issue: Selections from *Transition,* 1961–1976," special issue, *Transition* 75–76 (1997): 342–49.

Adams, Bernard. *Denis Johnston: A Life.* Dublin: Lilliput Press, 2002.

Adiga, Aravind. *The White Tiger.* New York: Free Press, 2008.

Anderson, Benedict. *Imagined Communities: Reflections on the Origin and Spread of Nationalism.* London: Verso, 1991.

———. *The Spectre of Comparisons: Nationalism, Southeast Asia, and the World.* London: Verso, 1998.

Appadurai, Arjun. "Disjuncture and Difference in the Global Cultural Economy." In *Colonial Discourse and Post-colonial Theory: A Reader,* ed. Patrick Williams and Laura Chrisman, 324–39. New York: Columbia University Press, 1994.

Arendt, Hannah. *The Human Condition.* Chicago: University of Chicago Press, 1998.

———. *The Portable Hannah Arendt.* Ed. Peter Baehr. New York: Penguin, 2000.

Arnold, Matthew. "On the Study of Celtic Literature." In *Lectures and Essays in Criticism,* ed. R. H. Super, 291–395. Ann Arbor: University of Michigan Press, 1962.

Asbee, Sue. *Flann O'Brien.* Boston: Twayne, 1991.

Attridge, Derek, and Marjorie Howes, eds. *Semicolonial Joyce.* Cambridge: Cambridge University Press, 2000.

Auerbach, Erich. *Mimesis: The Representation of Reality in Western Literature.* Trans. Willard R. Trask. Princeton: Princeton University Press, 2003.

Banfield, Ann. "L'Imparfait de l'Objectif: The Imperfect of the Object Glass." *Camera Obscura* 24 (September 1990): 65–87.

———. *Unspeakable Sentences: Narration and Representation in the Language of Fiction.* London: Routledge and Kegan Paul, 1982.

Barnett, Gene A. *Denis Johnston.* Boston: G. K. Hall, 1978.

Beckett, Samuel. "First Love." In *The Penguin Book of Irish Fiction,* ed. Colm Tóibín, 558–69. New York: Penguin, 2001.

———. *Premier amour.* Paris: Éditions de Minuit, 1970.

Benjamin, Walter. *The Arcades Project*. Ed. Rolf Tiedemann. Trans. Howard Ei-
land and Kevin McLaughlin. Cambridge, MA: Harvard University Press,
1999.

————. "Theses on the Philosophy of History." In *Illuminations*, ed. Hannah
Arendt, trans. Harry Zohn, 253–64. New York: Schocken Books, 1969.

————. "The Work of Art in the Age of Its Technological Reproducibility." In
Selected Writings, vol. 4, *1938–1940*, ed. Michael W. Jennings, trans. Howard
Eiland et al. Cambridge, MA: Harvard University Press, 2003.

————. *The Writer of Modern Life: Essays on Charles Baudelaire*. Cambridge,
MA: Harvard University Press, 2006.

Berman, Marshall. *All That Is Solid Melts into Air: The Experience of Modernity*. New York: Penguin, 1982.

Bersani, Leo. "Against *Ulysses*." In *James Joyce's "Ulysses": A Casebook*, ed. Derek
Attridge, 201–30. Oxford: Oxford University Press, 2004.

Bhabha, Homi. "Sly Civility." *October* 34 (Autumn 1985): 71–80.

Bielenberg, Andy. "Seán Keating, the Shannon Scheme and the Art of State-
Building." In *The Shannon Scheme and the Electrification of the Irish Free
State*, ed. Andy Bielenberg, 114–37. Dublin: Lilliput Press, 2002.

————, ed. *The Shannon Scheme and the Electrification of the Irish Free State*.
Dublin: Lilliput Press, 2002.

Blackbourn, David. *The Conquest of Nature: Water, Landscape and the Making
of Modern Germany*. London: Jonathan Cape, 2006.

Bollas, Christopher. *The Evocative Object World*. London: Routledge, 2008.

Bourdieu, Pierre. "Pour un savoir engagé." *Le Monde Diplomatique*, February
2002, 3.

Bowen, Elizabeth. "Modern Lighting." In *People, Places, Things: Essays by Elizabeth Bowen*, ed. Allan Hepburn. Edinburgh: Edinburgh University Press,
2008. Originally published in *Saturday Review of Literature*, October 27,
1928, 294.

Bradshaw, Brendan, ed. *Representing Ireland: Literature and the Origins of Conflict, 1534–1660*. New York: Cambridge University Press, 1993.

Brady, Joseph. "Dublin at the Turn of the Century." In *Dublin through Space
and Time (c. 900–1900)*, ed. Joseph Brady and Anngret Simms, 221–81.
Dublin: Four Courts Press, 2001.

Brantlinger, Patrick. *Fictions of State: Culture and Credit in Britain, 1694–1994*.
Ithaca: Cornell University Press, 1996.

Briot, Marie-Odile. "Electra-mémoires: L'électricité en large de la modernité." In
*Electra: MAM, Musee d'Art Moderne de la Ville de Paris, 10 decembre 1983–5
fevrier 1984. Électricité et l'électronique dans l'art au XXe siecle*, ed. Frank
Popper, 258–61. Paris: Musée d'Art Moderne de la Ville de Paris, 1983.

Brooks, Peter. *Reading for the Plot: Design and Intention in Narrative.* Cambridge, MA: Harvard University Press, 1984.

Brown, Terence. *Ireland: A Social and Cultural History, 1922–1985.* London: Fontana Press, 1985.

Buck-Morss, Susan. *Dreamworld and Catastrophe: The Passing of Mass Utopia in East and West.* Cambridge, MA: MIT Press, 2000.

———. *Hegel, Haiti, and Universal History.* Pittsburgh: University of Pittsburgh Press, 2009.

Cairns, David. *Writing Ireland: Colonialism, Nationalism, and Culture.* New York: Manchester University Press, 1988.

Cameron, Charles, and Edward Mapother. "Report on the Means for the Prevention of Disease in Dublin." *Reports and Printed Documents of the Corporation of Dublin* 1 (1879): 343–52.

Carroll-Burke, Patrick. "Material Designs: Engineering Cultures and Engineering States—Ireland, 1650–1900." *Theory and Society* 31 (2002): 25–114.

———. "Tools, Instruments, and Engines: Getting a Handle on the Specificity of Engine Science." *Social Studies of Science* 31 (August 2001): 593–625.

Casanova, Pascale. *The World Republic of Letters.* Trans. M.B. DeBevoise. Cambridge, MA: Harvard University Press, 2004.

Casino Royale. Dir. Martin Campbell. Columbia Pictures, 2007.

Césaire, Aimé. "Cahier d'un retour au pays natal." In *Aimé Césaire: The Collected Poetry,* trans. Clayton Eshelman and Annette Smith. Berkeley: University of California Press, 1983.

Chamoiseau, Patrick. *Texaco.* Trans. Rose-Myriam Réjouis and Val Vinokurov. New York: Vintage Books, 1998.

Cheng, Vincent. *Joyce, Race, and Empire.* Cambridge: Cambridge University Press, 1995.

Claybaugh, Amanda. "Government Is Good." *Minnesota Review* 70 (Spring 2008): 161–66.

Cleary, Joe. "Introduction: Ireland and Modernity." In *The Cambridge Companion to Modern Irish Culture,* ed. Joe Cleary and Claire Connolly, 1–21. Cambridge: Cambridge University Press, 2005.

———. *Outrageous Fortune: Capital and Culture in Modern Ireland.* Dublin: Field Day Publications, 2006.

Cleary, Joe, and Claire Connolly, eds. *The Cambridge Companion to Modern Irish Culture.* Cambridge: Cambridge University Press, 2005.

Clissmann, Anne. *Flann O'Brien: A Critical Introduction to His Writings.* Dublin: Gill and Macmillan, 1975.

Connolly, S. J., ed. *The Oxford Companion to Irish History.* New York: Oxford University Press, 1998.

Corso, Molly. "Promises Still Power Georgia's Electricity System." EurasiaNet, January 24, 2005. www.Eurasianet.org.

Cronin, Anthony. *No Laughing Matter: The Life and Times of Flann O'Brien.* New York: International Publishing, 1998.

Cullen, Bob. "Some Notable Features of the Design and Operational History of Ardnacrusha." In *The Shannon Scheme and the Electrification of the Irish Free State,* ed. Andy Bielenberg, 138–54. Dublin: Lilliput Press, 2002.

Davis, Mike. *Late Victorian Holocausts: El Niño Famines and the Making of the Third World.* London: Verso, 2000.

———. "Planet of Slums." *New Left Review* 26 (March–April 2004): 5–34.

———. *Planet of Slums.* New York: Verso, 2006.

Davitt, Michael. *The Fall of Feudalism in Ireland.* London: Harper, 1904.

Dawson, Ashley. "Squatters, Space, and Belonging in the Underdeveloped City." *Social Text* 22 (Winter 2004): 17–34.

Day, Robert Adams. "Joyce's AquaCities." In *Joyce in the Hibernian Metropolis: Essays,* ed. Morris Beja and David Norris, 3–20. Columbus: State University of Ohio Press, 1996.

Dayan, Colin. "Out of Defeat: Aimé Césaire's Miraculous Words." *Boston Review,* September–October 2008, www.bostonreview.net/BR33.5/dayan.php.

Deane, Seamus, gen. ed. *The Field Day Anthology of Irish Writing.* Vol. 2. Derry: Field Day Publications, 1991.

———. "National Character and the Character of Nations." In *Strange Country: Modernity and Nationhood in Irish Writing since 1790,* 49–99. Oxford: Oxford University Press, 1997.

Delbourgo, James. *A Most Amazing Scene of Wonders: Electricity and Enlightenment in Early America.* Cambridge, MA: Harvard University Press, 2006.

Deleuze, Gilles, and Félix Guattari. *Kafka: Toward a Minor Literature.* Trans. Dana Polan. Minneapolis: University of Minnesota Press, 1986.

Derrida, Jacques. *Of Grammatology.* Trans. Gayatri Spivak. Baltimore: Johns Hopkins University Press, 1998.

Didion, Joan. "At the Dam." In *The White Album,* 198–201. New York: Simon and Schuster, 1979.

———. "Holy Water." In *The White Album,* 59–66. New York: Simon and Schuster, 1979.

Dillon, William. *Life of John Mitchel.* 2 vols. London: K. Paul, Trench, 1888.

District B13. Screenplay by Luc Besson and Bibi Naceri. Dir. Pierre Morel. TF1 and Canal+, 2004.

Dorn, Harold. "Hugh Lincoln Cooper and the First Détente." *Technology and Culture* 20 (April 1979): 322–47.

Dostoyevsky, Fyodor. *Notes from Underground.* Trans. Richard Pevear and Larissa Volokhonsky. New York: Vintage Books, 1994.

Duffy, Enda. "Disappearing Dublin." In *Semicolonial Joyce,* ed. Derek Attridge and Marjorie Howes, 37–57. Cambridge: Cambridge University Press, 2000.

Duffy, Paul. *Ardnacrusha: Birthplace of the ESB.* Dublin: Electricity Supply Board, 1990.

Edwards, Brent, and Ashley Dawson, eds. "Cities of the Global South." Special issue, *Social Text* 22 (Winter 2004).

Electricity Supply Board. "Electricity Does the Heavy Work." *Irish Statesman,* September 22, 1928, 53.

———. "Energy! 90,000 Horsepower." *Irish Statesman,* September 8, 1928, 2.

———. "Progress." *Irish Statesman,* October 20, 1928, 133.

Ellison, Ralph. *Invisible Man.* New York: Vintage Books, 1995.

Ellmann, Richard. *James Joyce.* Oxford: Oxford University Press, 1959.

Essig, Mark. *Edison and the Electric Chair.* New York: Sutton, 2003.

Ferguson, Frances. *Pornography, the Theory: What Utilitarianism Did to Action.* Chicago: Chicago University Press, 2004.

Ferguson, James. "Decomposing Modernity: History and Hierarchy after Development." In *Postcolonial Studies and Beyond,* ed. Ania Loomba et al., 166–81. Durham: Duke University Press, 2005.

Foster, R. F. *Modern Ireland, 1600–1972.* New York: Penguin, 1989.

Foucault, Michel. *Discipline and Punish: The Birth of the Prison.* Trans. Alan Sheridan. New York: Vintage Books, 1995.

Fournier, Jacques. "Public Services." Embassy of France in the United States, June 1, 2008, www.ambafrance-us.org/atoz/public_services.asp.

Fox, Robin. "The Kindness of Strangers." *Harper's Magazine,* November 2007, 15–21.

Freedman, Ariela. "Did It Flow? Bridging Aesthetics and History in Joyce's *Ulysses.*" *Modernism/Modernity* 13, no. 1 (2006): 853–68.

Friel, Brian. *Translations.* London: Faber and Faber, 1995.

Gallagher, Catherine. "War, Counterfactual History, and Alternate-History Novels." *Field Day Review* 3 (2007): 53–66.

Gaonkar, Dilip Parameshwar. "On Alternative Modernities." In *Alternative Modernities,* ed. Dilip Parameshwar Gaonkar, 1–23. Durham: Duke University Press, 2001.

Garvin, John. *James Joyce's Disunited Kingdom.* Dublin: Gill and Macmillan, 1976.

Gaslight. Dir. George Cukor. Metro-Goldwyn-Mayer, 1944.

Gibbons, Luke. "Ghostly Light: Spectres of Modernity in James Joyce's and John Huston's *The Dead.*" In *The Blackwell Companion to James Joyce,* ed. Richard Brown. London: Blackwell, 2008.

———. "Spaces of Time through Times of Space: Joyce, Ireland, and Colonial Modernity." *Field Day Review* 1 (2005): 71–86.

———. *Transformations in Irish Culture.* Notre Dame: University of Notre Dame Press, 1996.

Gibson, Andrew. *Joyce's Revenge.* Oxford: Oxford University Press, 2002.

Gifford, Don. *"Ulysses" Annotated: Notes for James Joyce's "Ulysses."* Berkeley: University of California Press, 1988.

Gilmore, Paul. "Romantic Electricity, or the Materiality of Aesthetics." *American Literature* 76 (September 2004): 467–94.

Goodman, Kevis. *Georgic Modernity and British Romanticism: Poetry and the Mediation of History.* Cambridge: Cambridge University Press, 2004.

Gordon, Michael R. "In Sadr City, Basic Services Are Faltering." *New York Times,* April 22, 2008.

Griffith, Arthur. Preface to *Jail Journal,* by John Mitchel, ix–xvi. Dublin: M.H. Gill and Son, 1913.

Griffiths, A.R.G. "The Irish Board of Works in the Famine Years." *Historical Journal* 13 (December 1970): 634–52.

Groden, Michael, ed. *James Joyce's "Ulysses," "Ithaca" and "Penelope," a Facsimile of Placards for Episodes 17–18.* New York: Garland, 1978.

Habermas, Jürgen. "Consciousness-Raising or Redemptive Criticism—The Contemporaneity of Walter Benjamin." *New German Critique* 17 (Spring 1979): 30–59.

Hamilton, Patrick. *Angel Street: A Victorian Thriller in Three Acts.* Los Angeles: Samuel French, 1966.

Hardt, Michael, and Antonio Negri. *Empire.* Cambridge, MA: Harvard University Press, 2000.

Hart, Clive. "Wandering Rocks." In *James Joyce's "Ulysses": Critical Essays,* ed. Clive Hart and David Hayman, 181–216. Berkeley: University of California Press, 1974.

Heidegger, Martin. "The Question Concerning Technology." In *The Question Concerning Technology and Other Essays,* trans. William Lovitt, 3–35. New York: Harper Perennial, 1977.

Hogg, Thomas Jefferson. *The Life of Percy Bysshe Shelley.* New York: Dutton, 1933.

Honeywood, St. John. "Poetical Address to the Citizen Adet." In *Poems.* New York: T. and J. Swords, 1801.

Howes, Marjorie. "'Goodbye Ireland I'm Going to Gort': Geography, Scale, and Narrating the Nation." In *Semicolonial Joyce,* ed. Derek Attridge and Marjorie Howes, 58–77. Cambridge: Cambridge University Press, 2000.

———. "How Many People Has Gretta Conroy Killed?" In *Colonial Crossings,* 79–93. Dublin: Field Day Publications, 2006.

Howes, Marjorie, and Derek Attridge. Introduction to *Semicolonial Joyce,* ed. Derek Attridge and Marjorie Howes, 1–20. Cambridge: Cambridge University Press, 2000.

Hughes, Thomas P. *Networks of Power: Electrification in Western Society, 1880–1930.* Baltimore: Johns Hopkins University Press, 1983.

Hugo, Victor. *Les Misérables.* Trans. Lee Fahnestock and Norman MacAfee. New York: Penguin, 1987.

———. *Les Misérables.* 4 vols. Paris: Éditeurs Nelson, 1930.

Hyde, Douglas. "The Necessity for De-Anglicising Ireland." In *Language, Lore and Lyrics: Essays and Lectures,* ed. Breandán Ó Conaire, 153–70. Dublin: Irish Academic Press, 1986.

Jackson, John Wyse. Introduction to *Flann O'Brien at War: Myles na gCopaleen, 1940–1945,* ed. John Wyse Jackson, 7–17. London: Gerald Duckworth, 1999.

Jameson, Fredric. "Third-World Literature in the Era of Multinational Capitalism." *Social Text* 15 (1986): 65–88.

———. "*Ulysses* in History." In *James Joyce and Modern Literature,* ed. W. J. McCormack and Alistair Stead, 126–41. London: Routledge and Keegan Paul, 1982.

JanMohamed, Abdul. "The Economy of Manichean Allegory: The Function of Racial Difference in Colonialist Literature." In *"Race," Writing and Difference,* ed. Henry Louis Gates, 78–106. Chicago: University of Chicago Press, 1986.

Jay, Martin. "Experience without a Subject: Walter Benjamin and the Novel." In *The Actuality of Walter Benjamin,* ed. Laura Marcus and Lynda Nead, 145–55. London: Lawrence and Wishart, 1993.

Johnston, Denis. "Let There Be Light." In *The Selected Plays of Denis Johnston,* ed. Joseph Ronsley, 93–98. Washington, DC: Catholic University of America Press, 1983.

———. *The Moon in the Yellow River.* In *The Selected Plays of Denis Johnston,* ed. Joseph Ronsley, 99–174. Washington, DC: Catholic University of America Press, 1983.

———. "Period Piece." In *The Selected Plays of Denis Johnston,* ed. Joseph Ronsley, 259–60. Washington, DC: Catholic University of America Press, 1983.

———. *The Selected Plays of Denis Johnston.* Ed. Joseph Ronsley. Washington, DC: Catholic University of America Press, 1983.

Joyce, James. *Dubliners.* New York: Penguin, 1996.

———. *Finnegans Wake.* New York: Penguin, 1939.

————. *A Portrait of the Artist as a Young Man.* New York: Penguin, 1992.

————. *Ulysses.* Ed. Hans Walter Gabler et al. New York: Vintage Books, 1986.

Joyce, Stanislaus. *Recollections of James Joyce.* New York: James Joyce Society, 1950.

Kavanagh, Patrick. *Self-Portrait.* Dublin: Dolmen Press, 1964.

Kennedy, Seán. "The Beckett Country Revisited: Beckett, Belonging and Longing." In *Ireland: Space, Text, Time,* ed. Liam Harte, Yvonne Whelan, and Patrick Crotty, 135–45. Dublin: Liffey Press, 2005.

————. "'In the street I was lost': Cultural Dislocation in 'The End.'" In *Beckett and Ireland,* ed. Seán Kennedy, 135–61. Cambridge: Cambridge University Press, 2009.

Kiberd, Declan. *Inventing Ireland: The Literature of the Modern Nation.* London: Jonathan Cape, 1995.

————. *Irish Classics.* Cambridge, MA: Harvard University Press, 2001.

Kincaid, Andrew. *Postcolonial Dublin: Imperial Legacies and the Built Environment.* Minneapolis: University of Minnesota Press, 2006.

Klein, Naomi. "Disaster Capitalism: The New Economy of Catastrophe." *Harper's Magazine,* October 2007.

————. *The Shock Doctrine: The Rise of Disaster Capitalism.* New York: Metropolitan Books, 2007.

Korea. Dir. Cathal Black. Black Star Films/Cathal Black Productions, 1996.

Langan, Celeste. "Mobility Disability." *Public Culture* 13, no. 3 (2001): 459–84.

Latham, Edward. *Famous Sayings and Their Authors.* London: Swan Shonnenschein, 1906.

Latour, Bruno. *Aramis, or, The Love of Technology.* Trans. Catherine Porter. Cambridge, MA: Harvard University Press, 1996.

Leach, Andrew. "Electricity, Writing, Architecture." *Mosaic: A Journal for the Interdisciplinary Study of Literature* 35 (December 2002): 35–50.

Lee, Joseph J. *Ireland, 1912–1985: Politics and Society.* Cambridge: Cambridge University Press, 1989.

————. "The Irish Constitution of 1937." In *Ireland's Histories: Aspects of State Society and Ideology,* ed. Seán Hutton and Paul Stewart, 80–93. London: Routledge, 1991.

————. *The Modernisation of Irish Society, 1848–1918.* Dublin: Gill and Macmillan, 1973.

Leerssen, Joep. *Remembrance and Imagination: Patterns in the Historical and Literary Representation of Ireland in the Nineteenth Century.* Notre Dame: University of Notre Dame Press, 1997.

Lloyd, David. *Anomalous States: Irish Writing and the Postcolonial Moment.* Durham: Duke University Press, 1993.

————. *Ireland after History*. Notre Dame: University of Notre Dame Press, 1999.

————. *Irish Times: Temporalities of Modernity*. Dublin: Field Day, 2008.

————. *Nationalism and Minor Literature: James Clarence Mangan and the Emergence of Irish Cultural Nationalism*. Berkeley: University of California Press, 1987.

Lodge, David. *Thinks . . .* New York: Penguin, 2001.

MacLaran, Andrew. *Dublin: The Shaping of a Capital*. London: Belhaven Press, 1993.

Maguire, Mark. "Socialists, Savages and Hydroelectric Schemes: A Historical Anthropological Account of the Construction of Ardnacrusha." *Irish Journal of Anthropology* 3 (1998): 60–77.

Mbembe, Achille. *On the Postcolony*. Berkeley: University of California Press, 2001.

McCarthy, Michael. *High Tension: Life on the Shannon Scheme*. Dublin: Lilliput Press, 2004.

McClellan, James E., and Harold Dorn. *Science and Technology in World History*. Baltimore: Johns Hopkins University Press, 1999.

Miller, D. A. *The Novel and the Police*. Berkeley: University of California Press, 1988.

Miller, Kerby. *Emigrants and Exiles: Ireland and the Irish Exodus to North America*. New York: Oxford University Press, 1985.

Mitchel, John. *Jail Journal*. Dublin: M. H. Gill and Son, 1914.

Morash, Christopher. *Writing the Irish Famine*. Oxford: Clarendon Press, 1995.

Moretti, Franco. *Modern Epic: The World-System from Goethe to García Márquez*. New York: Verso, 1996.

Mukerji, Chandra. "Intelligent Uses of Engineering and the Legitimacy of State Power." *Technology and Culture* 44 (October 2003): 655–76.

Nabokov, Vladimir. *The Annotated Lolita*. New York: G. P. Putnam's Sons, 1970.

Nesbitt, Nick. "Troping Toussaint, Reading Revolution." *Research in African Literatures* 35 (Summer 2004): 18–33.

Nolan, Emer. "Modernism and the Irish Revival." In *The Cambridge Companion to Modern Irish Culture*, ed. Joe Cleary and Claire Connolly, 157–72. Cambridge: Cambridge University Press, 2005.

————. "State of the Art: Joyce and Postcolonialism." In *Semicolonial Joyce*, ed. Derek Attridge and Marjorie Howes, 78–95. Cambridge: Cambridge University Press, 2000.

Norwood, John. "On the Working of the Sanitary Laws in Dublin, with Suggestions for Their Amendment." *Journal of the Social and Statistical Inquiry Society of Ireland* 6, no. 43 (1873): 230–42.

Nye, David. *Electrifying America: Social Meanings of a New Technology, 1880–1940.* Cambridge, MA: MIT Press, 1990.

O'Brien, Flann. *At Swim-Two-Birds.* London: Longman, Green, 1939.

———— [Myles na gCopaleen, pseud.]. *The Best of Myles.* Ed. Kevin O'Nolan. Normal, IL: Dalkey Archive Press, 1999.

————. *The Dalkey Archive.* Normal, IL: Dalkey Archive Press, 2006.

———— [Myles na gCopaleen, pseud.]. *Flann O'Brien at War: Myles na gCopaleen, 1940–1945.* Ed. John Wyse Jackson. London: Gerald Duckworth, 1999.

————. *The Poor Mouth.* Trans. Patrick C. Power. Normal, IL: Dalkey Archive Press, 1996.

————. *The Third Policeman.* Normal, IL: Dalkey Archive Press, 1999.

O'Connor, Laura. *Haunted English: The Celtic Fringe, the British Empire, and De-Anglicization.* Baltimore: Johns Hopkins University Press, 2006.

Ó Gráda, Cormac. *Black '47 and Beyond: The Great Irish Famine in History, Economy, and Memory.* Princeton: Princeton University Press, 1999.

O'Reilly, Veronica. "The Realism of Denis Johnston." In *Myth and Reality in Irish Literature,* ed. Joseph Ronsley, 281–95. Waterloo, Ontario: Wilfrid Laurier Press, 1977.

Otter, Chris. "Making Liberalism Durable: Vision and Civility in the Late Victorian City." *Social History* 27 (January 2002): 1–15.

Patterson, Orlando. *Slavery and Social Death: A Comparative Study.* Cambridge, MA: Harvard University Press, 1985.

Pélis, Yoann. *Les nouveaux défis de l'énergie à la Martinique.* Paris: Éditions Publibook, 2007.

Pike, David. *Metropolis on the Styx: The Underworlds of Modern Urban Culture, 1800–2001.* Ithaca: Cornell University Press, 2007.

————. *Subterranean Cities: The World beneath Paris and London, 1800–1945.* Ithaca: Cornell University Press, 2005.

Pound, Ezra. "Suffragettes." *Egoist* 1 (July 1, 1914): 255.

Power Trip. Dir. Paul Devlin. 2003.

Prunty, Jacinta. *Dublin Slums, 1800–1925.* Dublin: Irish Academic Press, 1999.

Rancière, Jacques. "Who Is the Subject of the Rights of Man?" *South Atlantic Quarterly* 103 (Spring–Summer 2004): 297–310.

"The Religious Note." *Irish Independent,* July 23, 1929.

Robbins, Bruce. "Modernism in History, Modernism in Power." In *Modernism Reconsidered,* ed. Robert Kiely, 229–45. Cambridge, MA: Harvard University Press, 1983.

————. "The Smell of Infrastructure." *boundary 2* 34 (2007): 25–33.

————. "The Sweatshop Sublime." *PMLA* 117 (January 2002): 84–97.

————. *Upward Mobility and the Common Good: Toward a Literary History of the Welfare State.* Princeton: Princeton University Press, 2007.

Rodgers, Daniel T. *Atlantic Crossings: Social Politics in a Progressive Age.* Cambridge, MA: Harvard University Press, 1998.

Ronsley, Joseph. Introduction to *The Selected Plays of Denis Johnston.* Washington, DC: Catholic University of America Press, 1983.

Rosner, Victoria. *Modernism and the Architecture of Private Life.* New York: Columbia University Press, 2008.

Roth, Henry. *Call It Sleep.* New York: Farrar, Straus and Giroux, 1991.

Rubenstein, Michael D. "Light Reading: Public Utility, Urban Fiction and Human Rights." *Social Text* 97 (Winter 2008): 31–50.

————. "A Portrait of the Artist as a Young Urban Planner: Joyce and Dublin's Engineering Cultures." In *Making Space in the Works of James Joyce,* ed. Valérie Bénéjam and John Bishop. London: Routledge, forthcoming.

————. "'The Waters of Civic Finance': Moneyed States in Joyce's *Ulysses.*" *Novel: A Forum on Fiction* 36 (Summer 2003): 289–306.

Rynne, Colin. *Industrial Ireland, 1750–1930: An Archaeology.* Cork: Collins Press, 2006.

Sailer, Susan Shaw, ed. *Representing Ireland: Gender, Class, Nationality.* Gainesville: University Press of Florida, 1997.

Schivelbusch, Wolfgang. *Disenchanted Night: The Industrialization of Light in the Nineteenth Century.* Berkeley: University of California Press, 1995.

Schoen, Lothar. "The Irish Free State and the Electricity Industry, 1922–1927." *The Shannon Scheme and the Electrification of the Irish Free State,* ed. Andy Bielenberg, 28–47. Dublin: Lilliput Press, 2002.

Schwartz, Roberto. Review of *City of God,* dir. Fernando Meirelles. *New Left Review* 12 (November–December 2001): 103–12.

Schwarz, Daniel R. *Reading Joyce's "Ulysses."* London: Macmillan, 1987.

"Scope for Irish Engineers: No Longer Necessary to Emigrate." *Irish Times,* September 10, 1928.

Seidel, Michael. *Epic Geography: James Joyce's "Ulysses."* Princeton: Princeton University Press, 1976.

Semple, Kirk. "As Iraqi Lights Flicker, 'Generator Man' Feels Heat." *New York Times,* September 25, 2006.

Sen, Amartya. "Capitalism beyond the Crisis." *New York Review of Books,* March 26, 2009, 27–30.

————. "Infrapoverty." April 20, 2009. Regional Academy for Research and Renaissance. www.rarre.org/documents/sen/Sen-%20Infra%20Poverty.pdf.

"The Shannon Scheme." *Irish Independent,* July 23, 1929, 1.

Shiel, Michael. *The Quiet Revolution: The Electrification of Rural Ireland, 1946–1976*. Dublin: O'Brien Press, 2003.

Shklovsky, Victor. "Art as Technique." In *Russian Formalist Criticism: Four Essays*, ed. Lee T. Lemon and Marion J. Reis, 3–24. Lincoln: University of Nebraska Press, 1965.

Simon, Linda. *Dark Light: Electricity and Anxiety from the Telegraph to the X-Ray*. New York: Harcourt, 2004.

Slaughter, Joseph. "Enabling Fictions: The *Bildungsroman* and International Human Rights Law." *PMLA* 121 (October 2006): 1405–23.

Sloterdijk, Peter, and Gesa Mueller von der Haegen. "Instant Democracy: The Pneumatic Parliament." In *Making Things Public: Atmospheres of Democracy*, ed. Bruno Latour and Peter Weibel, 952–57. Cambridge, MA: MIT Press, 2005.

Smith, Adam. *An Inquiry into the Nature and Causes of the Wealth of Nations*. Ed. R.H. Campbell and A.S. Skinner. 2 vols. 1776. Reprint, Indianapolis: Liberty Fund, 1981.

———. *The Theory of Moral Sentiments*. Indianapolis: Liberty Fund, 1984.

Spencer, Andrew. "Many Worlds: The New Physics in Flann O'Brien's *The Third Policeman*." *Eire-Ireland* 30 (Spring 1995): 145–58.

Spivak, Gayatri. "Can the Subaltern Speak?" In *Marxism and the Interpretation of Culture*, ed. Cary Nelson and Lawrence Grossberg, 271–313. Champaign: University of Illinois Press, 1988.

———. "The Subaltern and the Popular: The Trajectory of the Subaltern in My Work." Paper presented at the University of California, Santa Barbara, February 7, 2008, video posted at www.youtube.com/watch?v=2ZHH4ALRFHw&feature=channel_page.

Stiegler, Bernard. *Technics and Time*. Vol. 1. *The Fault of Epimetheus*. Trans. Richard Beardsworth and George Collins. Stanford: Stanford University Press, 1998.

Stillman, Chris, Robert Barklie, and Cathy Johnson. "Viking Iron-Smelting in Dublin's Temple Bar West." *Geology Today* 19 (November–December 2003): 216–18.

"Success of the Shannon Scheme: Mr. Cosgrave Hopes for the Unity of Ireland." *Irish Times*, September 10, 1928, 5.

Synge, J.M. *The Playboy of the Western World*. New York: Penguin, 1997.

Szalay, Michael. *New Deal Modernism: American Literature and the Invention of the Welfare State*. Durham: Duke University Press, 2000.

Tanoukhi, Nirvana. "The Scale of World Literature." *New Literary History* 39 (2008): 599–617.

Taylor, Lucien. "Créolité Bites: A Conversation with Patrick Chamoiseau, Raphaël Confiant, and Jean Bernabé." *Transition* 74 (1997): 124–61.

Theall, Donald F. *James Joyce's Techno-Poetics.* Toronto: University of Toronto Press, 1997.

The Third Man. Dir. Carol Reed. British Lion Film Corporation, 1949.

Toer, Pramoedya Ananta. *This Earth of Mankind.* Trans. Max Lane. New York: Penguin, 1990.

Trumpener, Katie. *Bardic Nationalism: The Romantic Novel and the British Empire.* Princeton: Princeton University Press, 1997.

Valéry, Paul. *The Outlook for Intelligence.* Trans. Denise Folliot and Jackson Mathews. New York: Harper and Row, 1962.

Wacquant, Loïc. "Habitus." In *The International Encyclopedia of Economic Sociology,* ed. Jens Beckert and Milan Zafirovski, 315–19. London: Routledge, 2005.

Walkowitz, Rebecca L. *Cosmopolitan Style: Modernism beyond the Nation.* New York: Columbia University Press, 2006.

Warner, Michael. "The Mass Public and the Mass Subject." In *Habermas and the Public Sphere,* ed. Craig Calhoun, 377–401. Cambridge, MA: MIT Press, 1992.

Whelan, Kevin. "The Memories of 'The Dead.'" *Yale Journal of Criticism* 15, no. 1 (2002): 59–97.

Whelan, Yvonne. *Reinventing Modern Dublin.* Dublin: University College Dublin Press, 2003.

Wilde, Oscar. "The Soul of Man under Socialism." In *The Soul of Man under Socialism and Selected Critical Prose,* ed. Linda Dowling, 125–62. New York: Penguin, 2001.

Wills, Clair. *That Neutral Island: A Cultural History of Ireland during the Second World War.* Cambridge, MA: Harvard University Press, 2007.

Woloch, Alex. "Partings Welded Together: The Character-System in *Great Expectations.*" In *The One vs. the Many: Minor Characters and the Space of the Protagonist in the Novel,* 178–243. Princeton: Princeton University Press, 2003.

Yeager, Patricia. "Introduction: Dreaming of Infrastructure." *PMLA* 122 (Winter 2007): 9–26.

Yeats, W. B. "The De-Anglicising of Ireland." *United Ireland,* December 12, 1892. Reprinted in *Yeats's Poetry, Drama, and Prose,* ed. James Plethica, 261–62. New York: W.W. Norton, 2000.

Žižek, Slavoj. "Knee Deep." *London Review of Books,* September 2, 2004.

INDEX

MICHAEL RUBENSTEIN

is assistant professor of English
at the University of California, Berkeley.